RUSSIA and IRAN
1780 – 1828

Publication of this book
was assisted by a grant from the
IRAN-AMERICA FOUNDATION

RUSSIA and IRAN 1780 – 1828

Muriel Atkin

The University of Texas at San Antonio

University of Minnesota Press, Minneapolis

Published by the University of Minnesota Press
2037 University Avenue Southeast
Minneapolis, Minnesota 55414
Printed in the United States of America.

Library of Congress Cataloging in Publication Data
Atkin, Muriel.
    Russia and Iran, 1780-1828.

    Bibliography: p.
    Includes index.
    1. Russia — Foreign relations — Iran.
2. Iran — Foreign relations — Russia. I. Title.
DK68.7I7A84   327.47055   80-10391
ISBN 0-8166-0924-1

To my mother and the memory of my father

Contents

Preface

Russian expansion has been a subject of deep concern to European and Asian states ever since Peter the Great established his country as a major power. This process of expansion transformed the map of two continents and sparked a host of sometimes violent rivalries from Peter the Great's first war with the Ottoman Empire (1695-1700) to the American "containment" policy of the mid-twentieth century. One of the areas in which Russian penetration has been particularly significant is Iran. For nearly two centuries, relations between these two countries have been characterized by mistrust, recrimination, and, occasionally, armed conflict. To Russian expansionists, this confrontation represented the honorable pursuit of national interests with regard to defense, commerce, and the advance of civilization in the face of opposition by a backward state oblivious to the common good. It also marked the opening of a new stage in the development of the Russian Empire. To the traditional pattern of annexation of contiguous territories was added the conquest of a remote, relatively populous, settled area analogous to western Europe's overseas colonies in Latin America and India. To many Iranians, the growth of Russian power at Iranian expense was gravely unsettling. They felt the humiliation of defeat in war and the loss of valued territory. This in turn compounded the country's serious economic problems which made its government vulnerable to pressure from Russia and Britain. All of this damaged the prestige of the Qājār dynasty (1796-1925), while causing some of its subjects to consider the desirability of borrowing from the West first in military and later in other matters. This era marked the beginning of a prolonged crisis in Iranian society that was characterized by discontent over foreign encroachments on national sovereignty and uneasy concern over the conflicting pressures of tradition and foreign-inspired change. Despite various efforts to deal with these problems, they have continued to exist down to the present day, as demonstrated in the Iranian Revolution of 1978-1979.

The people living in the disputed territory found themselves caught in the center of the struggle. They were brought, sometimes willingly, sometimes not, into the Russian Empire. That resulted in marked changes not only in local political systems but also in economic and social structures. Some outside observers, especially among the British, fit decades of Russian involvement in Iran into a pattern that added up to a drive toward India.

All these developments were rooted in the late eighteenth and early nineteenth centuries, from the 1780s, when Catherine the Great became seriously interested in having an influence in Iranian and Georgian affairs, to 1828, when the end of the Second Russo-Iranian War brought Russia the territorial, commercial, and political concessions it had sought for so long from Iran. For all the importance of this critical period, it has received comparatively little scholarly attention.

Quite a few books and articles dealing with various aspects of Russian expansion in this quarter were written during the tsarist era and by twentieth-century emigrés. However, the authors shared the views of the men who had shaped official policy. In fact, the two groups often overlapped. One of the most important studies of Russian imperial history, Boris Nolde's *La Formation de l'Empire Russe*,[1] was unfinished at the author's death and, therefore, covered nothing later than Tsar Paul's decision in 1800 to annex Georgia. There are a number of Soviet treatments of various aspects of this subject that are sometimes informative about certain particulars, but overall they suffer from biases that closely resemble those of the tsarist expansionist school. The ambivalence of Russian authors treating this subject is reflected in the comments of V. P. Lystsov in his study of Peter the Great's Iranian campaign during the 1720s. Lystsov explained that, even though Russian expansion led to the colonial enslavement of non-Russians, the harmful consequences of expansion were outweighed by the benefits—the Russian conquest of the Caucasian borderlands freed the inhabitants of the area from oppression by the Iranian and the Ottoman governments, and the natural resources of the area encouraged Russian industrialization.[2] Modern Iranian views on this unfortunate era of the country's history are presented in a few works, which still leave room for further discussion. Jamil Qozanlu has written two short narratives of the First and Second Russo-Iranian Wars.[3] There is also a more complex study of Iranian relations with Britain by Mahmud-e Mahmud, who makes extensive use of British publications, especially those of the late nineteenth and early twentieth centures; however, he does not share those authors' views.[4] The last book in English on Russian expansion in the Caucasus was John Baddeley's *The Russian Conquest of the Caucasus*, which was published in 1908. The author was primarily interested in affairs of the high Caucasus and treated the struggle for the Iranian and Ottoman borderlands in a few opening chapters. In any event, he shared many of the biases of the Russian empire builders. More recently there has been important work done on related issues such as developments in Georgia and Armenia about the time of the Russian takeover and Russian expansion (considered in a somewhat broader framework).[5] Yet there has not been a study of some critical issues of the formative period of Russo-Iranian relations: the motives for and methods of Russian expansion in the eastern Caucasus and the responses of the Iranian government and the inhabitants of the disputed territories.

In referring to the disputed border zone, I have used the term *eastern Caucasus* rather than the Russian name *Transcaucasia* or the Iranian names *Āzerbāijān* and *Dāghestān*. Eastern Caucasus is a politically neutral term describing the location of the kingdom of K'art'lo-Kakheti, known as Georgia, and the Muslim-ruled khanates that had been part of Iran and became part of Russia. In contrast, Transcaucasia reflects a Russian perspective, while the Iranian names, apart from presuming that country's hegemony over the region at a time when that was hotly contested, are subject to confusingly different interpretations. In Safavi times, Āzerbāijān was applied to all the Muslim-ruled khanates of the eastern Caucasus as well as to the area south of the Aras River as far as the Qezel Uzān River, the latter region being approximately the same as the modern Iranian *ostāns* of East and West Āzerbāijān. It seemed clearer to me to use Āzerbāijān only for the southern part of the province that has remained under Iranian control. The term *Dāghestān* was used occasionally by the Iranians and frequently by the Russians to refer to the territories on the northeastern slopes of the Caucasus, including Derbent and Qobbeh. (The Russians also applied it to Baku, Shirvān, and Shakki on the southeastern side of the high Caucasus.) The problem with this term is that it does not distinguish the khanates—which, despite the large number of their tribal inhabitants, had long traditions of sedentary urban culture and links to Iran — from the Avars, Lesghis, Qumuqs, and other tribes of the high Caucasus, whose traditions were markedly different. Moreover, these tribes were brought into the Russian Empire through a much longer process than the khanates were.

For other geographical names, I have used the anglicized form when one exists, such as Iran instead of Irān, and the more accurate anglicization where possible, as, for example, Tehran rather than Teheran. Some anglicized forms are far more cumbersome than a direct transliteration. Thus, the standard Gandzha is an anglicization of a russianization of an Iranian place name that may be more simply transliterated as Ganjeh. Some Caucasian places have names that take different forms in Persian, Russian, Georgian, and Armenian. The choice of form may imply a political judgment. The capital of Georgia is now officially known by the Georgian form of its name, Tbilisi, although the Iranians called it Teflis and the Russians, Tiflis. Similarly, the capital of Soviet Armenia is known in Armenian as Yerevan; as a part of the tsarist empire, it was called Erivan; and to the Iranians, who sometimes governed it, it was Iravān. In the case of both cities, I chose to use the version of the name used in the native languages. I have also used anglicized equivalents for nongeographical terms, such as *bazaar* and *shah* (rather than *bazār* and *shāh*), except when a title is quoted as part of a person's name, as in the case of Fath 'Ali Shāh. In transliterating unfamiliar Persian words (and loanwords), I have tried to indicate the way they are pronounced in Persian rather than impose the theoretical reconstruction of the pronunciation of classical Arabic.

The different calendars in use in Russia, Iran, and western Europe present a possible source of confusion. In the period considered here, Russia employed the Julian calendar rather than the Gregorian calendar used in western Europe. For clarity, I have given dates according to the Gregorian calendar in the text. In the footnotes, all dates are given as they appear on the documents. During the eighteenth century, the Julian calendar lagged behind the Gregorian by eleven days, and, in the nineteenth century, by twelve. In the same era, Iran used the Arabic lunar calendar of 354 days reckoned from the date of Mohammed's departure from Mecca for Medina in A. D. 622. Any dates given according to this calendar are accompanied by their equivalents according to the Gregorian calendar.

Acknowledgments

In doing the research and writing for this book, I have received advice from many experts to whom I am very grateful. Foremost among these people is my dissertation advisor, Firuz Kazemzadeh. A number of others have also been very generous in sharing their time and wisdom. Among these are Gavin Hambly, Amin Banani, Hafez Farmayan, Malcolm Yapp, Richard Tapper, John Perry, Fereydoun Adamiyat, Alexander Morton, Fred Donner, Geoffrey Wheeler, and Anne Sheehy. William Wood provided much valuable editorial advice and encouragement. Elizabeth Branch, Florence Thomas, and Gay Walker all played a vital role at various stages in the preparation of the manuscript. Through the generous assistance of a Fulbright-Hays fellowship, I was able to spend a year doing research in the United Kingdom, Iran, and France.

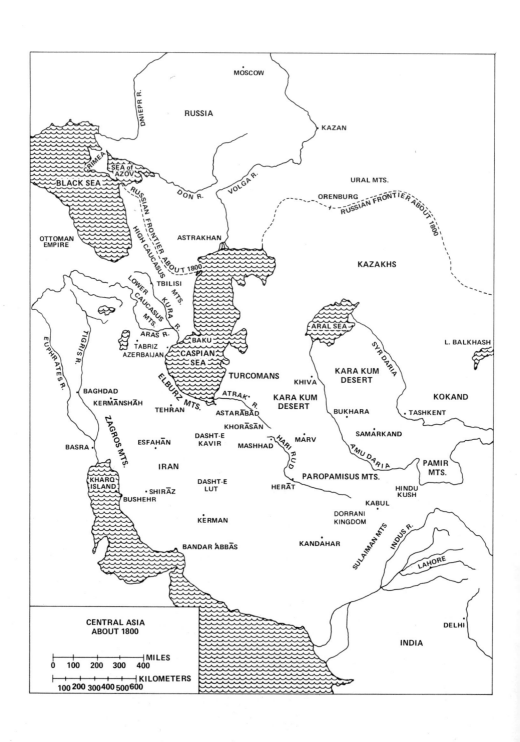

CENTRAL ASIA
ABOUT 1800

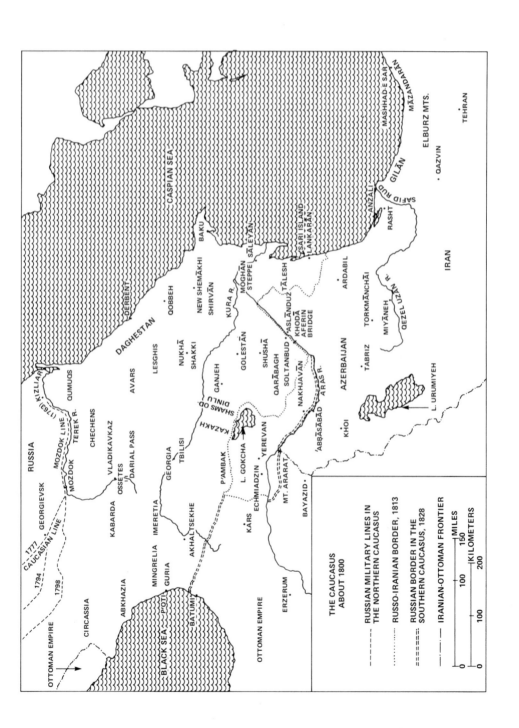

THE CAUCASUS
ABOUT 1800

- - - - - RUSSIAN MILITARY LINES IN
THE NORTHERN CAUCASUS

········· RUSSO-IRANIAN BORDER, 1813

======== RUSSIAN BORDER IN THE
SOUTHERN CAUCASUS, 1828

— · — IRANIAN-OTTOMAN FRONTIER

MILES
0   50   100   150
0   100   200
KILOMETERS

RUSSIA

OTTOMAN EMPIRE

1777 GEORGIEVSK
1794
CAUCASIAN LINE
1798

MOZDOK LINE
MOZDOK

KIZLIAR
(1763)

QUMUQS

TEREK R.

CHECHENS

VLADIKAVKAZ

OSSETES

DARIAL PASS

KABARDA

CIRCASSIA

ABKHAZIA

MINGRELIA

IMERETIA

GURIA

GEORGIA

TBILISI

BLACK SEA

P'OTI

BATUMI

AKHALTSEKHE

K'ARS

ERZERUM

OTTOMAN EMPIRE

BAYAZID·

MT. ARARAT·

ECHMIADZIN

P'AMBAK

L. GOKCHA

YEREVAN

KAZAKH

SHAMS OD DINLU

GANJEH

QARABAGH

SHUSHA

GOLESTAN

NAKHJAVAN

SOLTANBUD

ABBASABAD

KHOI

ARAS R.

DAGHESTAN

DERBENT

AVARS

LESGHIS

QOBBEH

NUKHA

SHAKKI

NEW SHEMAKHI

SHIRVAN

KURA R.

MOGHAN
STEPPE

SALEYAN

BAKU

CASPIAN SEA

DERBENT

TALESH

KHODA
AFERIN
BRIDGE

ASLANDUZ

SARI ISLAND

LANKARAN

ARDABIL

AZERBAIJAN

TABRIZ

TORKMANCHAI

MIYANEH·

QEZEL UZAN R.

L. URUMIYEH

ANZALI

RASHT

SAFID RUD

GILAN

MASHHAD-E SAR

MAZANDARAN

ELBURZ MTS.

QAZVIN·

TEHRAN·

IRAN

RUSSIA and IRAN
1780 – 1828

I

Introduction:
The Early Stages
of Russo-Iranian Relations

Commercial and diplomatic contact between Iran and modern Russia developed gradually from the second half of the fifteenth century, paralleling the reemergence of a Russian state under Muscovite hegemony. The first major increase in trade occurred during the sixteenth century, following Ivan the Terrible's conquest of Tatar-ruled Kazan (1552) and Astrakhan (1556), which opened the Volga-Caspian route between Muscovy and Iran. From that time until the latter half of the seventeenth century, Muscovy was a commercial magnet for Western merchants seeking Russian products (especially lumber, flax, and furs) and luxuries from Iran (notably silk and Indian goods available in Iranian markets). These luxury goods were also much sought after by the Muscovite elite. Tsar Alexei Mikhailovich (who ruled from 1645 to 1676) was particularly fond of Iranian rugs, jewels, and silks, as were many members of his court. The period of growing commercial relations also saw the first diplomatic contacts, the most important of which were the requests of several Georgian princes that Muscovy protect them from the Iranians and Ottomans, who competed for suzerainty over the Caucasus.

Whatever the potential for increased Russo-Iranian contacts, Russia was unable to turn the situation to greater advantage until it had strengthened its own domestic and international situation. Before the eighteenth century, Moscow of necessity had been preoccupied by other concerns: the period of upheaval known as the Time of Troubles in the late sixteenth and early seventeenth centuries; the schism of the Church in the second half of the seventeenth century; and the rebellion of Sten'ka Razin (1670-1671), which centered on the Volga region and severed communications between Muscovy and Iran. There were also recurring wars with Poland, Sweden, and the Ottoman Empire. Trade with Iran was also imperiled by marauding raiders along the lower Volga and in the Caucasus, as well as by the irregular exactions of Iranian officials. Despite numerous obstacles, Russo-Iranian trade, especially in silk, continued into the eighteenth century, although its international significance decreased after several Western nations established direct contact with the markets of India.

Peter the Great, having established Russia as one of the major powers of Europe, turned his attention to Iran. In 1717, as the Great Northern War neared its end, he sent Artemii Volynskii on a mission to Shāh Soltān Hosein, the last member of the Safavi dynasty to rule all of Iran. Volynskii was to explore the possibilities for increased trade with Iran and India and for military cooperation with Iran and Georgia against the Ottoman Empire. As a result of the treaty negotiated by Volynskii, Russia sent consuls to Esfahān (the capital), Shirvān (in the eastern Caucasus), and the Caspian coastal province of Gilān. Peter hoped the Gilāni establishment would be the start of a Russian colony that would stretch along the coast from Derbent in the west to Astarābād in the southeast and could rival the Western establishments in India. As the Iranian government weakened rapidly over the next few years, Peter became determined to intervene with or without the shah's consent in order to prevent Ottoman expansion to the shores of the Caspian.

The formal justification for Peter's Iranian campaign was an attack made in 1721 by several tribes of the eastern high Caucasus (Dāghestān) on Shirvān. Some Russian merchants who traded in the provincial capital, Shemākhi, were killed and perhaps half a million rubles' worth of their property was seized. (Iranian officials and other Shia Muslims in the city fared still worse. Between 4,000 and 5,000 of them were massacred by the Sunni mountaineers in reprisal for Iran's anti-Sunni policies.) As Peter gathered his forces for the coming campaign, the Iranian government entered the final stages of collapse. In October 1722, Shāh Soltān Hosein was overthrown by the Afghan tribal leader Mahmud Ghalzai, who had besieged Esfahān for eight months.

Two months before the fall of Esfahān, Peter led more than 100,000 Russian soldiers to the Caspian coast near the northeastern end of the Caucasus. The expedition's most significant achievement was the capture of the city of Derbent in September. This marked the end of the first stage of the Russian campaign. Peter still wanted to acquire more territory along the coast and march inland into north-western Iran to join forces with a Georgian-Armenian army. How-ever, a critical shortage of supplies, widespread illness (which account-ed for most of the campaign's 33,000 deaths), and the desire to avoid a direct confrontation with the Ottomans (who were also moving into Iranian territory) persuaded him to reduce the scale of his opera-tions. Two weeks after the surrender of Derbent, he returned to Rus-sia, leaving behind only a small garrison. Although the Russian army took the port city of Baku and part of Gilān in the next few months, Peter himself never returned to the area.

The final stage of Peter's involvement in Iran was the dismember-ment of the Safavi empire by two treaties, one with the Ottomans, the other with Shāh Tahmāsb II, a son of the late shah. By the Russo-Ottoman Treaty of 1724, Peter recognized Ottoman control over western Iran exclusive of the Caspian littoral. The Russo-Iranian Treaty was invalidated by Tahmāsb's refusal to make the extensive conces-sions desired by Peter and agreed to by Tahmāsb's negotiator. This fact was conveniently overlooked by the Russian authorities. The provisions that so angered Tahmāsb called for the cession to Russia of the western and southern Caspian coast (over which he had no control at the time). There were also provisions for the encourage-ment of trade and military cooperation. For its part, Russia did not cooperate with Tahmāsb against the Afghans but did maintain its garrisons in Derbent, Baku, and Gilān. These territorial gains proved much less advantageous than the Russians had expected. Silk-rich Gilān did not provide the desired revenues because there was consid-erable emigration from the Russian-occupied area and much of. the province lay outside Russian control. In addition, the occupying forces at various points along the coast suffered heavy casualties from disease. About 100,000 Russian soldiers died, almost all from dis-ease, during the occupation of the coastal provinces. No attempt was made to garrison the provinces of Māzandarān and Astarābād, which Russia had also claimed.

After the death of Peter the Great, Russian interest in Iran waned, while Tahmāsb and his able general, the future Nāder Shāh, began to reconquer the lost provinces. Finally, Tsaritsa Anna agreed in the treaties of Rasht (1732) and Ganjeh (1735) to withdraw all Russian forces stationed in the former Safavi provinces. Russian interest in Iran remained dormant until the reign of Catherine the Great late in the eighteenth century.

There are several points of similarity between Peter's and Cather-ine's Iranian ambitions. Both rulers justified Russian military intervention as vengeance for an unlawful attack on people under their protection by a party that was not the rightful government of Iran. In Peter's reign, the casus belli was the attack on Shirvān and secondarily the Afghan challenge to Safavi authority. Catherine justified her Iranian Campaign as a reprisal for the 1795 attack on Georgia by Āqā Mohammad Khān, the founder of the Qājār dynasty. She proclaimed to all the people of the region that her intention was not only to safeguard the Georgians (who had been under Russian protection, at least theoretically, since 1783) but also to protect all Iranian subjects, including Muslims, from the tyrannical rule of the usurper Āqā Mohammad Khān.[1]

Another common attribute of Russian policy toward Iran at the beginning and the end of the eighteenth century was the special interest in Armenians and Georgians. Peter and Catherine both toyed with the notion of liberating the Caucasian Christians from Muslim rule, an idea strenuously encouraged by the two Christian communities, which urged the Russians to send troops not only to take them under protection but also to conquer the central provinces of Iran. The Caucasian Christians promised military cooperation as well. In the 1720s, they gathered troops to join with Peter's army. However, he failed to take advantage of the opportunity. By the 1790s, neither the Georgians nor the Armenians were able to organize substantial military forces of their own. Nonetheless, spokesmen for both groups continued to promise cooperation with Russian troops should any be sent to the region. Peter and Catherine were also interested in the Armenians and Georgians as valuable commercial intermediaries in trade with Asia. A consistent trait of eighteenth century Russian policy toward these groups was the acceptance of their declarations of support unmatched by effective Russian protection. In Peter's campaign, King Vakhtang of Georgia was hopelessly compromised by his preparations to join forces with the Russians and as a result was forced into exile for the rest of his life. The Armenians who had cooperated with him took shelter in inaccessible mountain reaches. During Catherine's reign, the Georgians complained repeatedly of the inadequacy of Russian protection that had been guaranteed them by treaty, especially when nothing was done to prevent the sack of their capital, Tbilisi, in 1795.

Despite the immense prestige that eventually accrued to Peter's activities and the general similarities between Russia's Iranian interests at the beginning and the end of the century, Catherine's policy owed very little to Peter's influence. The real beginning of Russia's modern interest in Iran occurred in Catherine's reign. She occasionally referred to Peter's activities and his treaty with Tahmāsb but only as secondary arguments. Her campaign in the eastern Caucasus was not designed as an imitation of Peter's. Instead, she formed her Iranian policy on the basis of her analysis of conditions that existed in her own time. Peter's example served to legitimize a policy already formulated. For example, in her 1796 manifesto to the Iranian and Caucasian peoples announcing the war against Āqā Mohammad Khān, she cited the Petrine precedent but placed far greater emphasis on more recent events, especially Russia's obligation to protect Georgia and the evils of Āqā Mohammad's brutal misrule. Therefore, she argued, Russia had a duty to destroy the tyrant and establish justice in the afflicted territories.[2] Catherine's references to Peter's achievements studiously avoided any mention of his treaty with the Porte, according to which the latter was recognized as overlord of Georgia and most of the other territories Russia then claimed. Anna's two treaties were also conveniently forgotten until Alexander's war with Iran, at which time the Ministry of Foreign Affairs argued that the concessions were made only because Nāder Shāh had temporarily reestablished law and order, which, by implication, subsequent Iranian pretenders had failed to do. In any event, Russia argued that it was not bound by the treaties since Iran had failed to live up to certain provisions.[3]

Peter's activities on the Caspian coast influenced later generations by raising the possibility of using Iranian territory as a base for expanded trade with Asia. For half a century, the idea lay dormant while his successors gave their attention to other matters. Catherine the Great, who was as vigorous an advocate of Russian expansion as Peter had been, also developed an interest in that quarter. In so doing, she responded far more to contemporary attitudes about imperial greatness and to political turbulence in Iran than to her predecessor's accomplishments. The one precedent that seems to have influenced her greatly was the apparent similarity between Iran's political fragmentation at the beginning and end of the century and, therefore, the likelihood of easy Russian success against a weak opponent. However, the similarity proved deceptive, and the obstacles to duplicating Peter's achievements were many.

II

The Iranian Empire
and the Caucasian Borderlands
at the End
of the Eighteenth Century

The most salient feature of late eighteenth century Iran was its disunity. No shah ruled unchallenged over all the provinces that had comprised the Safavi domains. After the fall of Esfahan, the Afghans controlled most of the south, center, and east; the Ottomans, the west; and the Russians, part of the Caspian coast. At the same time, Turcoman raids from across the northeastern frontier contributed to the breakdown of order in the eastern and central provinces. Tahmāsb, who had fled north from the capital, proclaimed himself shah and attempted to rebuild the empire. He was abetted in this by the Afshār tribal chieftain Tahmāsb Qoli Khān. In 1732, once most of Iran was reunited under Tahmāsb's suzerainty, Tahmāsb Qoli deposed the shah and ruled under the guise of regent for the shah's infant son. Four years later, he seized the throne outright and proclaimed himself Nāder Shāh, first ruler of the Afshār dynasty. His reign was dominated by warfare: conquests, as in the northwest, where he forced the eastern Caucasus into submission; raids, notably on India and Central Asia; and the suppression of domestic opposition. With his assassination in 1747, central authority collapsed.

For the next half century, the provinces that had comprised the Safavi empire were governed by a variety of local rulers, some of whom used puppet Safavi princes to legitimize their authority, though without seriously intending to restore the fallen dynasty. The most successful of these local rulers was Karim Khān, leader of the Zand tribe, whose power was based on the southern province of

Fārs. He gained control of most of the Iranian plateau (except for Khorāsān, which was controlled by Nāder's grandson), the southern coast of the Caspian, and southern Azerbaijan. His reign was characterized as much by constructive domestic policies as by the quest for power, but, when he died in 1779, the political turmoil resumed with such vigor as to eclipse all other issues. Several Zands fought among themselves, while Afshārs controlled parts of Khorāsān, Māzandarān, and Azerbaijan. The Afghans also played a role in Khorāsāni affairs. The individual who emerged victorious from this struggle was Āqā Mohammad, who belonged to a faction of the Qājār tribe that had unsuccessfully opposed the extension of Karim's authority to the southeastern coast of the Caspian.

The Qājārs were Turcomans who had come west with the Mongol armies from Central Asia and settled in Syria and Anatolia. They moved eastward to Iranian territory during Tamerlane's reign and later joined the Qizilbash confederation of tribes, which was the mainstay of early Safavi military strength. By Safavi times, the Qājārs had split into several factions. One, the Ziādoghlu (Ziādlu), controlled the east Caucasian principalities of Ganjeh and Yerevan (Iravān, Erivan). Two other factions, the often hostile Qoyunlu (Qāvānlu) and the Davālu (Devehlu), settled in various parts of northeastern Iran. Āqā Mohammad's father, Mohammad Hasan, was chief of the Qoyunlu faction. His rise to power in the northeast paralleled Karim's in the south, but he was defeated and killed in the eventual confrontation with the Zands, in part because of opposition from the Davālu branch. Later clashes between the Zands and both the Qājār factions ended in the defeat of the latter and the execution of several Qājār leaders.

Āqā Mohammad's youth was marred by the turbulence of the era. As a child, he had been captured and castrated by an Afshār pretender who briefly controlled Māzandarān. Āqā Mohammad later returned to his father's camp but had to flee after his father's death. Eventually, he was made a prisoner at Karim's court, where he remained for nearly twenty years. Here his circumstances improved. Though nominally a hostage, he in fact enjoyed Karim's favor and was frequently employed by the khan as an adviser. This situation gave the astute Qājār a valuable political education. In the disorders that followed Karim's death, Āqā Mohammad returned to Māzandarān to build up his own power, while the Zands weakened each other through internecine warfare. The contest dragged on as Āqā Mohammad extended his authority in the northern and central provinces without being able to crush Zand opposition. During the early 1790s, a pattern began to emerge as Āqā Mohammad steadily whittled away at the domains of the last important Zand, Lotf 'Ali, Karim's grandnephew. Finally, in 1794, Lotf 'Ali's last stronghold, Kermān, fell to Āqā Mohammad, who punished the city dwellers for their support of his rival by killing, blinding, or enslaving thousands of their number. Lotf 'Ali was captured and killed soon after. Āqā Mohammad was then master of most of Iran. He chose Tehran as his capital because, among other reasons, it was well situated as a center for operations against the two most important areas that remained outside his control—Khorāsān and the eastern Caucasus. He attempted but failed to subjugate these areas in the last three years of his life. In Khorāsān the separatist forces were on the wane, but in the Caucasus he was opposed by local rulers who wanted to preserve their independence and by Russia, which had its own imperial designs on the region. His campaign there in 1795 marked the beginning of a generation of fierce competition for hegemony.

The disputed borderlands extended from Georgia and Yerevan east to the Caspian Sea and from the southern slopes of the Caucasus to the Aras (Araxes) and Kura rivers, although along the coast the zone exceeded these limits in both directions, from Derbent in the north to Tālesh in the south. The region could be subdivided into three broad zones: Georgia, Iranian Armenia (Ganjeh, Qarābāgh, Yerevan, and Nakhjavān), and the Shirvāni successor states (Shirvān, Shakki, Derbent-Qobbeh, and Baku). The small principality of Tālesh on the Caspian coast belongs in a category by itself.

Georgia had been at the apogee of its power in the late twelfth and early thirteenth centuries, but its fortunes declined after that period. In the fifteenth century, it broke apart. The western principalities soon came under Ottoman suzerainty, but the eastern ones were the object of a prolonged power struggle. The eastern area was subject to Iran for the last century of Safavi rule. As the province of Gorjestān (Georgia), it was ruled by its own kings of the ancient Bagration dynasty, who were simultaneously members of the Safavi administration as *valis* (governor-generals). The second quarter of the eighteenth century saw Georgia under Ottoman and then Iranian control once more, but for the rest of the century neither could enforce its claim. King Erekle (who ruled from 1762 until 1798) profited from the power vacuum and dominated the affairs of several neighboring principalities. At the height of Erekle's power, Georgia's position was still far from secure, being weakened internally by rivalries within the royal family and threatened from without by raids from tribes of the high Caucasus as well as the possibility of reconquest by the Ottomans or Iranians. Even before the rapid worsening of its fortunes in the last years of the century, Georgia was not strong economically and was thinly populated by perhaps 60,000 families.[1]

The rest of the east Caucasian principalities were under Muslim rule and occupied a larger area with a larger total population than Georgia. The population of the Muslim-ruled area may have been in the vicinity of 80,000 families representing diverse ethnic and religious groups. Yerevan was the most populous, with well in excess of 100,000 Muslim and Armenian inhabitants, while Baku and Tālesh were the least populous. Baku's small population was related in part to the khanate's small geographic size—it was virtually a city-state—and Tālesh was a remote area with few attractions.[2] The largest group of east Caucasians were Muslims belonging to Turcoman tribes, but this was not a homogeneous group. Some were semi-nomadic and in some cases migrated across borders, like the tribes living in the southern border districts of Georgia, who regularly crossed into Yerevan and Ganjeh, or the larger Shāhsavan tribe, who made camp at times south of the Aras and Kura rivers, at times north. Other tribes included sedentary farmers and town dwellers as well as nomads (as was the case with the Javānshirs of Qarābāgh). Shirvān and the four khanates of Iranian Armenia were controlled by Turcoman tribes (the Ziādoghlu Qājārs in Yerevan and Ganjeh, the Kangerlus in Nakh-javān, and the Khān Chopān in Shirvān), while elsewhere, including Qobbeh and southern Georgia, Turcomans were a subject minority. Several non-Turcoman tribes also played an important role in Caucasian affairs. There were Kurds living in various places along the Aras, including Yerevan and Qarābāgh, where they were valuable allies of the ruling Javānshirs. Tribes from the high mountains had also moved into the adjoining khanates. Some of the Lesghis (Lakz), who were feared for their frequent and often devastating plunder raids, lived as nomadic pastoralists in the higher reaches of several khanates. Qobbeh and Derbent were governed by a branch of the Qaitāqs, relatives of the Avars, who moved in from the high mountains in the eighteenth century and another Avar group dominated Shakki. In addition, there were sedentary Persian speakers in several areas, particularly Yerevan and Baku.

The nomadic tribes were neither aloof from nor wholly a part of affairs of the khanates in which they lived. Tribes that controlled the government of a khanate enjoyed special privileges, but other tribes paid taxes comparable to those imposed on the sedentary population. Since the nomads engaged in animal husbandry on a large scale and in certain other lucrative activities (such as sericulture in Shirvān), the khans would have deprived themselves of an important source of revenue had they not taxed the tribes. Furthermore, tribal cavalry provided the backbone of most of the khans' armies. The tribes' military skills and habitual mobility were a volatile factor in the struggle for domination of the eastern Caucasus.

There were also non-Muslims living in all parts of the region, except Tālesh. Ganjeh had a Georgian minority. Armenians constituted about a fifth of Yerevan's population and their coreligionists were to be found throughout the eastern Caucasus. All the Shirvāni successor states (except Shakki) had Jewish communities as well. Armenians and, to a lesser extent, Jews played a central role in the economic life of all the khanates as farmers and artisans and, above all, as merchants. In every major commercial center, including Baku (the most important), Armenians dominated trade. Baku's commercial significance made it an especially cosmopolitan place, with inhabitants from many parts of the Caucasus as well as from Iran and India.

Given the religious diversity of the region, sectarian differences were always a potential source of friction. The Muslim population was divided between the Sunni and Shia, sects, but this division did not correspond to ethnic or political divisions. Most of the Turcomans and Kurds were Shii, although the ruling Khān Chopāns of Shirvān and some of the smaller nomadic tribes of Iranian Armenia were Sunni. The tribes that had their origins in the high Caucasus were mostly Sunni. One notable exception in this case was the Qaitāqs of Derbent-Qobbeh who became Shii in order to obtain the endorsement of the Safavis. All of the principalities, except Shirvān and Shakki, were ruled by Shii khans, but all of the subject populations included members of both sects. There was no recurrence of the bitter religious wars that had gripped Shirvān and Shakki in the first half of the century, but Sunni-Shia relations continued to be sensitive. The Shii khans of Derbent-Qobbeh made a special point of trying to conciliate the Sunni majority. In the nineteenth century, conflict between the two groups would greatly hamper the Russian takeover of Shakki.

Non-Muslims lived under certain disadvantages, notably a higher rate of taxation, but they do not seem to have been actively persecuted. In the countryside, Christians and Jews lived in their own villages and enjoyed certain advantages, especially the local governance of their coreligionists. Some of the Armenian village chiefs were extremely powerful and had an influential voice in a khanate's affairs, for example, in Qarābāgh, where they supported the establishment of the Javānshirs as khans. The Christians and Jews, as "people of The Book," were able to maintain their houses of worship, obtain religious literature, and employ the clergy of their faith for their congregations. The capital of Armenian Christiandom was Echmiadzin (Uch Kelisia) in Yerevan, where the Catholicos resided. There were reports from Christian sources of the persecution of Qarābāghi Armenians in reaction to King Erekle's alliance with Russia in 1783, but the issue in this case was political, not religious, since the Qarābāghi Armenians had asked Russia to take them under its protection and overthrow the ruler.[3]

Political and military leadership in each principality was in the hands of a khan. (The title conveys a variety of meanings, including tribal chieftain, military commander, and notable.) The khans' powers were extremely broad, including final judgment in all matters subject to secular common law (*'urf*) and the authority to decide the life or death of the accused. Yet there were also certain constraints on their authority. In some khanates, they were expected to consult with a council of notables before deciding matters of political and military import or judging criminal cases. Moreover, when a khan violated traditional norms, he might be exposed to the wrath of his subjects. In the eighteenth century, there were successful uprisings against harsh or otherwise unpopular rulers in Shirvān, Shakki, and Ganjeh.

A khan was not only the ruler of his territory, he was to a considerable extent its owner. Inhabitants engaged in farming or animal husbandry paid the khan a fraction of their harvests or flocks as rent for the use of the land. Hunting, fishing, and the exploitation of mineral resources were farmed out as concessions that often proved valuable sources of the khan's revenue. Commercial activities, such as the export of a valuable commodity and the ownership of shops, also belonged to the khan. He also levied taxes such as import and export duties, a sales tax on most domestic staples, and the head tax on adult males. In keeping with Islamic tradition, Christians and Jews paid a higher tax, about double what the Muslims paid. There were also unofficial sources of revenue, including widespread gift giving by people seeking a khan's favor.

In theory the office of khan was inherited through the male line in each principality, but political rivalries and chance occurrences disrupted the succession in most khanates. Although there was a preference for succession by the eldest son, the issue was more often resolved on the basis of who was sufficiently strong and experienced to take and hold power. Power struggles among members of the ruling families led to bitter feuds in Baku, Shirvān, Shakki, and Qarābāgh, while rivalries with neighbors led to the deposition and murder of khans of Shirvān and Ganjeh.

There is little information about the khans' conceptions of their office—whether, like the ideal of the Islamic ruler, they aspired to promote justice and prosperity or whether they viewed their territories as sources of private wealth and bases for further conquests. In the second half of the eighteenth century, their energies were devoted, either by choice or necessity, to struggles with domestic and external rivals. Many khans came to power by force; those who were strong enough tried to expand their domains by conquest. Furthermore, most khans were tribal chiefs whose first loyalties were to their tribes not to the khanates. Given the disruptive effect of the wars, epidemics, and famines that wracked the Caucasus during this era, it would have been very difficult for a khan to afford to play the public benefactor had he been inclined to do so.

Below the khans were the notables (*begs*), a term applied to a khan's brothers or sons as well as to administrative officials. When a khan was strong enough to enforce his will, the *begs* were expected to serve him in whatever capacity, civil or military, he required. They were often employed as governors of districts of all sizes. Some of the *begs* could be powerful figures whose authority within a district was similar to a khan's. In return for his service, a *beg* enjoyed certain benefits and privileges. His khan paid him either a direct cash salary, a portion of the harvest, a grant of income from land, or outright land ownership. The *begs* were also exempt from most taxes, including the head and land taxes (on land they owned) and levies on various commercial activities. The rest of the public offices in the khanates were staffed by scribe-bureaucrats, village headmen, the headmen's subordinates, (who were in charge of a quarter), and tax farmers. Khans also had a variety of courtiers and servitors as well as guard corps that were separate from the army. *Begs* had their own retainers who, in addition to serving their master, also served in the khan's army. Many members of these groups as well as others, such as prosperous peasants, enjoyed tax-exempt status. This exemption was given on a hereditary basis to people who served the khan, including tribes that fought in the khan's army, and also to people who had no role in government but paid the khan to make them exempt.

Muslim holy men—experts on religious law, teachers, and descendants of Mohammad—also enjoyed special status. They were exempt not only from taxes but also from government service, and they received income from grants of revenue from farming villages, caravanserais, and shops (*vaqf*). The mosques of Shushā, the capital of Qarābāgh, held particularly large *vaqf* grants. The religious establishment does not seem to have been particularly influential. The only theological college known to have existed in the region was in Derbent. Even if it functioned as an instructional center for local Muslims, it could not have served adherents of both the Sunni and Shia sects. Nor do the local chronicles give any example of religious authorities playing a role in the turbulent events of the eighteenth century. On one occasion when the dispute between a khan and his subjects was largely religious—the oppression of Sunni inhabitants of Shakki by a Shii khan who ruled with the support of Nāder Shāh—it was not the religious leaders but the *begs* and village administrators who rallied the opposition and eventually started a rebellion.

The largest social group in the eastern Caucasus was the peasantry. Since the land itself was considered the property of the khans or *begs*, all peasants were tenants. Still, the more numerous category of peasants, the *ra'yats*, had some property of their own. They usually owned their own homes, tools, and animals. In at least one khanate, Qarābāgh, there was an attempt to bind the *ra'yat* to the land. However, such a change was virtually unenforceable since depopulation produced much vacant farmland and there was always the possibility of flight to the forests, mountains, or another khanate. The less advantaged peasants, the *ranjbars*, were bound to the landlords and could be moved from village to village. They owed the same rents and corvée services as the *ra'yats* and in addition had to work the landlord's demesne, the entire product of which belonged to the landlord.

Slavery also existed in east Caucasian society. The leading slave raiders in the late eighteenth century were the Lesghis and other tribes of Dāghestān. Georgian women in particular were highly sought after as slavewives. Three late-eighteenth-century khans married Georgian slaves, and one of the most persistent foes of Russian expansion in the Caucasus, Sheikh 'Ali Khan of Derbent-Qobbeh, was the son of an Armenian slavewife. Although boys were also enslaved, there is no indication that they were used to fill administrative posts or serve in the army as they were in other parts of the Islamic world.

Although some of the principalities of this region were stronger and more prosperous than their neighbors, the overall impression produced by this region in the late eighteenth century was one of decay. Qobbeh and Yerevan were the most prosperous khanates in the region. By the 1790s, Shirvān had made a surprising recovery from decades of external and internal warfare. The other economic leader was Baku, but it had to spend a large proportion of its considerable wealth to import food and pay "protection money" to powerful neighbors. At the low end of the economic spectrum were Nakhjavān and Tālesh. Cities were poorly maintained, and their reduced populations lived surrounded by the ruins of unoccupied buildings. In many rural areas, arable land lay fallow for want of peasants to work it. There was a special irony in this unimpressive economic picture because Russia was attracted to the region largely on the basis of its economic assets. Agriculture and animal husbandry were the dominant economic activities of the eastern Caucasus. The most widely grown crops were cereals; in most areas, these were produced in subsistence quantities, but Qarābāgh and Qobbeh were the breadbaskets of the region. In contrast, Nakhjavān and Baku were especially weak agriculturally. Baku at least produced modest quantities of the valuable saffron and, more important, could compensate with nonagricultural resources, but Nakhjavān had not recovered from devastation caused by the Safavi-Ottoman border wars. The area northeast of the Kura produced fruits and vegetable dyes, while Yerevan produced cotton and tobacco for export. Sheep and goats made up most of the herds, but cattle, buffalo, and horses were also raised. Shirvān derived considerable profits from locally grown silk, which the inhabitants made into carpets and fabrics. These manufactures were exported to Russia and throughout western Asia, although the prevailing opinion was that the silk itself was decidedly inferior to that produced in Gilān. Furthermore, during the 1760s political upheavals and an outbreak of plague disrupted the silk industry for a time.

Several extractive industries along the Caspian coast were among the most lucrative economic activities in the whole area. Baku and Shirvān were bases of large scale fishing and seal hunting. Baku obtained enough salt from lakes and mines to meet the needs of most of the eastern Caucasus and several Iranian provinces. Above all, Baku produced oil, *naft*. *Naft* was used not only for heating, lighting, and cooking but also for lubricating machines, encouraging silkworms to produce cocoons and waterproofing the flat-roofed buildings and as medicine for human consumption. About one-third of the annual production was used locally; the rest was exported to other parts of the Caucasus and especially to Iran.

Baku's other great economic strength was its role as the foremost commercial center of the eastern Caucasus. The khanate was the source of valuable commodities as well as a market for the many necessities it could not produce for itself in sufficient amounts. In addition, the capital city was located beside the only good harbor on the western Caspian coast. Only Baku could offer shelter from most of the sea's winter storms and a deep enough port for boats to be able to dock along the shore. As a result, the city functioned as the primary regional trade center for neighboring khanates, Gilān, and Astrakhan. Even most of the Russo-Iranian trade went via Baku. No other east Caucasian city could compete. Yerevan was a poor second to Baku. It was a market for slaves and domestic agricultural products. The capital of Shirvān had been a serious rival until the early eighteenth century, but that was ended by a series of military disasters: the anti-Shia massacre in 1721, the looting by Nāder Shāh's army and Avar raiders from the high mountains, and the political collapse of the 1770s and 1780s. Two other places Russia believed to be important for trade, the city of Derbent and Sāleyān (a district near the mouth of the Kura), had no harbor facilities at all. In its days of greater strength, Derbent had maintained stone jetties to create an artificial harbor, but these had been in ruins since the sixteenth century. Derbent conducted a modest level of trade with Russia, but Baku was the intermediary in most of this. Astrakhan merchants made semiannual fishing trips to the waters around Sāleyān. These regular visits encouraged the development of an impromptu market as nomads who pastured their flocks in the vicinity and inhabitants of several khanates came to sell their wares to the Russians and buy goods brought from Astrakhan. Yet there were serious obstacles to the development of Sāleyān as a great market even apart from its lack of a proper harbor. There was no town, but there were many poisonous snakes and lethal endemic diseases. The Russians discovered some of Sāleyān's liabilities when they occupied the area on the orders of Peter the Great. In a single year, an entire Russian garrison of 400 men was killed by disease. However, that did not deter Russian hopes of developing Sāleyān as a great commercial center.

The eastern Caucasus' uneven economic picture was matched by widespread political turbulence. Many of the ruling dynasties had only recently gained power. Every khanate, except the peripheral Nakhjavān and Tālesh, was the scene of savage domestic power struggles, attacks from without, or both. The most important principalities of earlier times were reduced in size and strength. Shirvān had been an independent or at least autonomous principality from the ninth century to the sixteenth, when the Safavis made it an integral part of their empire. Over the centuries, it lost more than half of its territory. Derbent broke away during the Mongol era; the Ottomans severed Baku and Shakki during periods in the sixteenth and seventeenth centuries when they took the region from the Safavis. In the second half of the eighteenth century, Shirvān's political fortune reached its nadir. The leader of the Khān Chopān tribe seized power in the early 1760s with Zand support, but later in that decade he was ousted through the intervention of Qobbeh and Shakki. For the next twenty years, Qobbeh dominated Shirvān, sometimes through direct rule, sometimes by backing feuding Khān Chopāns. During the 1790s, Qobbeh weakened and lost control of Shirvān, but the internal warfare persisted several more years. Not until the middle of the decade did the khanate show signs of recovery.

Baku, Derbent, and Shakki were not strong as independent khanates. In the mid-eighteenth century, Baku came under the rule of descendants of the Iranian garrison commander of 1723. There was a heated power struggle among members of the ruling family during the early 1790s. With the small size of the khanate's population and the cost of the internecine warfare, Baku was at the mercy of its neighbors. Qobbeh forced Baku to pay tribute, but by the end of the century Baku's ruler looked for protection from an alternate source, at first warily from Shirvān, then more enthusiastically from the revived Iranian state. Derbent was even weaker. It was ruled by a local family for eleven years after the breakup of Nāder Shāh's empire and conquered by Qobbeh. The ruling dynasty in Shakki seized power during the 1740s as the representative of Sunni interests against the Shii incumbent. In the middle of the century, the second ruler of the line was killed by tribesmen from the high mountains who were in league with a rebellious *beg*. There ensued a bloody war among members of the ruling dynasty that continued until the end of the century.

In the second half of the eighteenth century, Qobbeh was the strongest of the Shirvāni successor states and a dominant force in the region as a whole. Qobbeh's rise was facilitated not only by the weakness of potential rivals but also by its strategically advantageous terrain; its dense forests and numerous swift-flowing streams were valuable defenses against invaders. The Qaitāq khans had survived the claims of Peter the Great and Nāder Shāh by submitting to both, but during the 1760s Fath 'Ali Khān began to subdue his neighbors, forcing Shakki and Baku into submission and conquering Derbent and Shirvān and in the process taking control of Sāleyān. Fath 'Ali went on to extend his suzerainty south of the Aras and Kura to Ardabil, Tālesh, and parts of Gilān. He also struck at the power of his greatest rivals, Georgia and Qarābāgh, by helping the people of Ganjeh oppose those two principalities and by defeating Qarābāgh in battle. However, he died in 1789, soon after achieving this victory. Qobbeh's power began to decline immediately. A few years later, one of Fath 'Ali's younger sons, Sheikh 'Ali, rebuilt much of the khanate's strength just as Russia and Iran renewed their claims to the eastern Caucasus.

Developments in Iranian Armenia bore a resemblance to developments north of the Kura in that established powers of earlier times declined in importance while a former subject became strong. During the Safavi era, Iranian Armenia was divided into two administrative units, Yerevan (then called Chukur-e Saʻd) and Ganjeh. Nakhjavān was part of the former, Qarābāgh of the latter. Shifting fortunes of the Iranian Empire as a whole led to the emergence of the two subject districts as independent khanates. In the case of Nakhjavān, important connections with its former master endured as the khanate shared Yerevan's political stance and looked to it for protection. The situation in Qarābāgh was strikingly different. The death of Nāder Shāh gave the leader of the locally powerful Javānshir tribe an opportunity to seize power. As Zand power weakened after 1779, Javānshir power grew rapidly. The khan, Ebrāhim Khalil, improved his position by making an alliance with King Erekle of Georgia. The two rulers forced Ganjeh and Yerevan into submission, deposing khans in the former, pillaging the latter, and extracting a heavy tribute from both. Furthermore, Ebrāhim Khalil opposed Qobbeh's aspirations, claiming sovereignty over Shirvān, Shakki, Tabriz, Khoi, and the Shāhsavan tribe. According to some stories, he hoped to rule all of Iran but was thwarted by the rise of the Qājārs. To this is attributed his determined hostility toward that dynasty's designs on the eastern Caucasus.[4]

Āqā Mohammad wanted to add the Caucasian borderlands to the Iranian Empire he was trying to revive. His first campaign to the northwestern frontier, in 1791, was a largely successful effort directed at the lands south of the Aras and the Kura. In the course of the undertaking, his troops raided Tālesh and carried off much booty without enforcing Qājār suzerainty. A second campaign, in 1795, was aimed primarily at subduing the territories north of the two rivers, including Georgia. All of the principalities, except Georgia, Qarābāgh, and Tālesh, submitted, although some only did so after considerable fighting. Local political rivalries played a significant role in several khans' decisions. Baku looked to Āqā Mohammad for support against Shirvān and Qobbeh. Ganjeh hoped not only for protection but also for gains at Georgia's expense to make up for the losses suffered during the 1780s. Therefore, the Ganjevis actively welcomed Āqā Mohammad and participated in his attack on Georgia. In Shakki, a contender in the long-standing dynastic feud turned the 1795 campaign to his own advantage by obtaining Āqā Mohammad's support for a coup d'état.

Qobbeh's motives are less clear, but the ruling dynasty had traditionally allied itself with strong Iranian governments and Sheikh 'Ali Khan had recently been involved in some commercial disputes with the Russians. The khans of Yerevan and Shirvān resisted for a time but then submitted to superior military force. The allies Georgia and Qarābāgh refused to submit and particularly bloody warfare resulted. Faced with Qarābāghi opposition, Āqā Mohammad plundered the countryside and left part of his forces to besiege the capital, Shushā, while he proceeded to Georgia. After fierce fighting in an unequal contest, Āqā Mohammad entered Tbilisi, the capital, which his men plundered for nearly two weeks. The approach of winter signaled the end of the traditional campaigning season, so he left the region without fully consolidating his position there.

The 1975 campaign had a serious disruptive effect on various aspects of Caucasian life. One of the major results was the further depopulation of a region that was already underpopulated. In addition to battle casualties, there were wholesale massacres of anti-Qājār elements in Georgia and Qarābāgh. Many survivors in both principalities, soldiers as well as civilians, were carried off as slaves. An official Iranian source claimed that 500 Qarābāghi boys were enslaved. In Georgia, the losses were even greater, involving perhaps 10,000 to 15,000 women and children.[5] The number of people under the jurisdiction of established authorities was further reduced by the flight of sedentary farmers as well as nomads to remote areas, where they hoped to find shelter. This problem was particularly acute in Qarābāgh and Shirvān. The economic life of the principalities suffered as a result of the Qājār army living off the land, plundering herds of animals and objects of value, and destroying crops as a military tactic. Tbilisi and New Shemākhi, the capital of Shirvān, suffered especially severe damage from the Qājārs' scorched earth policy. Moreover, the Qājār army remained in the Caucasus during the harvest season and must have interfered with the gathering of crops and seeds for the next planting. All these setbacks came on top of an existing famine in Qarābāgh and Ganjeh, not to mention the raids, local wars, and outbreaks of plague that had caused so much suffering in the recent past.

None of the rulers of the eastern Caucasus survived 1795 unscathed. After years of pursuing their own aggrandizement and endeavoring to throw off any master, they were subjected to extreme pressure to acknowledge Āqā Mohammad as their suzerain. Those who attempted to resist did so at considerable cost. Those who submitted were burdened with tribute payments at a time when their revenue was reduced by the devastation of war. Although the khan of Shakki was the only ruler to be ousted, all had been given disquieting examples of their own vulnerability. This was the weakened, frightened condition in which the border rulers found themselves just as the struggle for control of the region reached a new level of intensity.

III

Russian Expansion
under Catherine the Great

Russia in the era of Catherine the Great expanded at a prodigious rate. In some ways, this was a unique achievement. No other European state of the late eighteenth century added 200,000 square miles to its territory. Russia was the newest of the major powers, still regarded as a barbaric parvenu by some western Europeans. However, the sheer magnitude of the territorial gains ought not to obscure the fact that Russian expansion was also a very normal process in terms both of the empire's own historical development and of the diplomatic attitudes of the time. Long before this period, expansion had become a habit of Muscovite statecraft. As Marc Raeff has observed, there was a very thin line between Moscow's gathering the Russian lands, the principalities that had once been part of the Kievan Federation, and the subjugation of alien people, especially since some of the other Russian lands had already established control over non-Russians. Techniques used in the gathering of Russian lands were later extended to non-Russian principalities.[1] The fundamental motives for Russian expansion from the gathering period on closely resembled those found elsewhere: the quest for protection against hostile neighbors; the need for more agricultural land; and the search for other natural resources, such as fur-bearing animals and minerals. Moreover, an eighteenth-century European statesman would not have felt that expansion needed any explanation. Expansion was good because it made states stronger. The Anglo-French rivalry in India; Prussia's drive to take Saxony and Bohemia in the Seven Years' War; and the partition of Poland among Austria, Prussia, and Russia all reflect the pervasive desire for territorial expansion during the second half of the eighteenth century. Henry Brougham, the publicist critic of slavery and the indiscriminate acquisition of colonies, expressed the prevailing sentiment when he wrote, "In the same manner as a state will naturally people up to its resources, it will naturally extend its dominions as far as those resources permit."[2] Russia differed from the other European powers in that it had greater opportunity for success because it was so much stronger than some of its immediate neighbors.

The existence of a "Greek project" might indicate the existence of a distinctly Russian messianic expansionism, but it is highly doubtful that Catherine ever meant the project as seriously as others thought she did. The tone of Catherine's reign was decidedly pragmatic, with little room for farfetched schemes like the expulsion of the Turks from Europe and the creation of a Greek kingdom with its capital at Constantinople. Her actions at many times during her reign indicated her ability to recognize when she could not proceed with her ambitious plans. She backed away from some of her boldest plans for reform when the Legislative Commission of 1767-1768 revealed the intensity of noble opposition. If she occasionally devised implausible panaceas, such as enlarging the middle class with specially trained orphans, she usually recognized when to abandon unsuccessful experiments. The "Greek project" was probably nothing more than an idea briefly entertained and quickly discarded.

In fact, the substance of the project was quite tenuous. It was based on a rather vague remark in a letter to the Habsburg emperor, Joseph II, referring to the possibility that, if Austria and Russia were to be successful in a war against the Porte, then the Turks might be driven from Europe. The rest of the evidence for the plan comes from the testimony of her secretary and political counselor Alexander Bezborodko and Gregory Potemkin, who was in charge of Russia's relations with the Porte and the development of southern Russia. However, the fact that two of the important members of Catherine's government were enthusiastic about the plan does not mean that she shared their feelings. Both these men had reasons of their own to favor a "Greek project" even when the tsaritsa did not. Potemkin was an extremely ambitious man who had risen from the lesser provincial gentry to become one of the most powerful men in Russia. He looked forward to becoming king of "Dacia," a country to be formed from the Ottoman Empire's Danubian provinces. Bezborodko was a Ukrainian who viewed the Turks as Russia's greatest enemy because of their repeated attacks on Russian and, especially, Ukrainian territory. Nonetheless, Catherine did not allow her advisers to dominate her. Potemkin would have preferred a more forward policy in the Caucasus as well as the Balkans, but in the former Catherine clearly restrained him. Bezborodko in his fragmentary memoirs expressed the opinion that Catherine was committed to the "Greek project," but that is clearly what he wanted to believe. Moreover, he used the account of the "Greek project" to show what an important role he played in Catherine's government.[3]

For all Catherine's professed concern over Christians living under Muslim rule, her actions in the Caucasus showed that she never allowed that issue to force her along a course that was not chosen first and foremost on the basis of Russia's best interests. She certainly did not care for the Greeks in their own right. In her opinion, they displayed an "innate tendency toward slavery and the utter frivolity of their character."[4] In any event, many of the Balkan Christians would become subjects of Austria, not Russia, if the Turks were expelled from Europe. That may reveal something about what Catherine meant by the project. It may well have been used by her to entice Joseph II into agreeing to the Austro-Russian alliance she so earnestly desired as a replacement for the discredited "Northern System." The naming of one of her grandsons Constantine and the occasional employment of Greek motifs do not in themselves prove anything. Apart from the fact that this was a Grecophile age in Europe, Catherine was a shrewd manipulator of public opinion, as her correspondence with various philosophes showed. Therefore, she may have used the pseudo-Greek panoply to keep people guessing about her intentions regarding the Porte without formally committing herself to anything. Whatever she really thought about the project, she never tried to put it into operation, not even in her next war with the Porte (1787-1792). Although international pressure toward the end of the war forced Russia to make peace on very moderate terms, even at the start of the war Russia's objectives had no direct relation to the expulsion of the Turks from Europe.[5]

While the significance of the "Greek project" has been exaggerated, there is a different sense in which Russian motives for expansion during this period were unlike those of other European countries. The distinctiveness lies in the ambition to acquire territory that would serve as the equivalent of the overseas colonies of western Europe. These colonies would enrich Russia and perhaps serve also as a badge of Russia's membership in the circle of great civilized powers. Of all the areas of Russian expansion during Catherine's reign, the one in which these considerations played an especially important role was

the eastern Caucasus. While hope of agricultural and commercial development was a factor in Russia's acquisition of the Crimea and the
north coast of the Black Sea, the primary concern was with the Turkish threat to Russian security. Siberia had been treated like a colony
ever since it was made part of the Russian Empire. Catherine once
made the telling remark that she considered it Russia's "India, Mexico, or Peru."[6] However, she did not pursue a very assertive policy in
this region. The same applies to the northwest coast of the Pacific
and trade with China even though she was interested in the economic
opportunities to be had in both places.

The initial motive for Catherine's involvement in the northern
marches of Iran was a traditional strategic one—the strengthening of
Russia's military position against the Ottoman Empire. In the early
1770s, during Catherine's first war with the Porte, the Russian army
used Georgia as a base of operations for attacks on Turkish strong-
holds in the western Caucasus. The Ottoman victory over the Russians in this campaign left Catherine wary of repeating the experiment.
In any event, the Pugachev Rebellion (1773-1774), the first partition
of Poland (1772), and the development of territory on the north coast
of the Black Sea acquired by the Treaty of Kuchuk Kainarja (1774)
preoccupied Catherine until the end of the decade. She still counted
the Muslim khanates of the eastern Caucasus among the shah's domains even though this was a time when political power in Iran was
fragmented and there was no shah. While she retained a general interest in the strategic uses of Georgia and adjoining territories, she studiously refrained from taking actions in the Caucasus that might provoke the Ottomans at the time of her second war against them (1787-
1792) or her 1796 Iranian campaign.

At the same time, the "colonialist" factor became increasingly important and led Catherine to an aggressive policy. Although there
were some commercial ties and a few diplomatic exchanges between
Russia and the Iranian borderlands in the Caucasus during Catherine's
reign, there were no steady communications and travel between the
two remained hazardous. There was no corps of marchwardens who
had known the inhabitants of the Iranian borderlands through generations of contact and had gradually extended Russian authority over
them, as happened elsewhere on the empire's eastern frontier. When
the Russian government turned its attention to northern Iran, it viewed
that area in light of the prevailing attitudes of the westernized Russian elite.

The Russian aristocracy of Catherine's reign was very different from
what it had been under Peter the Great, when a westernized life-style

was regarded with widespread loathing. By the second half of the eighteenth century, the westernization of the elite was an accomplished fact, whether it took the form of a superficial appropriation of status symbols or a deeper understanding of the intellectual heritage. Even those who yearned for the restoration of an idealized Muscovite past were themselves schooled in Western ways. Prince Michael Shcherbatov, the foremost reactionary of Catherine's reign, was fluent in French and wrote his first political treatise in that language. Most of the Russian elite favored not a rejection of the West but the recognition that their country had attained, or was capable of attaining in the near future, a level of achievement in the marshaling of human resources equal to that of the West. Russians were proud that St. Petersburg was, in their eyes, as impressive a city as any other European capital, that Russians produced artistic and scholarly works that met western standards, and that the empire had grown in size and military strength. One man who epitomized Russian intellectual accomplishments, the scientist-poet-historian Michael Lomonosov, viewed Russia's international achievements with pride and optimism. He determined that there were three criteria for a state's prosperity: internal peace, the defeat of enemies, and international commerce. He considered Russia to be extremely successful in the first two categories but behind western Europe in the last because of its lack of a navy prior to the reign of Peter the Great. Significantly, Lomonosov credited Peter's military reforms with establishing Russia as a great power and in so doing proving that Russia was not a colony of western Europe. The remaining task was to develop Russia's trade with Asia and thereby bring success in the third component of national well-being. His specific plan called for trade with China, Japan, India, and North America by a sea route across the Arctic and Pacific and the colonization of parts of the north Asian coast. One indication of Lomonosov's admiration for Western imperialism can be seen in his argument for the feasibility of his plan on the grounds that the British coped with similar difficulties in their trade with Hudson's Bay.[7]

There was good reason for the Russian elite to be interested in western Europe's overseas empires. Contemporary international developments and some of the most influential literature of the Enlightenment focused attention on colonial affairs. In the second half of the eighteenth century, Britain won victories in India over the French and Dutch as well as several Indian princes and established a dominant position in Bengal. The financial and administrative difficulties of the British East India Company and the loss of the thirteen North American colonies do not seem to have raised doubts in

Russian minds about the advisability of acquiring colonies in Asia. The prevailing wisdom asserted that colonies had made western Europe rich. That was certainly the lesson to be drawn from the treatise Catherine called her prayer book, Montesquieu's *The Spirit of the Laws.*[8] From the opening of book XXI, his discussion of commerce, the significance of trade with India was highlighted as a source of riches to those who conducted the trade. He regarded the commerce between Rome and India via Central Asia, the Caspian, and the Caucasus as beneficial to both parties, except for the degree to which it caused a drain on Rome's supply of precious metals. That need not have worried Catherine unduly, given her optimism that Siberia would be Russia's Mexico and Peru. He ascribed the decline of that trade to the shift in the course of the Oxus so that it no longer flowed into the Caspian and, more important, to the destructive impact of the Tatars. He went on to show that intermediaries in Europe's trade with India—Egypt and several Western countries with East India Companies—also prospered by that trade.

Russian imperialists could also draw encouragement from the most influential work on imperialism of the age, *Histoire philosophique et politique des établissemens et du commerce des Européens dans les deux Indes* by the Abbé Raynal and a number of other unnamed collaborators. The authors were basically opposed to colonies as artificial creations that often did not deliver the hoped for economic gains and frequently oppressed colonial inhabitants. Yet the authors occasionally revealed enthusiasm for the benefits of trade with Asia even when accompanied by colonialism. Raynal and his collaborators lauded the great widening of horizons caused by the interchange of goods and ideas between Europe and the outside world. This trade as well as the acquisition of territory had the authors' approval as long as the goods involved were useful items, such as spices, as opposed to sterile luxuries, such as tea. The right kind of trade was considered the source of great wealth for wise colonialists. For example, reforms of the British East India Company during the early 1770s had strengthened it greatly so that it could bring in immense profits at small cost to the mother country.[9] The authors' discussion of Russia's potential role in East-West trade constituted a brief for imperial expansion. Before the anarchic eighteenth century, Iran's Caucasian and Caspian provinces had played an important role in international trade as producers of silk and as transit points for Indian goods, some of which still reached Russia by an alternate route across Central Asia. There had also been a strong market for European goods in Iran, according to the authors. Peter the Great understood the significance of all this and, "guided by his genius," conquered part of the Caspian coast. There were still some obstacles to the realization of Peter's admirable goal of increased trade with Iran and India, particularly the misgovernment of Iran and Russia's unstable and tyrannical political system. However, Raynal believed Catherine was on the way to remedying Russia's problems.[10]

The tsaritsa had a low opinion of Raynal, who was a vehement critic of absolute monarchy, but she certainly knew his work. The *Histoire* was a *succès de scandale*, having been put on the Catholic Church's Index of condemned books and publicly burned in Paris. It was increasingly popular among the Russian elite from 1780 on, especially after 1789. Catherine knew enough of Raynal to recognize his influence on Alexander Radischchev's revolutionary *Journey from St. Petersburg to Moscow*. However much she disliked his republicanism, she held views much like his on the matter of Russian trade and expansion in Asia. She also devised her own solution to Iran's problems by advocating Russian tutelage of Iranian vassals and, later, direct rule of at least part of that country.

St. Petersburg's knowledge of Iranian affairs from sources other than Enlightenment theorists was limited and often inaccurate. For example, Platon Zubov, Catherine's favorite in her last years and a self-proclaimed expert on Iran, thought that the Iranian New Year's Day, *No Ruz*, was May 14 although in reality it falls on the vernal equinox.[11] As a voracious reader who took the responsibilities of her office seriously, Catherine made herself better informed about western Asia than many of her advisers were. She knew about the major events and personalities of eighteenth-century Iran, but, like the other St. Petersburg officials, she had to make policy decisions hampered by a dearth of reliable, detailed information.[12] Even in the early nineteenth century, when Russia had already added parts of the eastern Caucasus to its domains, several members of the Academy of Sciences expressed concern over the inadequacy of literature on that region available in St. Petersburg. A few important books on the eastern Caucasus and other parts of the Iranian Empire could be found in individual libraries, but it is difficult to judge who actually read them. The best work on Iran known to have been available in St. Petersburg was the Huguenot traveler Jean Chardin's massive study of Safavi Iran, *Voyages du Chevalier Chardin en Perse, et autres lieux de l'Orient*, first published in London in 1686. For information on the closing years of the Safavi era, there was a Russian translation of the account of John Bell, an Englishman who accompanied the 1717 Volynskii mission to the court of Shāh Soltān Hosein. The middle decades of the eighteenth century were covered by two anonymous and subsequently forgotten French works. Travel accounts of two German naturalists, Gmelin and Güldenstädt, were also published in Russia, although Güldenstädt's work was published posthumously and suffered from many inaccuracies.[13]

Russia's leaders relied less on books than on the information provided by contemporaries who had some direct contact with the provinces in which Russia was interested. Russian officials, such as General Ivan Gudovich of the Caucasian Line (who thought the differences between Sunni and Shii Islam were minor) or semiofficial agents, such as the adventurer Reineggs (who urged Potemkin to conquer the Caucasus) were unperceptive observers who reported their illusions with firm conviction. Armenians and Georgians were more knowledgable, of course, but their communications with the Russian authorities were often colored by the hope of obtaining aid from that country that would strengthen the position of Caucasian Christendom.

One of the Caucasians who was most active in counseling the Russians was an Armenian archbishop, Joseph Argutinskii-Dolgorukov, who lived in Russia. He was a fervent advocate of the Russian takeover of his homeland and argued that the security of the proposed Christian protectorate in that quarter necessitated the acquisition of all the khanates north of the Aras River, even those with few Christian inhabitants. This was a point of view Catherine and Potemkin shared, although with all the archbishop's advice it is difficult to tell how much he guided official opinion and how much he confirmed opinions arrived at by other means. Catherine and Potemkin both relied on him in a host of ways when major undertakings in the eastern Caucasus were planned. Potemkin ordered the publication of the archbishop's history of Russo-Armenian relations during the reign of Peter the Great.[14] The archbishop had the only Armenian and Persian type fonts anywhere in Russia at his Astrakhan press. Therefore, Catherine had him print her manifesto announcing the 1796 campaign to the Caucasian and Iranian peoples. He accompanied the campaign, vociferously proclaiming Russia's intent to deliver the Armenians from Muslim rule and serving as hostage for the safe return of a khan who went to negotiate at the Russian camp. When the head of the Armenian Church, the Catholicos of Echmiadzin, died in 1799, Russia obtained the office for Argutinskii Dolgorukov, who held it until his death in 1801.

King Erekle of Georgia also influenced Russian policy. From the 1770s on, he urged Catherine to take control of all of the territory between Georgia and the Caspian and argued that Muslims as well as

Christians earnestly desired to be ruled by Russia. When in the 1780s Russia had the opportunity to negotiate an agreement with a Zand pretender who controlled much of central Iran, Erekle's advice led the Russians to ask for the cession of the northwestern and Caspian provinces as a condition for supporting the pretender's claims elsewhere. Erekle also used his role as adviser to direct personal advantage, as when he convinced Russian authorities to support his claim of suzerainty over the neighboring khanates of Yerevan and Ganjeh. In this case, his success proved disadvantageous for Russia because it increased the reluctance of several khans to cooperate with that country.

The Russians' concern over the well-being of their fellow Christians in the eastern Caucasus played an important but extremely limited role in shaping St. Petersburg's policy toward that region. Caucasian Christians provided information about an unfamiliar area, and the Russians hoped to use Georgians and especially Armenians, with their legendary commercial prowess, to increase Russia's trade with Iran and India. However, in the implementation of the policy, Russia acted for motives based on its own interests and only coincidentally on those of the Caucasian Christians. Catherine did not make the takeover of the eastern Caucasus a high priority until 1795, when Āqā Mohammad's attack on that region cast doubt on the value of the protection Russia had guaranteed Georgia by treaty in 1783. When the tsaritsa sent an army to take control of the region, she proclaimed herself the liberator of Muslims as well as Christians. She intended leave in power those Muslim rulers who welcomed the Russian presence, which she expected to be the overwhelming majority. Even though the khanate of Qarābāgh had a sizable Armenian minority, Catherine praised its khan and ordered that his position be strengthened in light of his determined opposition to the Qājār attack. No troops were to be sent to Yerevan, despite its religious and historic importance to Armenians, for fear that such action so near the Ottoman border would provoke a declaration of war by the Porte. Even Ganjeh, for all its hostility toward Georgia, was left untouched because the khan submitted voluntarily. As Valerian Zubov, the commander of the 1796 expedition, remarked to one of his subordinates, it was necessary "to put off until the proper time" the liberation of Caucasian Christians.[15]

Catherine was not under any pressure to justify her secular, pragmatic approach toward foreign Christians to the Russian Orthodox Church because it was politically and spiritually weak at the time.

The patriarchate had been abolished by Peter the Great and replaced be a secular directorate, the Holy Synod, which administered the Church as a branch of state. In the first year of her reign, Catherine confiscated the property of the Orthodox monasteries. If she could strike with impunity directly at the power of the Church, she certainly did not have to answer to the Church about her attitude toward Georgians and Armenians. Even when the Church had been stronger, it traditionally emphasized the need to protect Russian Orthodoxy from foreign contamination rather than advocating increased contact of any sort with foreign Christendom. Among the many causes of the seventeenth-century schism in Russian Orthodoxy was the hostility toward Patriarch Nikon's attempt to make the Russian Church more like the Greek, which was judged heretical by many Russians.

One interested group that had no influence on the formulation of Russian policy toward Iran was the Russian middle class, specifically the merchants. There was no powerful lobby of Russian merchants involved in trade with Iran. That trade remained disappointingly small throughout the eighteenth century. Most of the business was not in the hands of Russians but of Armenians and to a lesser degree Iranians, Indians, and others. Russian merchants who did business in the Caspian region were more commonly involved in fishing and seal hunting than in trade with Iran. During the eighteenth century, St. Petersburg made repeated efforts to improve trade with Iran, but that did not necessarily mean favoring Russian merchants. During the 1750s, Elizabeth tried twice to set up chartered trading companies to deal with Iran. Some Russian merchants favored this but others, including one of those most active in the Caspian trade, were vehemently opposed. Neither company did well, and Elizabeth authorized others to trade with Iran in competition with the chartered companies. Among those who were allowed to enter into this trade were people of noble rather than merchant status like the courtier Lieutenant-General Roman Vorontsov. When Catherine, a firm believer in the advantages of free trade, came to the throne, she proclaimed that that principle should apply in dealings with Iran, thereby abolishing the chartered companies. This was counter to the interests of one of the wealthiest merchants in Moscow, a leading member of Elizabeth's Persian Trading Company. Catherine subsequently reversed attempts by the governor of Astrakhan to bar Armenians from building boats for the Caspian trade. She also rejected the advice of a commission set up to study trade with Iran that she establish a monopoly trading company. In any case, the commission had not intended to protect Russian merchants by the formation of such a company but rather wanted it to be open to anyone who wished to join.[16]

Catherine hoped that increased Russian involvement in Iran's northern marches would benefit all concerned. To the inhabitants of these provinces, Russia would offer the advantages of an enlightened state of laws. She believed this would be a marked advance over what she perceived as a cycle of usurpation, tyranny, and civil war in post-Safavi Iran. She was confident that the "example of this country's gentle proprietorship" would make the inhabitants of the region seek Russian overlordship.[17] The tsaritsa believed that Iran sorely needed the benevolent rule she offered. Like Raynal, she considered Iran a potentially wealthy country that had suffered from the depredations of "the greedy plunderers," such as Āqā Mohammad, who ruled it.[18] His brutal misrule and interference with Russian commerce had to be ended. Russia would then ensure stable government and personal security; the revival of commerce and prosperity would follow. That would provide Russia with a golden opportunity to become the new master of Europe's Asian trade. As Catherine explained to General Valerian Zubov (Platon's younger brother), whom she sent to establish Russian hegemony over Iran in 1796:

The establishment of peace and order in Persia will open to us rich markets not only along the shores of the Caspian Sea but within the borders of the Persian provinces. By means of the latter it would be easily possible to open the routes to India and, attracting this very rich commerce toward us by much shorter routes than those which all the European nations follow, going around the Cape of Good Hope, it will be possible to turn to our benefit all the advantages being obtained by the Europeans.[19]

Such hopes were widely shared among the Russian elite. Naturally the Zubov brothers' expectations about Russia's commercial prospects resembled Catherine's. There was widespread enthusiasm among the St. Petersburg aristocracy for the 1796 expedition and the economic gains that were expected to follow. Gabriel Derzhavin, the leading Russian poet of the age, expressed the prevailing mood in a poem celebrating Valerian Zubov's capture of Derbent. He compared the victory to the triumph of Alexander the Great over Darius and added:

Oh happiness! See already thronging to us
Elephants, laden with riches,
Covered with carpets from India!
Throngs of people!
Silver and gold flow like beneficient rain from heaven![20]

Despite Russian optimism, prospects for the rapid improvement of that country's trade with Iran and India were not very encouraging even before Catherine complicated the situation by sending 30,000 men to conquer Iran. The difficulties were many, ranging from political miscalculations and the insufficient development of a commercial infrastructure to a host of geographical obstacles.

The first problem was that Russia had to compete against well-established western European trading companies that did business in India and the Persian Gulf. By the late eighteenth century, Russia even imported Iranian silk from London.[21] Catherine's initial efforts to compete with the European East India companies hinged on establishing a major commercial center on the southern coast of the Caspian. (There were already a few Russian merchants living in small, unfortified settlements on the coast, at Anzali in Gilān and Mashhad-e Sar in Māzandarān.) She hoped that eventually the eastern Caucasus could also be used for the same purpose, but the danger of war with the Ottoman Empire over the annexation of the Crimea in 1783 forced her to postpone expansion in that area. (By the end of her reign, the situation had reversed. The power of the Qājārs proved greater than the Russians had expected, so the focus of Russian expansionism shifted from the south coast of the Caspian, which was subject to the Qājār shah, to the eastern Caucasus, where political hegemony was still hotly contested.) She made two attempts to attain her objective. Both failed, but the reasons for the failures were important because they were related to the worsening of relations with Āqā Mohammad Khān Qājār and because Russian mistakes on these two occasions were symptomatic of basic problems in that country's attitude toward Muslims in the Iranian Empire.

The first attempt to set up a Russian trading "factory" was directed toward the southeastern corner of the Caspian in the vicinity of Astarābād Bay in 1781. That area was attractive because the Russians thought it was fairly near India. (As it happened, they underestimated the distance from there to the Indus by more than half.) The leader of the expedition, Count Voinovich, soon encountered opposition from Āqā Mohammad, then a local princeling. The khan mistrusted the Russians. He had heard rumors that the expedition was really directed against him, which the Russian construction of a large fort seemed to confirm. Voinovich attempted to win the khan's cooperation through intimidation, which only made matters worse. Finally, Āqā Mohammad made the Russians his prisoners until they agreed to return to Russia which they did in 1782. Catherine regarded the khan's actions in the affair as an offense for which he deserved punishment.

Russia next had the opportunity to recoup its losses on the south-western coast of the Caspian. The ruler of Gilān, Hedāyatollāh, was a rival of Āqā Mohammad's. When the latter attempted the conquest of Gilān in 1785, Hedāyatollāh asked for Russian help. However, Russia, as it would often do in the future, required compliance with extensive demands before it would protect a khan. In this case, the most provocative demand was for the cession of the port city of An-zali. The Russians' actions convinced Hedāyatollāh that they were as much a threat as the Qājārs. When the expected attack from the lat-ter did not materialize, Hedāyatollāh lost all interest in becoming a Russian vassal. At this point, another phenomenon reoccurred: con-trol of affairs slipped out of the hands of higher officials. The consul in Anzali (Skilichii), with the aid of his predecessor (Tumanovskii), conspired to bring Gilān under Russian suzerainty and destroy Hed-āyatollāh. Skilichii considered Hedāyatollāh a typical Iranian, "inso-lent and uncouth; he does not understand gentleness and has grown arrogant because until now he has not been punished."[22] The consul and former consul encouraged Āqā Mohammad to conquer Gilān in 1786 and gave him Russian weapons to facilitate his conquest of the province. The besieged Hedāyatollāh eventually became sufficiently desperate to agree to all Russia's demands of the preceding year but could obtain no help from Skilichii and Tumanovskii except the of-fer of asylum after his defeat. When Hedāyatollāh took refuge on a Russian ship, the Russians turned him over to another local ruler, a long-time enemy, who killed him. Gregory Potemkin was displeased with the officials' actions in Gilān when he first learned of these de-velopments. However, the consul and former consul soon persuaded Potemkin to accept their grossly distorted account of events. Their account portrayed Hedāyatollāh as a treacherous enemy of Russia; they did not disclose their own provocations. As was often the case in Russia's dealings with Iran, preconceived notions of Asiatic barbarism and the dearth of alternate sources of information meant that higher ranking officials lacked the inclination or the means to scrutinize their subordinates' reports.

While Āqā Mohammad's power was on the rise in the parts of Iran in which Russia was interested, Russian officials repeatedly missed the opportunity to improve relations with him. During the 1780s he still had many rivals to defeat before he could claim the throne of Iran. Russian cooperation could have been an asset; Russian hostility, yet another obstacle. The year after he expelled Voinovich, he sent an ambassador to St. Petersburg with a message of good will. Cather-ine refused to receive the ambassador, stating that she did not regard

Āqā Mohammad as the legitimate ruler of Gilān and Māzandarān and warned that his actions put him in danger of her "stern punishment."[23] Nonetheless, when Skilichii and Tumanovskii urged Āqā Mohammad to conquer Gilān, he agreed and voiced his desire for good relations with Russia. Then, when the khan and the consuls had realized their objective, the burgeoning cooperation broke down. Āqā Mohammad was a man of far different mettle and ambition from Hedāyatollāh or the other khans who tried to make an agreement with Russia. Āqā Mohammad's communications with Russia reveal that he perceived cooperation with that country in terms of an alliance between two sovereigns rather than the submission of a vassal to his suzerain. He favored the growth of Russo-Iranian trade, but he suspected that Russia was not content with unimpeded commerce and planned to restrict his political authority. The most conspicuous symbol of that threat was the Russian intention to build forts inside his realm, especially near Astarābād and at Anzali. The possibility of his reaching an accord with the Russians was further reduced by Tumanovskii's greed. The ex-consul demanded a large bribe for his help in the conquest of Gilān but was turned down by Āqā Mohammad, who was annoyed that the two Russian agents had already seized Hedāyatollāh's treasures and refused to share the spoils of victory. A last attempt in 1787 to reach an agreement failed under obscure circumstances. Thereafter, Russia dealt with the khan's rebel brother, Mortezā Qoli, whom it intended to install on the Iranian throne as the tsaritsa's vassal. Catherine delayed putting this plan into operation until the 1796 campaign, which failed to achieve most of its objectives. The most noticeable result of Russia's endorsement of Mortezā Qoli's pretensions was the further estrangement of Āqā Mohammad, who ordered in reprisal that the small Russian settlement in Anzali be blockaded. This disrupted Russian commerce and caused considerable hardship for the isolated community.

Russo-Iranian commerce faced a host of other obstacles that would have been difficult to overcome even if political relations between the two countries had been better. Travel between the two had to be conducted by boat across the Caspian because the formidable barrier of the high Caucasus and the danger of attack made the overland passage of merchant caravans impossible. The sea route was not a great improvement. The violent storms to which the Caspian is subject made shipwrecks a real hazard for those who sailed it. Few points along the southern or western coasts offered a safe harbor. Anzali, the most important commercial center on the south coast, had no harbor at all. Ships had to anchor several miles offshore in open waters.

Russia's merchant fleet on the Caspian was barely adequate. The ships were too few and too small to sustain more than a light volume of traffic. Most were designed so that they could only travel with the wind. Many had flat bottoms, which aided passage through shallow coastal waters at the cost of decreased maneuverability. The crews were usually men of few nautical skills. For all the shortcomings of the Russian merchant marine, it played a central role in the trans-Caspian trade. The alternative was the Iranian merchant craft, the *karaji* (called *kirzhim* by the Russians). It was a small, flat-bottomed vessel sheltered only by bundles of branches along its sides. A sack of stones did duty as the anchor. The *karaji* was used more for fishing and local coastal travel than for the main commercial routes. The few Russians who did journey to Anzali found its hot, humid climate and its swamp-bred diseases to be at least as great a menace as the political instability.

Russia exported to Iran iron and steel, a variety of textiles, dyes, and perfumes, as well as goods from western Europe, including British and Dutch textiles and sugar from the British West Indies. The most important of Iran's exports was Gilāni silk. Its other exports included cotton, rice, fruits, spices, and opium. In light of the many difficulties, it is not surprising that the volume of Russo-Iranian trade was quite small. Attempts to stimulate it by establishing chartered companies modeled after the East India companies or by abolishing them were of no avail.

All of this would make it seem as though the only people who could believe in the practicability of Russia's ambition to rival the British East India Company were those who knew very little about Asia. Yet the French agent G. A. Oliver, who traveled across the Levant and reached Iran about the time of Catherine's 1796 expedition, viewed Russia's commercial opportunities in the same light as the tsaritsa. He, too, was convinced that, if Russia could secure its turbulent southeastern marches, then it would in all probability succeed in replacing Britain as the purveyor of Indian luxuries to Europe.[24]

Although the drive to emulate the great empires of western Europe provided the theoretical underpinning of Russian expansionism, that consideration was not the sole determinant of Russia's policy toward the lands to the southeast. Paralleling but only occasionally coinciding with the theory was an ad hoc approach in which Russia rarely took the initiative but instead reacted to the changing political alignments in a disunited Iran. Most of Russia's actions in these episodes did not produce the desired results, but they had a long-term significance anyway. These occasional engagements influenced officials' ideas about which local rulers would make cooperative vassals and which were enemies. This became important as the seriousness of Russian involvement in Iran's northwestern marches increased. In return, local rulers formed their own impressions of Russia, some perceiving it as a threat, others as a support in local rivalries.

While Russia was never truly enthusiastic about dealing with Āqā Mohammad Khān Qājār, nor he with them, there were other local rulers who were as eager as the tsaritsa to reach an accord. After Russia's first contact with Āqā Mohammad ended with mutual recriminations, Russia turned its attention to the Qājār leader's principal rival, 'Ali Morād Khān Zand, who was interested in using Russian aid to increase his domains. From his capital in Esfahān, he ruled over much of central and southern Iran. In 1784, he negotiated with Russia about the possibility of yielding the Caspian and northwestern provinces in return for Russian recognition of his claim to the rest of Iran. He did not control the northern provinces anyway and would rid himself of the Qājār stronghold on the southeastern Caspian coast by ceding this territory. Russia in turn would obtain rights to the parts of Iran it most wanted and hoped furthermore to convince 'Ali Morād to join forces against the Ottoman Empire. The Zand leader began to have second thoughts as the negotiations continued; when he died in 1785, the projected alliance had come to nought.

Negotiations with another local ruler were more successful in the sense that an agreement was concluded, although it is arguable that, ultimately, neither side derived what it had expected from that agreement. King Erekle of Georgia was eager to obtain Russian protection and, through his own persistence, eventually obtained a treaty to guarantee it. During Catherine's first war with the Ottoman Empire, Erekle asked to be taken under the tsaritsa's protection. She took a skeptical view of his request, determining that the advantages of such an arrangement would be lopsidedly in Erekle's favor. Her attitude changed during the early 1780s when she became interested in expansion in the Iranian marches. Then Erekle's renewed entreaties were favorably received. He asked for Russian protection and recognition of his authority, with Russian backing for his chosen heir against the many expected rivals. Gregory Potemkin, who supervised the Russian side of the negotiations, found Erekle's terms acceptable and the Treaty of Georgievsk was signed in 1783.

Erekle encouraged his neighbor and ally Ebrāhim Khalil, the khan of Qarābāgh, to follow suit and offer his own submission to Russia. The khan had mixed feelings, perceiving the recent establishment of a Russian garrison in Georgia as a potential menace, but in the end he decided it was more prudent to try to ingratiate himself with Russian authorities. This time the negotiations failed. The reason for the failure lay once again in the Russians' fundamental biases. The problem reemerged many times as Russia took control of the eastern Caucasus. Many Caucasian Muslims perceived the bias and became increasingly mistrustful of Russia's proclaimed benevolence. However, the Russians did not understand the nature of the problem and viewed the Muslims' uncooperativeness as contumely. In the case of Qarābāgh, the specific problem was that the Russian negotiator gave the impression that he would as soon have conquered the khanate as negotiate its submission. In fact, that is exactly what Prince Potemkin and his grandnephew Paul, who as commander of Russian forces in the northern Caucasus communicated directly with Ebrāhim Khalil, really wanted. When the khan tried to begin negotiations, he found that the Russians treated him very differently from King Erekle. In the khan's case, no genuine negotiations would be allowed; he had to submit unconditionally and accept whatever terms Russia imposed. Moreover, Paul Potemkin made clear he would take Erekle's side in any dispute with Ebrāhim Khalil and at the same time communicated with Qarābāgh's Armenian inhabitants behind the khan's back. When Ebrāhim Khalil sought some reassurance that Russia's interest was not hostile, the younger Potemkin rebuffed him, threatening to conquer Qarābāgh unless the khan submitted immediately. No military action was taken since Catherine opposed it, and Ebrāhim Khalil kept trying to initiate negotiations. His last letter to Paul Potemkin was sent in 1784, and he received no reply.[25]

There was no Russian military activity in the eastern Caucasus at that time or for the next decade, because Catherine did not give her ambitions in that part of Asia a sufficiently high priority to justify diverting resources from more urgent problems. In fact, when she finally did order the conquest of Iran, she was once again reacting to an outside stimulus rather than taking the initiative to realize her long-range goals. That stimulus was the devastating attack on Georgia by Āqā Mohammad Khān. When Catherine learned of the sack of Tbilisi, she was outraged. Āqā Mohammad had dealt a blow to Russia as well as to Georgia. The tsaritsa had thought that no Iranian prince was strong enough to oppose her expansionist ambitions, but Āqā Mohammad had brought great suffering to many Caucasians and had made a mockery of Russia's promises to protect Georgia. Moreover, the Qājār chief had to be destroyed because he was a "long-time, open, wicked enemy of Russia" who might yet pose a direct threat, perhaps by spurring the tribes of the high Caucasus to attack Russian positions north of the mountains. In all of these protestations of righteous wrath, Catherine never mentioned that Russia had not lived up to its commitment to Georgia. Once again the problem lay in the unwise decision of an official in the field and St. Petersburg's inability to control such officials. The man most responsible for the failure to aid Georgia was General Ivan Gudovich, the commander of the Caucasian Line (Russia's forts in the northern Caucasus). King Erekle had begun to warn him of the likelihood of a Qājār attack as early as the spring of 1795, but the general dismissed the request for help as alarmist and predicted that an alliance between Erekle and his neighbors would prevent Āqā Mohammad from reaching Georgia. There were many flaws in Gudovich's argument, not the least being that the small forces Erekle and his neighbors could muster were no match for Āqā Mohammad's 60,000-man army. There was a kind of peevishness about the way Gudovich exercised power. Unlike most of the officers who served in the Caucasus (who sought opportunities to stage daring operations even when St. Petersburg advised restraint), Gudovich's principal ambition seems to have been to hoard his resources and do nothing. In 1793, Catherine had given him blanket authorization to use Russian troops to defend Georgia, but, on the eve of Āqā Mohammad's entry into Tbilisi, Gudovich still insisted he could do nothing unless Catherine ordered it specifically. He displayed a similar attitude the following year when he sent insufficient reinforcements from the Caucasian Line to the Zubov expedition only after much delay.[26]

When Gudovich heard about the sack of Tbilisi, he informed Catherine that such action was the equivalent of a direct attack on Russia and recommended as a countermeasure a campaign against Āqā Mohammad. Catherine liked the idea and, with the aid of Platon Zubov, made preparations for such an undertaking. However, she chose to entrust its command to an officer of greater prestige than Gudovich. Zubov and the Armenian archbishop Joseph Argutinskii-Dolgorukov recommended General-in-Chief Suvorov, whose reputation had recently been enhanced by his suppression of the Polish uprising of 1794. Suvorov was unimpressed and rejected the offer. Therefore, Catherine gave the command to Platon Zubov's twenty-five-year-old brother, Valerian.

High hopes prevailed when the campaign began in 1796. According to various estimates, Catherine allocated millions of rubles to it from a near-empty treasury, thousands of cavalry horses and pack animals, and between 10,000 and 30,000 soldiers.[27] Catherine ordered the younger Zubov to obtain the submission of the east Caucasian khans, overthrow Āqā Mohammad, and enthrone the latter's brother Morte-zā Qoli, who had been kept in Russia for such an occasion. Valerian Zubov predicted he would reach Esfahān by September. In fact, he never came close to that city, nor did he jeopardize Āqā Mohammad's position south of the Aras; but he did obtain the nominal submission of most of the east Caucasian khanates and in so doing justified, in Russian eyes, the conquest of those territories a few years later. The problems of the Zubov expedition reappeared during the later conquest, but the commander's methods were surprisingly moderate when compared with those of his successors.

Valerian Zubov did not attempt to transform the political systems in the eastern Caucasus. Any khan who was willing to become a Russian vassal was left in power; only those who offered violent opposition were dealt with by military means. In this way, Zubov obtained the submission of all the khans, except Mohammad of Yerevan. Even when Zubov discovered a conspiracy among three khans to assassinate him, he was not provoked. Instead, he gave them a chance to back down. Two, the khans of Qarābāgh and Shakki, submitted, and the conspiracy was forgotten. The third, the khan of Shirvān, decided to fight; when he took shelter in a mountain stronghold, Zubov seized his capital. The only other khan who was deposed was Sheikh 'Ali of Derbent-Qobbeh, who also refused to submit. Although the siege of the city of Derbent lasted about two months, the pressures were mostly on the defenders' morale. There were no heavy casualties associated with this battle. In both cases in which Zubov deposed local rulers, he chose their successors from the rulers' families. No attack was launched against Mohammad Khān of Yerevan, although he continued to reject Zubov's overtures. The expedition lacked the military resources to stage such an attack, which had, in any case, been forbidden by Catherine, who did not want to risk troop movements so near the Ottoman border.

Zubov, like his successors, never understood why the khans submitted to Russia or opposed it. To Zubov, the issue was simple: he was offering benevolent enlightenment as an alternative to Oriental despotism. For the khans, the issue was much more complex. Basically, all the khans would have preferred not to submit to any outside power. The khans of Yerevan, Qarābāgh, and Shirvān all tried to oppose Āqā Mohammad in 1795 and Zubov the following year. The khans' military strength determined the range of options open to them. For example, Javād Khān of Ganjeh, who had welcomed Āqā Mohammad's arrival in the Caucasus in 1795, realized that he had no hope of resisting the Russians when Āqā Mohammad was far away in Khorāsān. Therefore, he submitted to the Russians. In addition, many khans did not see Russia as a benefactor. Above all, they feared that Zubov intended to overthrow them and persecute Islam while favoring the Armenians. It is not surprising that they suspected this when Zubov did oust the first khan he encountered, Sheikh 'Ali, and demanded that Russian garrisons be allowed into the citadels of the various capital cities at the same time. Archbishop Argutinskii-Dolgorukov did his best to offend Derbenti Muslims.

The Zubov campaign had little impact on the Caucasians in the short run. The Russian occupation lasted less than a year, in some places only a few months; in other places there were no Russian garrisons at all. It brought few changes except when one member of a ruling family was substituted for another. The sedentary inhabitants had little opportunity to voice their preferences and, living unarmed in walled settlements at the mercy of Russian artillery, could not risk an armed contest with the Russians. Some peasants in Qobbeh fled to the forests and mountains, from which they staged guerrilla raids. More opposition came from nomadic tribal cavalry living in the mountains of Derbent, Shirvān, and Shakki. When Āqā Mohammad returned to the Caucasus in 1797, all the khans, except Ebrāhim Khalil of Qarābāgh and Salim of Shakki, submitted to him. The Qarābāghis overthrew their khan and submitted to the Qājār ruler. Salim had obtained power two years earlier by persuading Āqā Mohammad to oust the current khan of Shakki. Āqā Mohammad learned later that he had been tricked by false evidence and in 1797 reinstated the man he had ousted.

The Russians themselves, not the khans, were their own worst enemies in 1796. The combination of inadequate information and terrible planning made it harder for Valerian Zubov to accomplish his objectives. Only luck saved him from any major calamities. The years of warfare, famine, and disease in the region; the miscarriage of several anti-Russian plans; the failure of the Ottomans to capitalize on the situation; and the preoccupation of Āqā Mohammad in Khorāsān made it possible for the Russians to have some success in spite of their mistakes. Like many of the campaigns of the Russo-Iranian War a decade later, Zubov's triumphs only narrowly escaped being disasters. The expedition had too few troops to garrison even a small fraction of the projected area of operation. The further Zubov advanced, the more troops he had to assign to protect the rear. Even though there were recent published descriptions of the eastern Caucasus, Zubov was not prepared for the terrain he encountered. The narrow mountain roads, the swift-flowing streams, the dense forests, and the coastal desert around Baku all put the Russians at a disadvantage. They moved much more slowly than they had expected they would; the cavalry could not operate; and the supply-laden carts had to be left behind at Derbent. The supply problem was magnified by the fact that the deliveries to the expedition were in a shambles. The officials in St. Petersburg who should have organized supply delivery did nothing.[28] The delivery of such emergency supplies as could be gathered was impeded by the difficulty of the terrain, the shortage of pack animals, and the small size of Russia's Caspian fleet (even when it was supplemented by merchant ships, the fleet was inadequate). Gudovich's obstructionism added to the problem, and Zubov's excessive optimism made matters still worse. Although in most cases he observed the guidelines set by Catherine, Zubov disobeyed her when he selected his main supply delivery point. Catherine wanted Baku, but Zubov was so confident that he would sweep quickly through the Caucasus and proceed to the Iranian plateau that he had most of the supplies that could be gathered sent to an island further south off the Tālesh coast. Therefore, most of the supplies were beyond his reach. The use of local fruits to make up for the shortage of expected rations made many of the soldiers ill.

In the end, all the miscalculations and difficulties left Zubov in a strategically weak position, with his forces strung out along the edge of the battle zone from Derbent to the confluence of the Aras and the Kura. The second branch of the Russian forces was split between Georgia, which was too exhausted by the 1795 attack and too disunified by internal hostilities to be capable of defending itself, and Ganjeh, which was of doubtful loyalty to Russia. For want of ships and men, Zubov was not able to make a diversionary attack on Gilān as he had intended. He also relied on the cooperation of the khans who had submitted to Russia but whose desire as well as their ability to fight the shah was questionable. Zubov was saved from a confrontation with Āqā Mohammad by his benefactress's death on November 17. Paul, the new tsar, halted the expedition the day after Catherine's death. Russian troops were out of the Caucasus by the spring of 1797, weeks before Āqā Mohammad's return.

Russian expansionists drew several important lessons from Catherine's involvement in Iranian affairs. The first was that such involvement was desireable. Much of the support for this belief came from intellectual trends that were stimulated by the westernization of the Russian elite, many of whom saw their country as the equal of the great Western powers. Russia was powerful not only militarily but also culturally and had a great civilizing mission to perform. In so doing, it would also become rich, as had the West through trade with exotic lands. Thus, Russia would acquire the badge of membership in the circle of great powers—"overseas" colonies. This attitude led to a habit of involvement in the Iranian marches whenever the status of Russia's domestic and foreign affairs permitted. During one of those episodic involvements, Georgia sought and obtained a Russian promise of protection. At the time, there was no pressing threat and the matter was taken rather lightly by Russia whose leaders thought of the agreement mostly in terms of its potential usefulness in some vaguely defined operations against the Porte and secondarily as the nucleus of a colony in western Asia. However, the factor most responsible for making permanent Russia's involvement in Georgia was an event that, by default, was outside Russian control—the sack of Tbilisi in 1795. From this time on, Russia had to play a role in Georgia for Russia's sake as much as Georgia's. Catherine and her advisers quite rightly perceived this attack as a blow to Russian prestige. While some might have questioned whether Georgia's relation to Russia ought to be closer than the existing vassalage, every official believed that the continuation of the present relation was the minimum consonant with Russia's might and dignity. Russia was permanently committed to a role in the Caucasus.

This emphasis on Georgia prompted a redefinition of the territory that Russia ought to bring into its orbit. The southern coast of the Caspian, where Catherine's efforts had been so unsuccessful, was reduced to peripheral significance. Peaceful commercial relations at Anzali were desirable, but the establishment of Russian protectorates along the coast was a distant prospect. After 1796, the region figured mostly in Russian deliberations as a second front in wars against the Qājār shahs. With the decline of interest in the southern coast, the economic significance of the eastern Caucasus took on new importance. That area could become the site of the much-desired center of East-West trade. In addition to Georgia, the khanates with comparatively large Armenian populations (Yerevan, Qarābāgh, and Ganjeh) would be valuable assets because of the Armenians' commercial connections elsewhere in Asia. As far as St. Petersburg was concerned, these khanates should rightfully become subject to Russia because of Erekle's claim to suzerainty over them (on the basis of his alliance with Qarābāgh and his attacks on the other two during the 1780s). Shirvān would be important for its silk and Baku for its oil and excellent harbor. In fact, all the khanates between Georgia and the Caspian would have to be brought into the Russian orbit because communications with Georgia made a corridor to the sea necessary. There was an overland route linking Tbilisi and the Caucasian Line, but it was narrow and steep even after Paul Potemkin made improvements since it crossed the high Caucasus. Even the key pass, the Darial, was almost 8,000 feet high. The road was blocked by snow half the year and vulnerable to rock slides and floods. It was also liable to be cut by hostile mountain tribes, as the Russians discovered when their garrison in Tbilisi was cut off from the line between 1785 and 1787 by the Chechens, who were then at war with Russia. The Tbilisi garrison received no pay or material from Russia as long as the road was cut. The hard-pressed commandant warned St. Petersburg of the need for a link to the Caspian.[29] Finally, the 1795 attack persuaded the expansionists of the need to shield Georgia with a buffer zone comprised of the neighboring khanates. In fact, Catherine determined that Russia needed to have suzerainty over all the territory up to the Aras River, which she believed would provide a clearly defined and strategically defensible border.[30] Moreover, she believed that this goal was nearly fulfilled by the 1796 expedition since Zubov obtained the submission of most of the khans in that region. In the minds of the expansionists, this gave Russia a legal claim to those khanates, no matter how unwilling or temporary the submission had been.

Despite the scarcity of information about the border provinces, the expansionists were convinced by recurring contacts with those areas over a sixteen-year period that they knew how to deal with "Persians," a term they used indiscriminately to describe speakers of Persian, Kurdish, or Āzeri Turkish; Qājār shahs and their subjects or autonomous marchwardens. "Persians" were exceedingly venal—that had been proven to Russian satisfaction by consul Tumanovskii's accusations against Āqā Mohammad when the latter conquered Gilān in 1786. Thus, General Gudovich quite blithely assumed in 1795 that he could make Āqā Mohammad leave Tbilisi by offering him a bribe. The offer was not accepted, but there is no indication that St. Petersburg disagreed with the approach, which fitted in with Catherine's belief that Iranian rulers in general cared only for personal enrichment at public expense. In addition to being corrupt, "Persians" were militarily inferior to Russians. The plausibility of this conviction stemmed to a considerable degree from the fact that there had been no battles between Russian and Qājār armies. (The capture of the Voinovich mission to Astarābād had been accomplished without fighting.) Russians consistently underestimated the effectiveness of Iranian (and Caucasian) methods of warfare, which seemed so unorganized to people reared in the Western military tradition. Thus,

when Gudovich heard rumors that Āqā Mohammad planned to subdue the eastern Caucasus in 1795, the general belittled the threat because he considered the Qājār army weak, primitive, and disorganized.
Although Āqā Mohammad enjoyed a number of successes in the campaign, they were against much smaller armies from the same military
tradition. Thus, Russians had little cause to modify their assessment
of the Qājār forces. Officials of Catherine's reign and later repeatedly
underestimated the number of soldiers needed to fight the "Persians."
With the single exception of Catherine's son Paul, no high-ranking
government figure realized how unsuccessful the 1796 campaign had
been. No one in St. Petersburg knew how much trouble the guerilla
raids be Sheikh 'Ali of Derbent-Qobbeh caused Zubov, tying down
about 2,000 Russian soldiers and harassing the Russians until their
complete withdrawal in May 1797. Yet St. Petersburg thought the
campaign was a triumph. Valerian Zubov claimed, shortly after he
had reached Baku, that he had taken all the territory to the Aras and
along the Caspian coast to Gilān, and he was believed. Derzhavin put
the official assessment of the expedition into poetic form in his ode,
"On the Return of Count Zubov from Persia," in which the hero
strides effortlessly from victory to victory.[31]

Zubov's exaggerated claims point to a salient characteristic of Russian involvement in the Iranian borderlands during and after Catherine's reign—officials in the field repeatedly evaded or directly disobeyed the wishes of their superiors. St. Petersburg was not averse to
allowing considerable leeway to its officers in the field. That seemed
a reasonable thing to do in light of the slowness of communications
and their limited knowledge of exotic lands. However, the effect was
to eliminate many of the restraints St. Petersburg had built into its
policies. During the 1780s, this excessive aggressiveness had made an
enemy of Āqā Mohammad at a time when he might have become an
ally. The negative consequences of such behavior were not discern-
able in the 1796 campaign because of its abrupt termination. Unrec-
ognized, the problem continued unchecked as Russia pursued its
expansionist goals.

IV

Russian Policy:
Questions and Continuity

Catherine died before she could fulfill her plan to conquer the eastern Caucasus and turn Iran into a puppet state, so her successors, Paul and Alexander, had to decide whether to proceed along that course. Both tsars began their reigns by questioning aspects of Russian policy toward Iran and Caucasian borderlands. Paul accepted the motives for Russia's involvement there but disagreed with the methods Catherine had employed at the close of her reign. Alexander briefly reexamined his country's objectives but soon adopted an approach that was as expansionist in its goals and as aggressive in its methods as his grandmother's had been. Russia's policy toward the Caucasus and Iran had acquired under Catherine a momentum that carried it forward despite the change of rulers.

One of the most important reasons for the continuity in Russian policy toward this region was that the people who provided the advice and information that shaped policy decisions came from a small, inbred group that had changed very little since Catherine's day. Although both Paul and Alexander, and not their advisors, made their foreign policies, the options each entertained were effectively limited by the kinds of information they received. This was especially true in dealing with such areas as the Caucasus and Iran, which were remote from the traditional interests of most of the Russian elite. Few people understood, or even claimed to understand, those areas, so Paul and Alexander had little choice but to rely on many of the same ignorant or biased people that Catherine had.

Paul openly disapproved of many of the people and policies his mother had favored. He ordered a halt to the Zubov expedition on November 7, 1796, the day after Catherine died, and canceled the undertaking one month later. The Zubov brothers soon fell from favor and remained in eclipse until the last months of Paul's reign. He also downplayed the importance of New Russia, the territory Catherine had acquired on the Black Sea's northern coast, where Gregory Potemkin and later Platon Zubov had exercised broad authority. Although Paul had bitter memories of Potemkin, he appointed as chancellor Alexander Bezborodko, who rose to prominence through his connection with Potemkin. Bezborodko had been an advocate of Russian expansion in Asia (including the Iranian marches in the Caucasus) when he was Catherine's vice chancellor. In 1797, at the height of his power, he emphasized the primacy of Russia's domestic concerns over involvement in the war against France. Bezborodko's influence declined as his health worsened over the next two years. When he died in 1799, the role of foreign policy adviser was divided among a number of people, of whom the most important—especially with regard to Russia's position in western Asia—was Fedor Rostopchin, who became chancellor in August 1799.

Rostopchin had served in Catherine's second war against the Ottoman Empire and had gained diplomatic experience under Bezborodko, including his role as Bezborodko's assistant in the negotiations that ended the war. During Paul's reign, Rostopchin saw the members of the Bezborodko circle as his adversaries, but his views on the desirability of Russian expansion in Asia closely resembled those his former mentor had once championed. Even though Rostopchin became the foremost of Paul's foreign policy advisers, he did not dominate the tsar. Paul was determined to be the model autocrat who was actively involved in every facet of government and, therefore, insisted on direct scrutiny of the minutiae of Russian diplomacy. Under such circumstances, Rostopchin could play a leading role in foreign affairs because he told Paul what he wanted to hear. Like Bezborodko, Rostopchin favored Russian involvement in Georgia because that kingdom could provide a base of operations against the Ottoman Empire. He also looked further afield to the use of Georgia and the khanates to the east as a commercial center for trade with India.[1] In 1800, when the king of Georgia began to urge St. Petersburg to make his realm a province of the Russian Empire, Paul chose Rostopchin to negotiate the terms of annexation with the king's emissaries. The chancellor was quite enthusiastic about the emissaries' proposals: creation of a Russian province of Georgia with a member of the Bagration dynasty as governor and the extension of Georgia's boundaries to include territory it had ruled in earlier times when it was stronger. He submitted a plan based on these concepts to Paul, who endorsed it, although unforseen events later caused the tsar to curtail the role of the Bagrations.

Another, less prominent official who played an important role in informing Paul was the consul Skibinevskii who had first been appointed by Catherine in 1793 to promote Russia's commercial interests in the Iranian port of Anzali. He continued to serve in that capacity, although the deterioration in Russo-Iranian relations had forced him to move to other Caspian ports. One example of the way ideas were transmitted from Catherine's reign to Paul's can be found in Skibinevskii's report on Āqā Mohammad's seizure of Anzali in 1786, an act that increased significantly the hostility between Russia and the Qājār leader. The two consuls who had been directly involved in that event were no longer in a position to influence their superiors. Tumanovskii was dead and Skilichii was in disfavor because of his ineffectiveness after the conquest of Anzali. However, the former consuls' self-serving distortion of events was accepted by Skibinevskii and, through him, found acceptance in St. Petersburg. The State Council did not doubt Skibinevskii's report that the former consuls were the innocent victims of Āqā Mohammad's unprincipled rapacity. The rest of Skibinevskii's report set forth the attitudes toward Iranian trade that had developed during Catherine's reign: that Russia could derive great economic benefit from such trade and that Russia ought to establish its own "factory" at Anzali in imitation of the commercial "factories" of various European countries in several parts of Asia. The State Council agreed with all the main points of the memorandum, as did Paul, who tried to revive Russo-Iranian trade by sending Skibinevskii back to Anzali in 1800.[2]

Two of the people who were particularly influential in transmitting ideas about Asia from Catherine's reign were the Zubov brothers, Platon and Valerian. Their comeback began with Paul's general amnesty of November 1800, but Alexander was the one who particularly valued their advice. Both brothers championed the argument for extensive Russian involvement in the Caucasus and Iran to Alexander and the State Council. The tsar put great trust in Platon Zubov's opinions about Caucasian affairs. It was Platon who wrote the manifesto, issued in Alexander's name, announcing the incorporation of Georgia into the Russian Empire. The tsar also chose him to help devise an administrative system for that new province. Until Platon's death in 1822, he continued to argue in favor of Russian expansion in the eastern Caucasus and increased commerce with that region, Iran and India. He wrote a number of books on those themes, all published posthumously.[3]

Valerian Zubov's ideas made a particularly vivid impression on Alexander. It may well be that the younger Zubov's arguments in favor of the annexation of Georgia were the ones that confirmed Alexander's determination to follow that course. That seems to be the most plausible inference to be drawn from the tsar's deliberate concealment of Valerian's proannexation memorandum from two articulate critics, Alexander Vorontsov and Victor Kochubei, who were otherwise among the tsar's most trusted advisers. Another indirect reflection of Valerian's influence on Alexander is the way Kochubei fawned on Valerian after the decision in 1801 to annex Georgia. In a strange display of humility, Kochubei, then president of the College of Foreign Affairs, not only accepted all the ideas in Valerian's memorandum but also praised its author as an expert on Asian affairs to whose judgment Kochubei felt compelled to defer. One of the strongest arguments Valerian Zubov used in favor of annexation of Georgia was that such an action was morally incumbent on Alexander. The tsar echoed this theme when he justified annexation on the grounds that it represented the wish of the suffering Georgians as well as their only hope of security. The younger Zubov also repeated an argument formulated during Catherine's reign and destined to have great importance in Russia's relations with Iran for the next thirty years: that, in order to protect Georgia, it was essential to secure the Kura and Aras rivers as the border with Iran.[4]

Valerian Zubov's other major concern was trade with Asia. He recapitulated for Alexander all his old arguments about the desirability of encouraging trade with Iran and India and the significance of Baku and Astarābād in that connection. Like most of the other members of the small circle Russians interested in Asia, he was blithely overoptimistic about the ease with which such ties could be established. For example, he informed Alexander that an excellent and safe road had been built by Shāh 'Abbās the Great (who ruled from 1588 until 1629), linking Baku with Tabriz, Tehran, Esfahān, the southern province of Fārs, and the Persian Gulf.[5] Apart from the fact that a host of public works were spuriously attributed to Shāh 'Abbās by later generations of Iranians is the fact that the road that linked the Caucasus and the commercial centers of Iran was beset with obstacles, especially rough terrain, exposure to extremes of weather, and risk of attack by tribal marauders. Alexander was impressed with Valerian's opinions on Asian trade. The tsar informed Prince Paul Tsitsianov, whom he had just appointed commander-in-chief in the Caucasus, that the realization of Zubov's recommendations was "highly desirable," even though he did not expect that it would be accomplished immediately.[6] Years later, Alexander again singled out Zubov's recommendations on Russo-Iranian trade as something his new ambassador to Iran, General Alexis Ermolov, should try to attain in his forthcoming negotiations.[7] The younger Zubov remained in Alexander's favor until Zubov died in 1804.

Both Paul and Alexander, as well as the officials who served them, continued Catherine's practice of relying on Caucasian Christians for information. When Paul first decided to annex Georgia, he not only agreed to restore its lost territory but also decided to judge which territories were at issue solely on the basis of claims presented to him by Georgia's emissaries. The area included a number of khanates to which Iran also had a claim and that were actually independent at the time. Alexander placed greater value on information from Armenians than from Georgians, especially since many Georgians complained of Russian misrule. The Russian-backed candidate for the Catholicos of Echmiadzin (Daniel) and other Armenians, especially those who had family in Iran or did business there, repeatedly provided Russian officials with information. In 1808, Alexander rewarded Daniel with the Order of St. Anne, First Class.

Another factor in the continuity of Russian policy was the inaccuracy of much of the information the tsars received. Sometimes the mistakes were unintentional, as in the case of Valerian Zubov's underestimation of the difficulties of trading with India via Iran. Sometimes deliberate misrepresentations were made to ensure the victory of a certain point of view and the personal advantage of the informants. That was the case with most of the arguments presented to Paul and Alexander in favor of the annexation of Georgia. The College of Foreign Affairs, under Rostopchin's leadership, prepared a report for Paul on conditions in Georgia and, in the process, wildly overestimated that kingdom's strength. According to the report, Georgia had a population of 800,000 and was capable of raising an army of 25,000. The implication was that, while Georgia needed Russian protection, it was strong enough not to be a burden. Yet there was much evidence available at that time that showed that Georgia was not nearly as strong as the college's report claimed. On the specific issue of population, the commander of the Caucasian Line, Karl Knorring, reported that the kingdom had only 160,000 inhabitants.[8]

Knorring himself was involved in a similar deception when Alexander revived the question of what Russia's role in Georgia ought to be. The general had a personal stake in the decision, because he hoped to become the first governor of the territory when it became a Russian province. He submitted a report in which he warned that, unless Georgia were annexed, it would collapse and that annexation would guarantee Russia great economic benefits. When his opinions were challenged by members of the Secret Committee, Knorring admitted that he had deliberately slanted his report to favor the proannexation view and gave the excuse that he thought that was what Alexander wanted to hear. He added that annexation was not essential after all and that the needs of both Russia and Georgia could be served just as well by continuing the old protectorate arrangement.[9]

Similar misrepresentations permeated the reports of another "expert" in the field, Count Apollo Musin-Pushkin, whom Paul had sent to investigate Georgia's mineral resources and who hoped to be put in charge of the mines. In his reports to Paul and Alexander, Musin-Pushkin emphasized the rich mineral deposits that Russia would acquire if it annexed Georgia. While the economic argument did not in itself determine the outcome of the controversy, it was a contributing factor. Alexander showed his interest in Musin-Pushkin's plans for the exploitation of Georgia's ores and at the same time fulfilled the count's ambition by making him head of mining operations there. In fact, the mines had been unprofitable for years. Musin-Pushkin was a singularly unobservant man who believed the mines were prospering when he was surrounded by disorganization, war, and starvation. He ran the mines with a disastrous lack of success until his death in 1805. Those who followed him produced equally disappointing results.[10]

Even though Paul and Alexander were more closely bound to Catherine's expansionist goals that they realized, each tsar tried to begin anew with a policy of his own making. Both were compelled to reappraise the existing policy when they had to resolve the status of their predecessors' incomplete projects. Paul had to decide whether to proceed with the campaign begun in 1796. Alexander had to decide whether to annex Georgia since Paul's sudden death had left the new province in an ambiguous position within the empire. Even though it was Alexander who questioned the fundamental principles of Catherine's Asian policy, it was Paul whose change of methods came nearer to altering the nature of Russia's involvement in the eastern Caucasus and Iran. Paul chose to recognize that there were problems with Russia's conduct in Asia. Alexander asked searching questions, but, when the answers indicated that there were problems, he chose to shut himself off from the distressing information.

Paul never doubted that Russia ought to play an active role in Asia. Like his mother, he valued the Iranian marches for their strategic and economic usefulness. Paul, too, was determined to keep the Turks out of the area. This wariness of the Ottomans was part of Paul's fundamental outlook, not a reaction against any present Turkish threat. In fact, Russo-Ottoman relations were uncommonly cordial during Paul's reign. Even at the start of his reign, when he seemed bent on doing the opposite of whatever his mother had done, he accepted the role of protector of Georgia and made preparations to shield it from the Iranian attack expected in 1797. He also shared Catherine's focus on Georgia as the keystone of Russia's Caucasian policy. Thus, he not only wanted to make several khanates subject to Georgia but also expected the neighboring khans to be willing to cooperate in Georgia's defense. Like Prince Potemkin, he regarded the Armenians as valuable allies in the realization of Russia's goals. He hoped to use them to bolster Georgia's defenses and economy by offering land grants, cash bonuses, and local autonomy to Armenians who would move to Georgia from neighboring khanates. He also shared the hope that Russia would be able to organize lucrative equivalents of the trading establishments of several European countries in southeast Asia. His president of the College of Commerce, Peter Soimonov, stated the underlying ambition forthrightly when he argued that, if Russia were to build a permanent and secure outpost at Anzali, it would be able to trade with Iran the way Western countries traded with India. The tsar considered the possibility of rivaling the highly valued textiles of India with the products of silk and cotton mills he contemplated establishing at Baku. In his first, generally conciliatory message to the second Qājār shah, Paul insisted that the shah take measures conducive to increased Russo-Iranian trade.[11] The lure of the India trade came to the fore again near the end of Paul's reign when he sent an expedition to dispossess the British East India Company from the Subcontinent. The tsar wrote to the General of the Cavalry Vladimir Orlov, the commander of the expedition, that

the English have their commercial establishments [in India], which were obtained either by money or by arms; the goal is to destroy all this and liberate oppressed rulers and win [them] over to the same dependence on Russia as they have on England, and turn their commerce toward us. . . .[12]

(However, Paul's motive for attempting the conquest of India lay in the clash of English and Russian interests in Europe and was not a direct outgrowth of his attitude toward Asia.)

If Paul's objectives in Iran and the Caucasus were not innovative, his methods of achieving them certainly were. One of his first official acts was to recall the Zubov expedition, not only because the project was connected with the circle of Catherine's favorites so personally loathsome to him but also because he rightly perceived what those favorites refused to admit—that the expedition had been ill-conceived and incompetently executed.[13] He followed this first step by endeavoring to change the whole tone of Russia's dealings with Iran and the Caucasian states from intimidation to cooperation. This change of tactic was not simply an indication that Paul was uninterested in affairs in that quarter. On the contrary, his statements and actions throughout his reign show how much he believed Russia could gain from involvement there. Moreover, this restraint in the use of force was more than an expedient necessitated by more pressing demands on Russian resources elsewhere. Paul began his reign with the determination to keep Russia out of war. Once the Zubov expedition was recalled, Russia was at peace, and Paul set about improving relations with France, Britain, and the Porte. For the rest of his reign, he followed a consistent policy toward the Caucasus and Iran, regardless of whether he was at war elsewhere. His cautiousness in the matter of adding Caucasian territory to his empire was part of his basic diplomatic outlook in which service of a higher good was put ahead of self-interest. He adhered to this policy in the idealistic crusading spirit he brought to the War of the Second Coalition, and there can be no question of the seriousness of his commitment in that undertaking. Paul's diplomacy was guided by what Norman Saul has described as an "acute, though sometimes unbalanced, sense of justice."[14] In dealing with the Caucasus and Iran, that sense of justice showed remarkable balance, especially when compared with the actions of his mother or his son.

Although Paul's east Caucasian policy centered on the Georgians and Armenians, he also tried to win the good will of the region's Muslims. He took Georgia's side in territorial disputes, but he wanted to be certain that the Tbilisi government treated its Muslim neighbors fairly. Catherine had deliberately kept aloof from Caucasian and Iranian Muslims. Even her candidate for the Iranian throne, Mortezā Qoli Khān, was denied permission to journey to St. Petersburg and was kept in southeastern Russia throughout his years of waiting to be made shah. When Ebrāhim Khalil Khān of Qarābāgh had tried to negotiate the terms of his submission to Russia in 1783, he was brusquely informed that the only permissible course of action was for him to wait for Catherine to grant him whatever terms she thought best. In contrast, Paul favored closer contact with the Muslims of this region. Six months after his accession, he granted an audience to a representative of Ebrāhim Khalil and sent a cordial letter to the khan. Later, when the khans of Nakhjavān and Shakki voiced an interest in putting their territories under Russian protection, they received encouraging replies from Paul's officials, who assured the khans that Paul was likely to agree to their requests. The khan of Nakhjavān was specifically encouraged to send his request directly to Paul.[15]

At the heart of Paul's benevolent disposition toward east Caucasian Muslims was the pragmatic recognition that he would not make the strategic and economic gains he sought there if he had to fight to impose his authority on khans who did not want to be his vassals. He had before him the example of Valerian Zubov's difficulties with Qobbeh, Qarābāgh, Shirvān, and Shakki to demonstrate the hazards of coercive tactics. Late in his reign, when his enemies at home and abroad considered many of his actions proof of his detachment from reality, he warned his political agent in Tbilisi, "Do not seek to make acquisitions other than those who will willingly seek my protection. It is better to have allies who are interested in the alliance than untrustworthy subjects."[16]

Paul was unique among high-ranking members of the Russian government of the late eighteenth and early nineteenth centuries in that he could conceive of Iranians and Caucasians as having their own legitimate self-interests apart from those of Russia. This realization, combined with the tsar's desire to keep Russia out of war at the start of his reign, caused him to relent from Catherine's determination to destroy Āqā Mohammad. Paul would not yield an iota on the matter of the two empires' conflicting claims in the Caucasus, but he also saw the conflict as limited to a few specific, soluble disputes, not as a fundamental confrontation between the forces of enlightened civilization and Asian barbarism, as Catherine had come to view the matter. Shortly after coming to the throne, Paul sent Gudovich a very interesting message to be transmitted to the shah. The central theme was that Āqā Mohammad's position would never be secure so long as he persisted in claiming territory north of the Kura and the Aras or acted in a hostile manner toward Russia.[17] Apart from demonstrating Paul's preference for deterrence over head-on confrontation, the message also showed Paul's willingness to accept Āqā Mohammad as the legitimate ruler of Iran south of the two rivers and his desire for amicable dealings with those who would reciprocate. This attempt to find a modus vivendi for Russia and Iran depended on a territorial concession neither side was willing to make. Unpredictable developments spared Paul from having to find a way to reconcile that con-flict with the conciliatory diplomacy he favored. Āqā Mohammad launched another campaign in the Caucasus in the spring of 1797. He advanced as far as Qarābāgh but was assassinated on June 17, a few days after the fall of Shushā, by two slaves whose execution he had ordered for the next day. His army disbanded and a struggle for the throne broke out.

With the removal of Āqā Mohammad, greater opportunities emerged for Paul to follow a conciliatory policy toward Iran. The task was facilitated by the new shah, Fath 'Ali, who sometime at the end of 1798 or the beginning of 1799 sent several cordial notes to Paul. There were a number of other indications that this was an opportune time to improve Russo-Iranian relations.

The Russians believed that Fath 'Ali was not strong enough politi-cally or militarily to threaten Russian interests. In the context of eighty years of political warfare in Iran, there seemed to be a good reason for Paul and those around him not to expect the new shah, who had to battle several rivals, to be secure in his position. (In reality, the fighting was one-sided and the issue was resolved by August 1798.) Reports to Russian officials indicated that Fath 'Ali was too weak to establish his authority as far north as the area claimed by Russia and that he was preoccupied by a serious challenge at the northeast-ern end of his domains in Khorāsān, which the Afghan ruler Zamān Shāh Dorrāni also claimed.[18] To Paul, Fath 'Ali was just one of several men who ruled some part of Iran. The tsar directed his agents to deal with "all other Persian rulers" as well as Fath 'Ali and addressed the shah by his precoronation name, Bābā Khān, and the nonroyal title, sardār (general).[19] Since Russian authorities tried to keep abreast of current developments in Iran and the tone of Paul's letter was friendly, neigther ignorance of the change of name—which took place the year before Paul wrote the letter—nor a desire to insult the shah suffices to explain the form of address. In addition to the fact that Russian authorities considered Fath 'Ali's position less exalted than the latter claimed, they also received information that he might well lose the territory then under his control. According to a report by Kovalenskii, a Russian political agent in Georgia, Fath 'Ali's army was turbulent and cumbersomely large and would overthrow him at the first sign of weakness. Other reports led the Russians to believe that the Qājār army, regardless of its disruptive potential in Iranian politics, was an ill-trained, ill-supplied, undisciplined mob that could be disposed of easily by a small number of Russian troops. The shah was believed to be a drunkard who was "not suited to great undertakings" and who allowed others, including his mother and boon companions as well as some able people, to run the government.[20]

While Paul believed he was dealing from strength in his relations with Fath 'Ali, he never tried to browbeat the shah. Instead, he made gestures of good will in the hope of establishing mutually beneficial relations between the two countries. Even before he received Fath 'Ali's letters, Paul took steps to counter the belligerent tone of Catherine's dealings with Iran. He discontinued his mother's ban on the navigation of the Caspian by Iranian naval vessels, insisting that nothing be done to hamper their movement as long as they did not interfere with Russian shipping. As much as he anticipated the riches to be derived from Russo-Iranian commerce, he rejected the advice of his officials that it was essential that the Russian commercial base at Anzali include a stone fort. It had been the construction of such a fort there in the 1780s that had done so much to persuade Hedāya-tollāh and Āqā Mohammad that Russia was their enemy. Character-istic of Paul's attempt to be fair and reasonable in his dealings with Iran was the way he instructed Fath 'Ali in the duties of a good neighbor, requiring that the shah take no action hostile to Russia while also setting the same standard for himself and his allies, includ-ing the king of Georgia and Kovalenskii, who were to be good neigh-bors to the shah.[21]

This did not mean that the tsar shrank from defending Russia's in-terests. In military matters, he demanded the punishment of Iranians who had encouraged anti-Russian actions during the Zubov campaign and required the shah to allow the use of any Caspian port by any Russian vessel in need, even warships. In commercial matters, he in-sisted that the shah had no right to interfere with a Russian consul's exercise of his duties anywhere in Iran and wanted the shah to guar-antee that Russian merchants would no longer be required to pay im-port tariffs once they had paid at the port of entry. Even in pressing these demands, Paul tried to show that he was not being unfair. He promised that no warships would approach Iranian ports unless they were in difficulty and cited Russian practice in taxing imports by Iranian merchants as the basis for the treatment he wanted for Rus-sian merchants in Iran.

In addition, Paul made a number of friendly gestures toward Iran. He ordered the release of Iranian merchants who had been caught trying to leave Astrakhan with gold currency and metal wares, the export of which had been prohibited by law until 1798. He further agreed to the shah's request that Iranian merchants be allowed to buy thousands of tons of iron and steel, which were still subject to export restrictions. The official reply to Fath 'Ali's letter was accompanied by a number of gifts, including a jewel-studded clock and some sable pelts. Later, Paul sent consul Skibinevskii back to Anzali to promote Russo-Iranian trade. The instructions to the consul emphasized that he was not to do anything that might antagonize the Iranians but, instead, was to win their "trust and love." Paul did not expect the Iranians to do anything antagonistic, but, if any difficulties did develop, Skibinevskii was not to adopt a hostile stance, still less to call in the Russian military; instead, he was advised to appeal to higher officials in the Iranian government or, at worst, move to another location.[22]

The most striking example of Paul's moderation in dealing with Iran was the way he responded to the likelihood of an Iranian attack on Georgia in 1800. Paul was willing to fight, if necessary, to prevent a repetition of the horrors of 1795, but he did not believe matters would ever become that desperate. When rumors of the impending attack reached him in 1799, his first reaction was to look for a way to reduce Iranian hostility instead of assuming that armed conflict was inevitable. With that in mind, he twice sent word to the shah that there was no cause to fear Russia and that he, Paul, desired only good relations and increased trade. In 1800, when the Iranian campaign in the eastern Caucasus was imminent, Paul began to prepare for military action; yet, he sought a way to minimize the conflict or avoid it altogether. He sent reinforcements to the Russian garrison in Tbilisi but hoped that the mere report of the strengthening of the garrison might deter an attack. Most of all, he did not want to jump to the conclusion that conflict between Russia and Iran was inescapable. Given his impression of Fath 'Ali as someone who was in the process of establishing his authority over various truculent provincial lords, Paul considered the possibility that the real target of the campaign might be not Georgia but some other border district to which the shah had a perfectly legitimate claim. In that case, Georgian soldiers might even cooperate with those of the shah to restore a part of his dominions.[23]

In fact, Paul was partially correct. The shah's objectives in 1800 did include territories like Khoi, which Russia did not claim, but they also included Georgia and its neighbors, which Paul would not recognize as part of Iran. However, Paul was saved once again by events outside his control from having to grapple with the conflict between his desire for amicable relations with Iran and the irreconcilable conflict between the two empires' territorial claims in the eastern Caucasus. That region was not the shah's principal target in

1800. His main force was sent to oppose the Afghans in Khorāsān. The smaller force sent to the Caucasus managed to besiege Khoi and Yerevan and to approach the borders of Georgia. However, the expected support from Turcoman tribes along the Georgian border and dissident members of the Bagration family failed to materialize. Georgia itself was not attacked. The Iranian army had no victories before its recall at the end of August. In the remaining seven months of his reign, Paul was not faced with any further attempts to enforce the shah's claim to disputed provinces. The Iranian army did not resume operations in the northwest until the summer of 1802, more than a year after Paul's assassination.

One aspect of Paul's attitude toward the disputed border territories that seems out of keeping with his general restraint is his decision to make Georgia an integral part of his empire, thus ending rule by the ancient line of Bagration kings. Yet, even in this case, Paul acted much less aggressively than the simple fact of annexation would appear to indicate. The most important factor in his decision lay outside his control—the critical weakness of the Georgian kingdom. King Erekle died early in 1798. Without that once strong and respected ruler in command, the country seemed on the verge of anarchy and civil war. Giorgi, the new king, evinced a desire to remedy his country's problems, but he was ineffectual and in failing health. His relatives prepared for the struggle for the throne that all expected to follow his impending death. There was a possibility that some of the pretenders to the throne might call upon Iran or the Ottoman Empire for support or that either state would on its own initiative move in to fill the vacuum resulting from Georgia's collapse.

Giorgi sent representatives to ask Paul to make the kingdom a Russian province, with the Bagrations to serve as its governors. At the same time, these representatives and Paul's Russian advisers held forth the picture of the increase in trade with Asia to be derived from the annexation.[24] However, Paul had cause to wonder whether annexation would be enough. While a Bagration remained the chief official in Georgia, there was a possibility that he could be the spokesman for fellow countrymen dissatisfied with Russian rule. Giorgi had tried to pressure Paul into establishing a large, permanent garrison in Tbilisi by threatening to submit to Iran unless Russia satisfied his defense needs. If a 1798 letter purportedly from Giorgi to Fath 'Ali is authentic, which a Georgian source seems to confirm, the king was quite serious about his threat. After lamenting the foolishness of Erekle's rebellion against Āqā Mohammad, Giorgi affirmed:

From the truth of ancient chronicles and the records of the Safavi state, I know that Teflis [Tbilisi] is a part of Iran and a dependency of the nation-conquering Qizilbash Sultans [Safavi shahs]. I consider myself one of the servants and dependents of the state of the most exalted 'Alid Shah of Iran.[25]

On December 18, 1800, Paul signed the decree making Georgia a part of the Russian Empire. Although the decree did not mention whether the Bagrations would be governors of the province, Paul sent word that he would recognize Giorgi's eldest son David as governor if David could obtain Georgian backing. Ten days later, Giorgi died. The Russian garrison commander acted in accordance with Paul's earlier instructions by setting up a temporary executive, which included himself, another of Giorgi's sons, and a member of the Georgian bureaucracy. This action was extremely unpopular with the rest of Giorgi's sons, who began attacking rival cliques. The situation rapidly became more and more confusing. In January 1801, the Georgian negotiators returned home from St. Petersburg carrying Paul's message about the possibility of recognizing Prince David as governor. Then in February, the annexation manifesto was finally published in Tbilisi, further complicating the situation since it made no mention of the Bagrations' official position. The negotiators had just arrived in St. Petersburg to work for a clarification of the new administrative system when Paul was assassinated on March 11, 1801. It remained for Alexander to decide the status of Georgia.

In terms of Russia's role in western Asia, the annexation meant more than the acquisition of Georgian territory. As Paul's letter to Fath 'Ali showed, the tsar was convinced that all the territory up to the Kura and Aras rivers constituted a zone that had to be under Russian influence at the very least if Georgia were to be defended. Moreover, discussions of Russia's role in Georgia were inseparable from discussions of the hoped-for expansion of Russia's trade with Iran and other parts of Asia. In a different sense, the annexation showed how little connection there was in official thinking between decisions regarding this region and developments elsewhere. Paul was concerned about the danger of Ottoman expansion eastward in the Caucasus even though his relations with the Porte on all other matters were excellent. The threat of French expansion in the Levant did not play a major role in shaping Paul's decision about Georgia. The French army and navy in the eastern Mediterranean had already suffered decisive defeats, which eliminated France as a powerful influence there. In fact, the removal of the French threat there was a principle factor in the creation of a Franco-Russian alliance in November 1800.[26]

Nor was the annexation part of a Russian plan, with or without French participation, for extensive conquests in Asia that were to culminate in the conquest of India. The purported Franco-Russian plan is most probably a forgery. Even if it were authentic, the plan called for an invasion route that did not involve any part of the Caucasus. The same is true for the expedition Paul really sent to expel the British from India. In fact, the decision to send Russian troops to India in 1801 was an outgrowth of Russia's conflicts in Europe. Russia and Britain were then at war, and Paul, like many of the British themselves, believed that the best way to strike at Britain would be to strike where it was most vulnerable—in India.[27]

The attempted conquest of India was but the latest in a series of Paul's unpopular actions in the foreign and domestic spheres. On the night of March 11, he was assassinated in a palace coup that put his twenty-three-year-old son Alexander on the throne. Like his father, the new tsar began his reign with the determination to keep Russia out of war. Therefore, while he continued amicable relations with France, he also achieved a reconciliation with Britain, Austria, and Prussia. The day after he came to the throne, he canceled the expedition, which was still far from reaching India. He refused to establish a Russian garrison on Malta but agreed to send troops to the Ionian Republic. In these two cases, the bases for his decisions were clear. Russia did not yet have any troops in Malta—which Alexander wanted restored to its former sovereign, the king of Naples—but Russia had occupied the Ionian Islands briefly under Paul and still had considerable political influence there..

In contrast, Alexander was uncertain about how to resolve the status of Georgia. At the heart of his concern was the issue of the legitimate rights of monarchs. He asked the State Council to decide whether he would commit an offense against the heirs to the Georgian throne if he approved the annexation of Georgia. The debate over the future of that kingdom was really about the whole of Russia's policy toward the Caucasus and Iran, so intimately connected had these themes become. The "experts"—the Zubovs, Knorring, and Musin-Pushkin—favored annexation, as did most members of the Council.[28] However, for the first time since the 1780s, there were trusted counselors who challenged all the standard assumptions of what Russia might gain by establishing a foothold in the eastern Caucasus. The debate marked the culmination of a crucial stage in the shaping of Russian attitudes toward Iran and the Caucasian borderlands. Once Georgia had been made an integral part of the Russian

Empire, there could no more be a retreat from the beliefs that justified annexation than there could be from the annexation itself.

Alexander chose two members of his closest circle of advisers,
Alexander Vorontsov and Victor Kochubei, to scrutinize all the
records of Paul's involvement in Georgia. Their report, presented
to the tsar in July of 1801, concluded that the annexation of Georgia was not in the best interests of that country or of Russia. In
their knowledgeable, well-reasoned argument, the two men deftly
undermined the expansionists' case. With regard to the defense of
European Russia's southeastern provinces, Vorontsov and Kochubei
asserted that the Caucasian Line, north of the mountains, was much
more advantageous strategically than an outpost in Georgia. That
kingdom would be better protected by stationing a Russian garrison
there as a deterrent and keeping the Bagration dynasty in power
than by annexation, which would only serve to provoke Iran or the
Porte. The authors showed how claims of Georgia's economic and
military strength and its inhabitants' desire to become Russian subjects were grossly distorted. They also exposed the fallacies of the
ambitious schemes for increased Asian trade based on a commercial
center along the Caspian coast. Apart from the unfavorable omen of
the long decline in Russia's Caspian trade, the authors pointed to
the high cost in men and money of Peter the Great's establishments
on the inhospitable Caspian coast. Above all, Vorontsov and Kochubei opposed expansion in this part of Asia because they believed it
would distract the government from its proper task of solving domestic problems. The rest of Alexander's Secret Committee—his
friends Adam Czartoryski, Paul Stroganov, and Nicholas Novosil'tsev
—endorsed these opinions.[29]

Alexander's reaction to the opinions of the people whose advice
he usually valued was quite remarkable. General Knorring had acci-
dentally hit on the truth when he stated his belief that Alexander
wanted to hear arguments in favor of annexation. The tsar accepted
the opinions of Knorring, who admitted to lying in his report, and
the Zubovs, whose arguments were corroborated only by their reputation as experts, while he rejected the report based on a perceptive
analysis of the documents of the preceding reign. In August 1801,
Alexander made it known that he believed the incorporation of
Georgia into the Russian Empire to be necessary because that was
the wish of the Georgian people and because the failure to take such
action would lead to Georgia's collapse. In addition, he took steps
to ensure that there would be no further criticism of the proannexa-

tion view. Not only did he conceal Valerian Zubov's memorandum from Vorontsov and Kochubei, he also gave Knorring complete control over foreign relations in the Caucasus when he assigned the general to win over the Armenians and the khans of that region.[30] Thus, Alexander bypassed the customary administrative organization, which would have made Knorring responsible to the College of Foreign Affairs, of which Kochubei was about to become president.

The Soviet historian A. V. Fadeev has asserted that Kochubei, Vorontsov, and Novosil'tsev all opposed the annexation of Georgia because they feared that the annexation would jeopardize Russia's improved relations with Britain.[31] It would be reasonable to expect some connection between Russian foreign policy in Europe and the Caucasus. Nonetheless, it is striking how little the major foreign policy concerns of the Napoleonic era affected Russia's actions in the eastern Caucasus or its relations with Iran. Kochubei and Vorontsov minced no words in enumerating the reasons not to annex Georgia, yet they never mentioned the possibility of damaging Anglo-Russian relations. Moreover, both men continued to favor amicable relations with Britain even after they reversed their stand on the Caucasus. Alexander himself endorsed annexation two months after the signing of the Anglo-Russian Convention (June 17, 1801), a major step in the reconciliation of the two countries. Russia's relations with Britain remained peaceful until 1807, even though Alexander pursued and expansionist policy in the Caucasus at the same time. In 1801, neither Russia nor Britain perceived the eastern Caucasus as an arena where their interests clashed. In fact, British authorities determinedly refused to share Iran's concern over the growth of Russian power in the Caucasus until several years after the start of the Russo-Iranian War. Even then, Britain was drawn into the conflict not to counter Russia but to prevent France from gaining influence over Iran by helping it wage the war.[32] Alexander separated Russia's diplomatic concerns in Europe from those in Asia, in direct contrast to Paul's attempt to weaken Britain by attacking India. In 1807 and 1808, when Russia was again allied with France against Britain, Napoleon pressed Alexander to join in a campaign, which would also include Iranians, to expel the British from India. Alexander foresaw a host of obstacles and concluded that the allied armies would be defeated by the difficulties of the journey before reaching India. Therefore, he avoided making a firm commitment by promising to reflect on the merits of the plan but hoping, in the meantime, to trade his assent for concessions from Napoleon regarding the Ottoman Empire.

No acceptable concessions were made, and the Indian campaign became a dead issue.[33]

In the year following Alexander's decision to incorporate Georgia into the Russian Empire, he elaborated his policy toward the eastern Caucasus and Iran. That policy, which advocated expansion in order to make Georgia secure and encourage trade with Asia, was consistent with the ideas that had developed over the preceding twenty years. Even though there were practical difficulties in reaching some of his goals, Alexander held to the same basic approach until Russia achieved victory over Iran.

During this year of policy formulation, the tsar repeatedly linked expansion with the upholding of Russia's imperial dignity, as he would do again many times in later years. He was deeply affected by Knorring's argument that countermanding Paul's annexation order would dishonor Russia in the eyes of Europe and Asia.[34] The 1801 manifesto that proclaimed the annexation of Georgia voiced a similar theme. Even though the words were Platon Zubov's, they were written with Alexander's approval. According to the manifesto, Paul had denied the Georgians the protection they were entitled to expect from Russia because he recalled the 1796 expedition. Then, Alexander, motivated solely "dignity, honor, and humanity," would once again fulfill the "sacred duty" of making Georgia safe.[35] Alexander returned to this theme of imperial dignity at the end of the formulative period when he demanded that Russia's candidate for the hotly contested leadership of the Armenian Church (the office of Catholicos of Echmiadzin) be supported by all interested parties as a matter of respect for Russian authority.[36]

A corollary of this concern over the imperial dignity was the desire to humble the shah. During the early stage of Alexander's involvement in Caucasian affairs, he did not expect the shah to be a serious opponent. In keeping with the axioms developed during the two preceding reigns, the tsar saw Iran as the victim of recurring civil wars from which one contestant emerged briefly as the strongest among the rivals. Accordingly, Alexander viewed Fath 'Ali Shāh as merely one of several regional despots. If Fath 'Ali were to attack Georgia, Alexander hoped to use the other regional chiefs against him. This view of the restricted nature of the shah's authority did not cause Alexander, as it had Paul, to be willing to risk a conciliatory approach toward a presumably weak opponent. Alexander regarded the shah as a troublemaker who would certainly pursue an anti-Russian policy if not kept in his place. Therefore, Alexander ordered Knorring to conquer Yerevan at the first sign that the shah planned to attack it, even if there were no indication that Georgia would be the next target, in order to guarantee that Fath 'Ali had no victories to embolden him. Alexander also refused to continue Paul's policy of tolerating the navigation of the Caspian by armed Iranian ships as long as they did not interfere with Russian shipping. He further looked forward to the time when his country's merchant fleet would be large enough to handle all the Caspian trade so that Iranian merchant shipping could be banned as well.[37]

Another facet of Alexander's belief in Russia's superiority was his confidence that the example of Russian rule in Georgia would persuade local Muslims that they should put themselves under his protection. Part of the attraction would lie in Russia's military might, which would make local khans realize that the best guarantee of their security would be the stationing of Russian garrisons in their capitals.[38] In a broader sense, he believed in the irresistible attractiveness of enlightened Russian rule. He predicted that, when the newly appointed governor-general—Paul Tsitsianov—established law and order in Georgia, people in neighboring khanates would want the same benefits for themselves. Tsitsianov's first objective

. . . must naturally be to clarify the confused system of affairs there [Georgia] and by mild and just but still quite firm behavior endeavor to gain for the Russian government the trust, not only of Georgia but of various neighboring states where they are accustomed to see only the cruelty of Persian power. They will regard every act of a strong state founded on justice and strength as, so to speak, supernatural. [In doing this you] ought to win their favor to it [Russian rule] quickly.[39]

The tsar's hopes of a mutually beneficial Russian presence in the eastern Caucasus led him to the conclusion that it was essential for Russia to take control of the entire region as far south as the Kura and Aras rivers, although that might involve vassalage agreements and not necessarily the elimination of all local governments. He was convinced that only a border defined by those two rivers would be strategically defensible. Pointing to a map, he told the Secret Committee that, if Russia did not fill in the gaps in its Caucasian holdings as far as the two rivers, the border would be too long and too irregular for his troops to prevent incursions.[40] He also wanted to make certain that each ruler in this zone followed a pro-Russian policy. Shakki, Shirvān, and Baku had to be under his suzerainty in order to establish a corridor linking Georgia and the Caspian. With that route secured, Russia would be spared the burden of sending supplies to Georgia "by the difficult route across the Caucasus Mountains."[41] Yerevan and Ganjeh had to have Russian garrisons in their capitals in order to create a buffer zone around Georgia, which in Alexander's opinion, had no natural defenses near its borders. Ironically, the tsar was especially concerned about the danger of an attack via Yerevan, which is separated from Georgia proper by the desert and mountains of the sparsely populated border district of P'ambak. In the next few years, when Russian generals made two unsuccessful attempts to conquer Yerevan, they blamed their failures on the difficulty thrown in their way by the harsh terrain separating that khanate from Georgia.[42]

Alexander's decision to embark upon an expansionist course in the eastern Caucasus was the first of many occasions when, in dealing with that area, he allowed himself to be won over by men who advocated aggressive policies. Two of the most important of these later occasions took place at the beginning and end of his war with Iran: when General Tsitsianov was given free rein to embark on a series of conquests that contributed materially to the outbreak of war; and, in the postwar negotiations, when General Ermolov persuaded Alexander not to make even a token territorial restoration to Iran.

When Alexander committed the Russian Empire to permanent and active involvement in Caucasian affairs, he was confident of easy success. He expected the Caucasians to welcome Russia as their benefactor and the Iranians to be incapable of threatening his secure and prosperous Caucasian domains. Russia, too, would prosper from its expanded trade with Asia. What he found as he pursued his chosen course was widespread opposition throughout the area he wished to control and a decade of war on four fronts that exacted a high toll in men and money.

V

Russia's Conquest
of the Eastern Caucasus

Russian historians of the nineteenth and twentieth centuries have generally characterized their country's acquisition of the eastern Caucasus as a progressive step that was welcomed by most of the region's inhabitants. As one author described it, the Russian takeover meant "the liberation of Transcaucasian peoples from a foreign yoke."[1] In reality, Russia's attempt to extend its border to the Kura and the Aras met with considerable opposition from local Muslims as well as from Iran. The principal factor in the Russian takeover was force, direct or threatened. After nine years of warfare, Iran recognized Russian sovereignty over most of the territory north of the two rivers as well as Tālesh, but it took fifteen years and another war with Iran before Russia acquired the last two khanates, Yerevan and Nakhjavān. While armed conflict between Russia and Iran influenced the course of events in every khanate, only in three—Yerevan, Nakhjavān, and Tālesh—was it the most important factor. Elsewhere the contest was primarily between Russia and the local leaders. For generations they had profited from the weaknesses of neighboring empires by asserting their own autonomy. They continued to pursue their traditional objective, then including Russia and Iran in their maneuverings. Thus, a khan might side with Russia if an Iranian threat seemed more pressing or the reverse if Russia seemed bent on controlling the khanate's affairs. For some khans, this strategy degenerated into a frantic struggle to appease both sides. Except for Mostafā Khān of Shirvān, every khan who submitted to Russia abjured that submission. A number of

66

would-be khans also tried to use one or both of the competing empires in order to supplant the incumbent. Some khans had very little
room to maneuver because of military weaknesses or the disaffection
of the governed. While the pattern of events after 1801 bore a resemblance to the Zubov era, there were also some very important differences. That year saw the beginning of permanent Russian involvement in the Caucasus. There would be no sudden disengagement as
there had been in 1796. Especially after the arrival of General Tsitsianov in 1803, Russia began to employ greater force and in more extreme formes than it had before. At the same time, the Qājār government of Iran was in a position to be more assertive of its own claim
to the region.

The period between Paul's decision to annex Georgia and the beginning of Tsitsianov's command was a transitional one in which Russia tried unsuccessfully to negotiate the submission of three of the four
khanates of Iranian Armenia: Ganjeh, Nakhjavān, and Yerevan.
Events of this period belie the truism that greater contact between
alien cultures always leads to greater understanding and good will.
Lieutenant-General Knorring, who represented Russia in the negotiations, could not understand why the khans were so uncooperative
and ascribed it to malevolence, while the difficulties in the negotiations made the khans increasingly mistrustful of Russia. As a result,
not only were specific points of contention left unresolved but the
whole climate of relations between Russian officials and Caucasian
Muslims worsened.

The essence of the problem was that the khans were looking for
an alliance that would bring them clear benefits in terms of protect-
ing the khanates from conquest by Iran and bolstering the khans'
position in local feuds, but each suspected that the kind of alliance
Russia offered would be one-sidedly in Russia's favor. This ought to
have been a golden opportunity for Russia to achieve an important
part of its objectives in the eastern Caucasus, since each of the three
khans was seriously interested in obtaining Russian protection. Nakhjavān was weak, vulnerable strategically to an Iranian attack, and at
that particular time, engaged in a dispute with the pasha of Kars.
Yerevan was involved in the same dispute and had been subject to
Iranian attacks aimed at forcing it into submission, most recently in
1800. Since members of the Georgian royal family were at odds with
Russia, Ganjeh was able to pursue its existing anti-Bagration policy
and give it a pro-Russian coloring by blocking the effort of one of
King Erekle's sons to seize the throne with the help of Avar tribesmen of the high Caucasus.

Russia was unable to profit from the favorable situation in Iranian Armenia because St. Petersburg put a higher priority on interests that clashed with those of the khans. Given Russia's commitment to Georgian territorial integrity, it could not possibly support the claims of Ganjeh and Yerevan to the districts along their borders with Georgia. The alliance between Russia and the Ottoman Empire was an enormously important part of Russia's foreign policy and could not have been jeopardized by supporting an attack by Yerevan and Nakhjavān on the border province of Kars. However, the fact that Russia followed these policies and the way in which it carried them out guaranteed the failure of negotiations with the khans of Iranian Armenia. As was often to be the case in Russia activities in the eastern Caucasus, the actions of officials in the border zone made St. Petersburg's policies even more aggressive than their superiors had intended. Knorring showed a certain favorable disposition toward Mohammad Khān of Yerevan. The frustration of trying to satisfy conflicting interests and his personal biases drove the general to fulminate against the chosen scapegoats for his dilemma. Although state policy obliged him to oppose Yerevani and Ganjevi claims to Georgian border districts, he received information from Kovalenskii in Tbilisi and the pro-Russian tribe of Qazzāq Turcomans (who lived along the disputed border) that indicated there was indeed a historic basis for the two khans' claims. Knorring would never acknowledge this either to the khans or to his superiors. In fact, his reports to his superiors cited these claims as proof of the threat both khans posed to Georgia's security. He first used this argument as a way to persuade Alexander that further delay in the annexation of Georgia exposed it to great peril but continued to present the khans' motives in a negative light even after that question had been decided.[2] Whatever the merits of the claims of Yerevan and Nakhjavān against Kars, Knorring sided with the pasha to the point of sending Russian troops to defend him from a Nakhjavāni attack. Several hundred of the khan's soldiers were killed in the battle.

Perhaps the Russians had counted on the three khans' fear of Iran to make them concede whatever Russia wanted in return for military protection. The opposite proved to be the case, and the khans turned away from Russia as a benefactor. Mohammad of Yerevan and Javād of Ganjeh protested against Russian favoritism, pointing out that the interests of some of Russia's friends were supported at the expense of other friends and that the promised benefits of submission to Russia were illusory. Moreover, they doubted whether Russian protection would be available no matter what concessions the khans might make. In light of a generation of cyclical engagement and disengagement by Russia, many Caucasians must have expected Alexander to reverse his father's expansionist policy. Kalb 'Ali of Nakhjavān voiced particular concern over this issue.[3] As a result of all these problems, the three khans turned against Russia. Javād supported the same Bagration prince he had lately opposed and died in 1804 while waiting for Iranian troops to save him from Russian conquest. Mohammad and Kalb 'Ali participated in Iran's Caucasian campaigns of 1802 and 1804.

One of the most striking indications of the Muslims' low estimate of the value of the Russian presence is that the fourth khan of Iranian Armenia (Ebrāhim Khalil of Qarābāgh), who as an ally of Georgia and a foe of the Qājārs should have been the most eager for Russian protection, did not even try to negotiate an alliance but sided with Iran instead. He had managed to regain control over Qarābāgh after Āqā Mohammad's assassination, but his realm was so badly weakened by the fighting and natural disasters of the 1790s that he could no longer be an arbiter of east Caucasian affairs. The khanate was further depopulated by the emigration of Armenians whom Paul had invited to settle in an uninhabited district of Georgia. Therefore, when Fath 'Ali Shāh demanded Ebrāhim Khalil's submission, the khan complied with every stipulation, including the sending of a son as hostage and a daughter to be the shah's wife. (She later became an influential figure at the Iranian court.) Ebrāhim Khalil made the symbolic gesture of submission by minting coins bearing the shah's name. In return, the alliance brought him demonstrable economic, political, and military benefits, which Russia seemed unable to offer. The fact that Āqā Mohammad had conquered Qarābāgh twice and that Fath 'Ali repeatedly campaigned in the eastern Caucasus made it seem plausible that Iran would defend its new ally. Moreover, the shah helped Ebrāhim Khalil compensate for the collapse of Qarābāgh's economy by giving him the revenue of a district across the Aras River. In 1802, the shah decided he would also support the return to power of Ebrāhim Khalil's ally and son-in-law Salim, who had ruled Shakki in 1796 and 1797. Ebrāhim Khalil not only accepted Iranian suzerainty but also embarked on a course of active hostility toward Russia and Georgia. He supported a Bagration pretender, raided Georgia several times, and participated in Fath 'Ali's 1802 campaign.

Thus, at the moment Alexander was ready to launch his new Caucasian policy, Russia's prestige there had fallen to a new low. Russia was not even feared, much less admired as Alexander earnestly hoped it would be. Knorring occasionally threatened khans with harsh punishment for their uncooperativeness, but he never made good his threat. Even in the dispute involving Kars and Nakhjavān, Russian action was limited to the defense of the *pashalik*; no punitive measures were taken against Nakhjavān. This situation changed dramatically once Paul Tsitsianov took charge of Caucasian affairs in 1803. There could no longer be any doubt about the permanence of Russia's involvement in Caucasian affairs. As for the style of that involvement, Tsitsianov was indifferent to the idea of making Russia admired but he was fiercely determined to make it feared.

Tsitsianov belonged to an inbred group whose members held key offices in the Caucasus for a generation. These men served under Valerian Zubov in the 1796 campaign and became great admirers of his. Tsitsianov added the severity of his methods to the goals he shared with Zubov in setting the tone of this group. Another member of the circle, Peter Butkov, returned to head the chancellery of the province of Georgia from 1801 to 1803 and helped Platon Zubov draft the plan for the administration of the province. He went on to hold a variety of administrative posts in European Russia and was eventually given the honors of membership in the Academy of Sciences and the Senate (a nonlegislative body with administrative and judicial functions). He spent many years writing a history of the Russian conquest of the Caucasus and justified the conquest in terms similar to the Zubovs'.[4] Next to Tsitsianov, the best known veteran of the 1796 campaign was Alexis Ermolov, who served with distinction in the war against Napoleon from 1812 on and returned to the Caucasus in 1816 as commander-in-chief and ambassador to Iran. Like Tsitsianov, he was arrogant, cruel, contemptuous of Muslims, and not nearly as great a commander as he believed himself to be. His career was ended in 1827 by a series of defeats inflicted by the Iranians at the start of the second war with Russia. A number of less prominent veterans of the Zubov-Tsitsianov circle also returned later to the Caucasus.[5] Other officers who did not participate in the 1796 campaign still had the opportunity to imbibe the Zubov-Tsitsianov spirit as they worked their way up through the ranks during years of service in the Caucasus. Foremost among this group was Peter Kotliarevskii, the victor over Iran at Aslanduz (1812) and conquerer of Tālesh, the decisive battles of the First Russo-Iranian War. He was the son of a village priest who had been persuaded to make the boy a soldier by Ivan Lazarev, who passed through the village. Kotliarevskii entered the army at fourteen, became Lazarev's adjutant when Lazarev was made commandant of the Russian garrison in Georgia (1799), and—after Lazarev's murder (1803)—became adjutant to Tsitsianov. He showed a reckless courage in battle as he rose through the ranks in the next few years and became a lieutenant-general at the precocious age of twenty-nine. He showed an aggressiveness worthy of Valerian Zubov or Tsitsianov and some of Tsitsianov's harshness in his eagerness to invade Iran and his refusal to spare the lives of the vanquished defenders of Tālesh.[6]

Continuity of a different sort was provided by the return to the Caucasus of Gudovich, who succeeded Tsitsianov as commander-in-chief in 1806 and held office for a little more than two years. He could hardly be called a member of the Zubov-Tsitsianov circle since he saw Valerian Zubov as a rival who had cheated him of the command of the 1796 expedition. Nonetheless, he had, on his own, developed many attitudes that resembled those of the circle—bellicosity, contempt for Asians, and faith in the assumption that there were simple solutions to complex problems.[7]

Of the four other commanders-in-chief who participated in the conquest of the eastern Caucasus, three had a brief period of experience as a subordinate to their predecessors. Alexander Tormasov (1809-1811) and Ivan Paskevich (1827-1831) were posted to field commands under their respective precessors, Gudovich and Ermolov. Philip Paulucci (1811-1812) spent a year as quartermaster under Tormasov before replacing him. Only Nicholas Rtishchev (1812-1816) moved directly into the position of commander-in-chief (after nine years of retirement from government service). All four of these commanders differed from the commanders from the Zubov-Tsitsianov circle in that they occasionally saw good sides to their Muslim adversaries and did not always prefer extreme force as the means to their ends.[8] In addition, Paskevich had the rare distinction of achieving substantial victories in the conquest of Yerevan and the defeat of Iran and the Ottoman Empire in the wars of the late 1820s. (He went on to be the ruthless suppressor of uprisings in Poland in 1831-1832 and in Hungary in 1849.)

Of all the commanders-in-chief who participated in the conquest of the eastern Caucasus, Tsitsianov acquired the most prestigious reputation. By comparison, Ermolov was hurt by his poor performance at the start of the second war with Iran and Paskevich by defeats in the growing war in the high Caucasus and the enmity of Ermolov's influential admirers. Tsitsianov had an unusual gift for persuading people to view all his actions in the most flattering light, and his reputation was sanctified by his "martyrdom" outside the walls of Baku in 1806. He was not only the hero of the struggle for the Caucasus, he was the individual who did the most to determine the character of the Russian takeover. He came to the Caucasus with unprecedented powers. In appointing him, Alexander gave him the previously separate offices of commander-in-chief in Georgia, civilian governor of Georgia, inspector of the Caucasian Line, and military governor of Astrakhan (important for naval reinforcements and supply deliveries). Even Ermolov and Paskevich did not hold all these commands. During the three and a half years Tsitsianov filled those offices, he reorganized the government of Georgia; fought tribesmen of the high Caucasus; endeavored to bring the west Georgian principalities under Russian control; signed treaties for the submission of Baku, Shakki, Shirvān, and Qarābāgh; attempted the conquest of Yerevan; and succeeded in conquering Ganjeh. In the process, he intensified the Muslim Caucasians' mistrust of Russia and contributed directly to the outbreak of war with Iran. Alexander was well pleased with his accomplishments and rewarded him with the order of St. Alexander Nevskii and later the same medal set with diamonds, as well as the order of St. Vladimir, First Class, and 8,000 rubles. He was promoted from lieutenant general, the third highest grade in the Table of Ranks, to general of the infantry, the second highest. Not surprisingly, he became the model for many an officer serving in the Caucasus. In 1805, he was recalled so that he could be given an even more prestigious command in the war against France, but he stayed at his current post until a successor could be named. In February of the following year, his career came to an abrupt end when he was shot after walking into a trap set for him by Hosein Qoli Khān of Baku.

In his personal attributes, Tsitsianov contrasted sharply with the model of the heroic world conquerer (for example, the Chingiz Khān, Timur, or Napoleon) who, by the audacity of his daring and the force of his will, builds an empire and inspires awe. Tsitsianov did not lack the ferocious drive to sweep all obstacles from his path, but his career shows us the other side of the conquering hero—the obstacles that cannot be overcome by the will to victory, the arrogant blunders of the self-enamored, and the sordidness that, on closer inspection, can be found underlying the triumph. His apparent success and his "martyrdom" at Baku caused him to be remembered admiringly by later generations of Russian imperial historians. N. N. Beliavskii and V. A. Potto wrote of his breadth of vision, determination, nobility of character, eloquence, energy, and enormous devotion to the service of Russia's interests.[9] Such admiration was not limited to proponents of Russian expansion in Asia. The standard English work on Russia's Caucasian empire, J. F. Baddeley's *The Russian Conquest of the Caucasus*, also praised the general in glowing terms:

[He] was a man of indomitable courage and extreme energy. . . . He was also endowed with administrative ability of a high order, coupled with an aggressive, over-bearing spirit, that served him admirably in his dealings with the native rulers, Christian as well as Mussulman though probably enough it contributed both to his own tragic fate and to that of one of his most valued subordinates. . . . [His wit] made him powerful enemies, yet taken with his soldierly qualities and care for those who served him well, secured him the love, the adoration almost of the army.[10]

To the Muslims of the Caucasus, Tsitsianov appeared in a very different light. One of his titles, inspector (of the Caucasian Line), was pronounced by Āzeri-speaking Caucasians as "ishpokhdor," which was given a Turkish etymology meaning "his work is dirt." He was given another name by the Iranian chronicler Rezā Qoli Khān Hedāyat: "the shedder of blood."[11] Beliavskii and Potto were mistaken. What they saw as Tsitsianov's devotion to Russia's interests was really overweening personal ambition; his eloquence was marred by bluster, just as his nobility of character was marred by deceit; the energy he spent was largely other people's; and his determination manifested itself in slaughter.

Like many officers who rose to prominence during Catherine's reign, Tsitsianov spent the years between 1797 and 1801 in retirement. When Alexander gave him the Caucasian command, he was forty-eight years old and determined to make up for lost time in advancing his career. Apparently, he had aged prematurely, for his associate, Major-General Sergei Tuchkov, assumed him to be a man about sixty years old although an unusually energetic man for that age. Tuchkov believed that Tsitsianov deliberately provoked confrontations with Muslim rulers because he wanted the opportunity to impress Alexander.[12] The accuracy of Tuchkov's comments about Tsitsianov might be questioned on the grounds that Tuchkov believed he was denied the honors due him because of Tsitsianov's spite. Although Tuchkov's memoirs contain some errors, the credibility of his judgments on his commander is strengthened by information derived from a variety of contemporary sources, including Tsitsianov's own letters.

The commander-in-chief capitalized on any opportunity to magnify his own importance. All his successors referred to their position as the office conferred on them by His Imperial Majesty. Tsitsianov spoke of *his* territory. Not content with the official goal of establishing the Aras and the Kura as the border with Iran, he argued that he should be allowed to take control of Khoi and Tabriz as well. Sometimes his self-aggrandizement had overtones of derangement. In 1804, St. Petersburg approved Tsitsianov's plan to force Fath

'Ali Shāh to make peace on Russia's terms by attacking Gilān. When Tsitsianov gave a subordinate his orders for the expedition, he referred to the plan as being determined by secret instructions known only to the tsar and himself. This was patently untrue. The Gilān campaign was treated by St. Petersburg like any other policy decision regarding that region. There was no special secrecy. Foreign Minister Czartoryski and Tsitsianov discussed the plan in correspondence, and no doubt other officials knew of it as well.[13]

Tsitsianov, a descendant of a Georgian prince of the Tsitsishvili family who had emigrated to Russia during the time of Peter the Great, could speak as the leader of a Georgian national revival when the occasion warranted. He was eager to reunify his ancestral homeland by extending Russian sovereignty over the western as well as the eastern Georgian principalities (which Alexander also favored) and over Ganjeh, which he claimed had been subject to Georgia since the reign of Queen Tamara (who ruled from 1184 to 1213). In a letter to Fath 'Ali Shāh, the general announced his intention to restore Georgia to its ancient greatness, with borders extending from Abkhazia, on the Black Sea, to Derbent.[14]

More frequently, Tsitsianov represented himself as the spokesman for European civilization in a world of Asian depravity. In fact, he reverted to this theme with such conspicuous regularity that it seems to have been an integral part of his obsession with having his way in all matters. Anyone who interfered with his wishes was contemptible, uncivilized, and, therefore, to be swept aside. His concept of European standards varied erratically. He offered Javād Khān of Ganjeh the opportunity to surrender and avoid bloodshed, saying he was acting "according to European customs and the Faith I profess," but, when Javad suggested that Tsitsianov lift the siege to avoid bloodshed, the general refused further discussion on the grounds that to pursue the subject was "unacceptable in any well mannered European writing."[15] Tsitsianov's pose as a European chauvinist nearly cost him the submission of one of the few khans who was genuinely eager to become a Russian vassal. Ja'far Qoli Khān Domboli had been ruler of Khoi, located south of the Aras near the Ottoman border, but had lost power because of his opposition to Fath 'Ali Shāh. Therefore, the khan hoped to be reinstated with the help of Russian arms, an idea Tsitsianov encouraged. They agreed that Ja'far Qoli and his supporters would cross the Aras to meet Tsitsianov, who planned to conquer Yerevan and then restore Ja'far Qoli to power in Khoi. The khan did not arrive at the appointed time because his stronghold on the Ottoman border was besieged by Turkish troops. His wife, who had taken shelter with her brother (the khan of Yerevan), wrote to Tsitsianov to assuage the general's wrath and explain her husband's predicament. Tsitsianov knew she was telling the truth (and soon after informed the tsar about the siege), but he told the wife that she was a liar and her husband a traitor, adding a nasty remark about the Persian treachery of her brother. He closed the letter with a reproof for her temerity: "Moreover, according to European custom, women do not meddle in men's business and if there is such a custom in Asia, it seems to me to be undignified and base."[16]

As these examples show, Tsitsianov's militant Europeansim was closely associated with his loathing for all things "Asian" and "Persian" (terms that he often used synonymously). His numerous fulminations against Asian ways were often used to persuade his superiors and all others that his tactic of intimidating, humiliating, and crushing anyone who opposed his will was the only suitable course of action. His letters abound in phrases such as "Persian scum" and "Asian treachery." His notion of "Asian treachery" makes clear the extent to which he followed a double standard of morality. On one occasion, he devised a strategy for the overthrow of Sheikh 'Ali Khān of Derbent-Qobbeh. The plan called for lulling the khan's suspicions by conspiring with him to overthow his old rival, Mostafā Khān of Shirvān, and by having a Russian official negotiate with Sheikh 'Ali's representative to St. Petersburg. In recommending this strategy to the tsar, Tsitsianov observed that "Persian" khans could never be trusted because "not a single nation exceeds the Persian in cunning and their inherent faithlessness."[17]

Alexander's confidence in the irresistible superiority of Russian civilization to "Persian" led him to suggest that new vassals from the Causasus deliver their tribute payments to St. Petersburg in person so that exposure to life in the capital could win them over to Russian values. Tsitsianov opposed the plan on the grounds that such exposure would be pointless because of the profound gaps between Muslim and Russian mores. This argument served a double purpose. First, it strengthened the image of the "Persian" as an immoral being and, consequently, justified the general's harsh methods. Second, he did not want local rulers to meet people in St. Petersburg to whom they could complain about him. Some members of the Georgian royal family were already doing that, much to Tsitsianov's distress. Therefore, he attempted to persuade the tsar that "Persians" were too barbaric to benefit from exposure to life in Russia. According to Tsitsianov, the only reason Caucasian Muslims submitted to Russia was that demonstrations of its military might led them to seek its protection against the threats to property and physical safety characteristic of Asian rule. Therefore, for the next thirty years (by which time Russian values would begin to be absorbed), the only way to deal with new Muslim subjects was by a policy of stern force because "among the Asians, nothing works like fear as the natural consequence of force."[18]

One of the reasons Tsitsianov resorted so frequently to insults in his dealings with subordinates and Caucasians was that his extraordinary ambition was not matched by his achievements. Any officer in his position would have had to grapple with imposing obstacles, but the general's own miscalculations increased his problems. His greatest weakness was his inability to anticipate factors that might stand in his way. When confronted with the resulting failures, he found scapegoats, whom he punished severely. These characteristics can be seen in two closely related events of the summer of 1804: the attempt to conquer Yerevan and the anti-Russian uprising in Georgia and the high Caucasus.

For about a year, Tsitsianov had been corresponding with Mohammad Khān of Yerevan about the terms of the khan's submission to Russia. However, the general demanded more than Mohammad was willing to concede. In addition to terms stipulated by St. Petersburg, such as the stationing of a Russian garrison in the citadel of Yerevan city, the general demanded a large annual tribute and increased the amount when Yerevan rejected the terms so that the final sum was 100,000 rubles (worth at that time more than £15,000). Mohammad was also under pressure from Fath 'Ali Shāh to be a more obedient vassal. Tsitsianov decided to abandon negotiations and conquer Yerevan. The fighting, which lasted from July to September, marked the opening clash in the war between Russia and Iran. After some battles around the monastery at Echmiadzin in which there was no clear victory for either side, both armies turned their attention to Yerevan City, which was besieged by the Russians, who were themselves besieged by a larger Iranian force. The Iranians fought much more bravely and effectively than the Russians had expected them to and managed to cut the Russians off from supplies and reinforcements while the citadel, garrisoned by the khan's troops and reinforcements from the shah, held off any direct attacks. While Tsitsianov was in difficulty at Yerevan, an anti-Russian uprising broke out in Georgia and adjoining districts of the high mountains. The Georgians had many grounds for dissatisfaction, including the abolition of Bagration rule, the corruption of Kovalenskii's administration, and various actions by Tsitsianov. One of the most important arguments in favor of the Russian presence was that it would provide security. However, Tsitsianov made one disastrously unsuccessful attempt in 1803 to stop Lesghi raids from the mountains northeast of Georgia and then turned his attention to the more attractive prospect of conquering Ganjeh and Yerevan. The Yerevan campaign left Georgia denuded of troops at at ime when Lesghi raids increased. Many Georgians were further aggrieved by Tsitsianov's use of peasant labor under extremely harsh conditions to improve the road across the high mountains. At the same time, a growing number of Georgians hoped for a Bagration restoration, to which the shah gave his military support. By September, five of the six generals accompanying Tsitsianov decided that his plan to storm Yerevan was unsound and forced him to abandon the campaign. The Russians returned to Georgia after an arduous journey as the end of summer brought the traditional campaigning season to a close.[19]

Tsitsianov saved his reputation and in the process upheld the validity of his methods by persuading Alexander that others were to blame for the year's reverses. Among those at fault were the generals who refused to storm Yerevan. The khan of that place was also a grave offender. Tsitsianov argued that "the annihilation of this treacherous khan" was crucial for Russia's glory and strategic position in the Caucasus. The person who bore the greatest share of "guilt," according to Tsitsianov, was Prince Volkonskii, whose failure to deliver supplies to the Russians at Yerevan caused the "disgrace" there.[20] (Tsitsianov did not mention that the Iranian control of the area between Yerevan and Georgia prevented Russian detachments from traveling between the two places or that Georgia was short of troops because of the Yerevan campaign.) These explanations were well received in St. Petersburg. Alexander praised Tsitsianov for his zeal in the imperial service and exonerated him completely. To console the general for his disappointment, the tsar gave him a medal and money. Prince Volkonskii was recalled. In contrast, when General Gudovich failed in his attempt to conquer Yerevan in 1808, Alexander called the campaign "stupid" (though not to Gudovich's face) and sent him into retirement without a word of consolation.[21]

No matter how effectively Tsitsianov shifted the blame for the setbacks of 1804 onto the shoulders of others, in retrospect it can be seen that the damage done to Russia's interests by his mistakes was extremely high. By the end of 1804, war-related deaths, as well as those caused by diseases contracted in the unfamiliar climate of the Caucasus, left the Russian force 2,554 men below strength.[22] There is no reliable information on the extent of civilian casualties or property destruction, but, given the extent of the fighting and raiding, some localities were probably hard hit. The issues over which the summer's battles had been fought remained unresolved. Georgia and the tribes of the high Caucasus were only temporarily pacified. In turn, this hindered Russia's efforts to take control of the khanates south and east of Georgia because it provided new grounds for the existing doubts about Russia's ability to enforce its demands or to oppose the Iranian army. At the same time, the harshness of Tsitsianov's methods made new enemies for Russia.

Tsitsianov's success in persuading St. Petersburg to praise him for his failures is representative of one of the most curious aspects of his career in the Caucasus, namely, his influence over Alexander. The tsar's benign exterior was often taken as a reflection of a malleable nature. However, his apparent vacillation was used at times as a deceptive ploy to create the appearance of a favorable atmosphere in which to elicit the opinions of those around him without revealing his true thoughts. In the end, Alexander made his own decisions. One of the few officials whom Alexander permitted to guide him was Tsitsianov. The tsar did not give him his way in all matters but to a considerable extent did allow his advice to guide imperial policy. Tsitsianov evaded inconvenient orders, afterwards presenting his superiors with a fait accompli and a carefully edited account of events designed to justify his actions. Alexander had deliberately created a framework within which Tsitsianov had unusual authority. Faced with a manifestly corrupt and ineffective administration in a remote corner of his empire, Alexander authorized the general to take whatever actions he felt were necessary without his having to request prior approval from St. Petersburg. This approach could have led to a situation in which the tsar transferred the responsibility for any unsuccessful actions from himself to Tsitsianov, yet the general was never held accountable for his mistakes and remained in favor until his death.

One of the areas in which Tsitsianov enjoyed his greatest successes was in the thwarting of St. Petersburg's policy directives. In 1803 and 1805, he was ordered to limit his activities—in the first case, so that he could concentrate on making Georgia secure; in the second, so that Russia could devote its maximum energies to the war against Napoleon. The general used several tactics to circumvent these limitations. He argued that it was imperative that he punish Mohammad Khān of Yerevan (for seizing the Russian candidate for Catholicos of Echmiadzin) and take Ganjeh (to eliminate the dangers it posed to Georgia). Then, all the other east Caucasian khanates would also have to be taken to provide a link to the Caspian and ensure the security of Georgia. At first, Alexander disagreed but then left the decision up to Tsitsianov out of respect for the general's knowledge of the region. The general also tried to persuade St. Petersburg that his planned expeditions were worth the effort because they were assured easy victory since the khans, he said, welcomed Russia as an alternative to Iranian tyranny and the Iranian army was cowardly and inept. The reverses of 1804 did not cause him to modify these claims. In 1805, once the war with Iran was a year old, Tsitsianov argued that it was not possible for Russia to limit itself to defensive actions as his superiors wished because the only alternative to continuing aggressive warfare was to negotiate a settlement. However, that was not a realistic alternative because the shah, according to Tsitsianov's prediction, would never agree to Russia's territorial demands unless compelled to do so by force of arms. St. Petersburg accepted this argument as well, even though the directive that Tsitsianov act only within the scope permitted by his available resources remained in effect.[23]

When it was necessary, Tsitsianov simply evaded St. Petersburg's restrictions and proceeded with his plans, regardless of orders. There is no indication that he ever changed his plans to comply with St. Petersburg's wishes, and the most striking example of his disobedience was the expedition to Gilān and Baku. The undertaking was a complete failure, but not for want of boldness. While Tsitsianov was obtaining the submission of Qarābāgh, Shakki, and Shirvān, Major-General Zavalishin, with 1,345 officers and men of the Caspian fleet, was to set sail from Astrakhan to Gilān. These troops were to occupy Anzali and Rasht until the shah agreed to the harsh and insulting terms contained in a letter from Tsitsianov. If the shah refused the terms, Zavalishin was to make Rasht break away from Iran and become a Russian vassal. Once this was accomplished, Zavalishin was to take Baku. Instead of reducing or postponing this expedition once he received the tsar's order to curtail his activities in 1805, Tsitsianov enlarged its scope. Not only was Zavalishin to take Rasht, he was also to march across the Alburz Mountains to Qazvin (100 miles northwest of Tehran on the main route to Azerbaijan) in order to frighten the shah into compliance. In addition, Zavalishin was to establish a garrison at Lankarān on the Tālesh coast.[24]

No question of the soundness of Tsitsianov's judgment was permitted during his "reign" or after his death. There were only two attempts to offer St. Petersburg a different evaluation of his actions. One was a report by Prince Roman Bagration, brother of the general killed at Borodino. Alexander sent this scion of the Georgian royal family to Georgia to look after that country's well-being under Russian rule. Prince Roman was appalled by conditions in Georgia and denounced Tsitsianov as a tyrant. After the general's death, Prince Roman was recalled. The other critical report was submitted to Alexander in 1806 by Collegiate Assessor Lofitsskii, secretary of the Executive Expedition (administration) of the civilian government of Georgia. General Gudovich informed St. Petersburg that the Lofitsskii report was highly inaccurate and that its author was a conceited troublemaker. Lofitsskii's reliability might be challenged on the grounds that Tsitsianov reprimanded him for supposedly keeping sloppy and deliberately falsified records to cover up for Kovalenskii's transgressions. However, Tsitsianov did not think Lofitsskii guilty enough to be dismissed along with others who had served under Kovalenskii.[25] Despite the attempts by Prince Roman and Lofitsskii to bring about a reevaluation of Tsitsianov's career, there were no official inquiries as there were in the cases of the Kovalenskii-Knorring administration or the conquest of Qarābāgh in 1806.

St. Petersburg did not express any preferences about the order or the rate at which the east Caucasian khanates were to be added to the Russian Empire. There also were no instructions about the form the administration of these newly acquired territories should take, except in the general sense that Alexander had no objection to allowing cooperative khans to stay in office as his vassals. Therefore, Tsitsianov was the one who planned the acquisition of the khanates. Perhaps *planned* is too strong a word since, except for Ganjeh and Yerevan (his first two targets) and Derbent-Qobbeh (which was geographically remote from his base of operations), he tried to take everything at once, relying on intimidation to bring the khans into line. When he encountered more resistance than he had expected, he responded on an ad hoc basis to the problems he found in each situation. Except for his reliance on the threat of force, there was no clear pattern to the way he dealt with the various khans. He seems to have been determined to oust the khans of Ganjeh and Derbent-Qobbeh (and probably Yerevan, had he conquered it), but he was willing to leave in office other khans who met his apparent criteria for ouster—active involvement in anti-Russian activity (the khan of Shirvān) or control of a strategic location (the khan of Baku). He used exorbitant tribute demands to provoke a fight in some cases and then chose not to force a confrontation (as in Qarābāgh). When local conditions provided the right opportunities, he tried to obtain the submission of khans or would-be khans by intervening in policial rivalries. After his death, the remaining khanates were added to the Russian Empire by force, partly because anger over Tsitsianov's death hardened the Russian officers' attitude toward Caucasian Muslims and partly because those khans who had not yet submitted had rejected previous Russian efforts to compel them to do so.

The ferocity of Tsitsianov's demeanor in dealing with various khans reflected not only his desire to humble them into submission but also the weakness of his own position. Even if he had felt inclined to compromise, he could not have afforded to do so without abandoning many of his goals. In the three sieges he initiated—at Ganjeh, Yerevan, and Baku—the Russian position was at least as perilous as the defenders'. On each occasion, the Russians' food supplies and ammunition were virtually exhausted and illness incapacitated a large proportion of the force. Thus, Tsitsianov was compelled either to attack immediately or to retreat, which would have been injurious to his reputation in St. Petersburg as well as humiliating to Russian self-esteem. At Ganjeh, he chose to attack; at Yerevan, his subordinates forced him to withdraw; at Baku, he was saved this bitter choice by the apparent last-minute submission of the khan.

Tribute was another issue on which Tsitsianov refused to allow the khans any leeway. Whenever a khan tried to negotiate for more favorable terms of submission instead of complying unquestioningly with Tsitsianov's demands, the general replied by increasing substantially the amount of tribute he demanded. If tribute were important only as a symbol of subjection to Russia and were scaled to each khanate's resources, as Alexander intended, then the size of the payments would have been less important than a khan's willingness to make them. However, for Tsitsianov, the issue was far more than symbolic. The cost of occupying Georgia and of taking the offensive against various Caucasion rulers and the shah of Iran exhausted the general's finances. Before the annexation of Georgia, advocates of annexation had portrayed that kingdom as a country whose mineral resources and other riches would support the Russian presence in the Caucasus. After annexation, it became clear that regardless of the country's potential, it was a depopulated, devastated land on the verge of anarchy. In 1802, Georgia's cash revenue was more than 30,000 rubles in arrears. Its grain taxes had not been collected at all. Especially after the resumption of the war against France in 1805, St. Petersburg was unwilling to make supplementary allocations for the Caucasian theater. Therefore, Tsitsianov believed that he had to exact the maximum in tribute from each khanate in order to finance his ambitious projects.[26] With his characteristic inability to appreciate other points of view, he failed to anticipate the degree of anti-Russian feeling his exorbitant tribute demands would create.

One of the khanates in which tribute was a particularly important issue was Ganjeh. This khanate was Tsitsianov's first conquest and his first big success. It was a logical choice not only because of its strategic proximity but also because of its decades of hostility toward Georgia. The fact that Tsitsianov achieved results that pleased him greatly encouraged him to continue using the same approach in dealing with the other khans even though he did not intend to press them all into an armed confrontation. At the same time, the fate of Ganjeh confirmed many Muslims' worst fears of Russia's intentions.

Tsitsianov's first move in the takeover of Ganjeh was to demand Javād Khān's submission in terms that implied that the khan could not legitimately refuse since he had already submitted in 1796 and his khanate was traditionally subject to Georgia. The general's specific requirements intensified Javād's belief that Russia would act against his best interests. Tsitsianov not only opposed Ganjeh's claim in the territorial dispute with Georgia, he also took no action against pro-Georgian inhabitants along the border who raided Ganjeh while he demanded that the khan make restitution for Ganjevi counterraids. The general added two particularly ominous stipulations: that Javād accept a permanent Russian garrison in his capital and that he pay the disproportionate sum of 20,000 rubles in tribute annually. The years of Georgian interference in Ganjeh's affairs and Russia's demonstrated preference for Georgia over Ganjeh must have weighed heavily on Javād's mind. He rejected the arguments Tsitsianov had used to justify the demands and showed his concern over Russian hostility by pointing out that his submission in 1796 had been obtained under duress but that at least Catherine had sent him an official patent of office. None was forthcoming in 1803. He closed on a note of defiance, stating that, when he had submitted before, the Iranian army had been far away but now, "thank God!" it was close at hand to protect him from Russia.[27] Tsitsianov made no effort to allay Javād's fears; the only alternative left was war.

Late in 1803, Tsitsianov invaded Ganjeh. He marched unopposed to the immediate vicinity of the capital, where Javād attempted unsuccessfully to block his advance. The khan then withdrew to his citadel, and a month-long siege began. The Ganjevis were cut off from their supplies of water and firewood; the Russians ran short of food and fell ill in large numbers from drinking the local water. As the siege wore on, an Iranian army under the command of the shah's favored son, 'Abbās Mirzā, marched to Javād's aid. Unable to continue the siege but unwilling to retreat, Tsitsianov ordered the storming of the citadel at dawn on January 15, 1804. At first, the defenders were able to repel the onslaught, but in the end the Russians broke through. Javād, his son Hosin Qoli, and several other relatives were killed in battle and with them many other Ganjevis. Tsitsianov put the number of inhabitants killed at 1,500; other Russian authors put the figure at 1,750; Ganjevi and Iranian sources referred to more than 3,000 casualties. Tsitsianov himself acknowledged that thousands of Ganjevis had been ruined by the conquest of the khanate. Ganjeh was made a district of Georgia and renamed Elizavetpol' in honor of Alexander's wife.[28]

Some of Tsitsianov's contemporaries believed that the violent resolution of Ganjeh's status was exactly what the general had intended, perhaps to demonstrate his prowess to St. Petersburg, perhaps to punish Javād for repudiating his submission of 1796.[29] Whatever his motives, circumstantial evidence makes it appear that Tsitsianov deliberately made his demands on Javād intolerably harsh. By Tsitsianov's own reckoning, all of Javād's regular revenue (except his share of the harvests and herds) came to only 16,430 rubles in the last year of the khan's reign, yet tribute was set at 20,000 rubles. Tsitsianov refused to discuss the merits of the khan's counterarguments, offering only the choice between submission and bloodshed. Moreover, at the end of November 1803, while Tsitsianov was still urging Javād to submit peacefully, the general issued a proclamation to the Armenians of Ganjeh that could easily have been interpreted as an attempt to undermine Javād's authority. The proclamation promised Russian protection for the Armenians from all Muslim coercion and robbery. Since Caucasian Armenians of that era frequently described Muslim rule as Muslim oppression, the protection the general offered was likely to be interpreted broadly. The general also gave Ganjevi Armenians permission to settle in any part of Georgia and, as an added inducement, offered them state peasant status instead of serfdom.[30] Ganjeh was already sparsely populated, and its Armenian community was an important source of the kahn's revenue, both through its payment of the extra tax on tolerated non-Muslims and its involvement in a variety of economic activities. Thus, Russian suzerainty would mean not only a substantial drain on the Ganjevi revenues in the form of tribute payments but also the reduction of the number of taxpayers.

Tsitsianov was well pleased with the way events developed in Ganjeh. After the conquest, he portrayed his actions as necessary for the maintenance of Russian prestige. He wrote to Chancellor Vorontsov that, if he had lifted the siege without taking the citadel, that "would have been, in my opinion, improper and the might of Russian arms would fall in the eyes of neighbors, who base their conduct solely on fear of the strong."[31] The fact that he took the citadel by storm rather than any other means gave him particular satisfaction since the structure had been considered impregnable. "The fortunate storming [of

Ganjeh] is an example of the moral supremacy of the Russians over the Persians and of that spirit of confidence in victory which I consider my primary goal to nurture and ignite among the soldiers."[32]

He was not afraid that someone would think the destruction of the old order in Ganjeh was deliberate. On the contrary, he did his best to persuade the khans of Yerevan, Qarābāgh, Baku, and Shakki that he would destroy them as he had Javād unless they complied immediately with his demands. When Mohammad Hasan Khān of Shakki informed Tsitsianov of his distress over the killing of Javād (his brother-in-law), the general replied by lauding Russia's generosity in giving Javād's widow a pension and added threateningly, "Can the fly fight the eagle or the rabbit the lion? Be certain that I need only give the order and the khanate Nukhā [Shakki] will cease to be, like the khanate of Ganjeh."[33]

Not only was Ganjeh eliminated as a political entity, there was a wholesale assault on the khanate's social and cultural life. It became a crime punishable by a fine of one ruble even to refer to the place as Ganjeh rather than Elizavetpol'. According to Iranian sources, Muslims were expelled from their homes within the citadel. The main mosque of the capital was turned into a church. Russian law replaced the Koranic law and common law. The jurisdiction of the Muslim lawyers was drastically reduced and their fees were eliminated. Within a year, they were destitute. Some of the most important among them were given salaries by the Russian government, which also agreed to maintain five mosques. In return for the salaries, these religious leaders were expected to serve as functionaries of the Russian government.[34]

Javād Khān's wives and other relatives who survived the battle but had not escaped to Iran (as had most of his sons) were arrested. They were held as prisoners in the citadel until 1812, when they were freed by Tsitsianov's successor Philip Paulucci, who held the view, novel among Russian officials, that Javād was a valiant man who died fighting to defend his interests.[35]

The conquest of Ganjeh and the changing of its name to honor the tsaritsa brought Tsitsianov the recognition he had sought from St. Petersburg. He was promoted to general of the infantry, and eight of his officers were decorated. All the other soldiers who participated in the undertaking were given a silver ruble each and the tsar's praise. The clement tsar praised Tsitsianov's use of harsh methods, which were said to be necessary because of Javād's obstinacy. The casualties, however regrettable, were the khan's own fault, said the tsar. In any event, only the guilty suffered. Most of all, Alexander was pleased that Tsitsianov had avoided backing down, which would have encouraged "Asiatic arrogance."[36]

The degraded position of Islam in Elizavetpol' casts some light on the religious aspect of relations between Russia and the east Caucasian Muslims, a problem that has generally been underestimated by European observers. When Consul Skibinevskii described the preaching of Muslim religious leaders in Shirvān and Baku against submission to Russia, he treated their arguments as scare stories told by fanatics. Although Russia did not attempt to abolish Islam in the khanates, its policies in Ganjeh and elsewhere gave the Muslims genuine cause for alarm. After the annexation of Georgia, Russia exerted social pressure to force Christian women in the new province to cease wearing the veil, a long-established custom that had developed as the result of Georgia's ties to the Muslim world. The change was not welcomed, but the wearing of this symbol of what was assumed by the Muslims to be a woman's correct status and demeanor gradually ended. The practice of billeting soldiers in the homes of less affluent Georgians also led to some problems involving Russian soldiers and Georgian women. If Russians treated their fellow Christians so contemptuously, Muslims must have been worried about the treatment they would receive. In fact, the small Muslim community in Tbilisi did suffer under Russian rule. They were allowed one mosque, but others were confiscated, as were the *vaqf* grants.[37] When these actions were followed by the conquest of Ganjeh, it is not surprising that Caucasian Muslims feared persecution by the Russians.

Russian rule also carried with it the threat of disrupting the traditional relationships between Muslim and Christian inhabitants of the khanates by using Armenians to undermine Muslim rulers. Russia's attempt to replace the Catholicos of Echmiadzin and the offer to resettle Ganjevi Armenians in Georgia could be interpreted in that light, as could the removal of 250 Armenian families from Qarābāgh by a Russian detachment shortly after the fall of Ganjeh. Equally ominous was Tsitsianov's letter to the Armenians of Qarābāgh demanding that they send some cavalry to join the Russians in fighting Iran. This demand was made in 1805, when the Muslims of Qarābāgh doubted Russia's ability to protect them from an Iranian attack. Therefore, the proclamation carried a triple threat. First, Tsitsianov was calling upon some of Ebrāhim Khalil's subjects to prepare for war without discussing the matter with the khan, thus belittling the khan's authority during the negotiations for Qarābāgh's submission to Russia. Second, many Muslim Qarābāghis were concerned that nothing be done to provoke another Iranian attack on their khanate.

Finally, the Armenians of Qarābāgh had a tradition of urging Russia to overthrow Ebrāhim Khalil, and the Armenians of Ganjeh were believed to have aided the Russians in the conquest of that khanate.[38] Therefore, the possibility existed that the Qarābāghi Armenians, once mobilized to fight under the Russian aegis, might play an active role in the forced abolition of Muslim rule in the khanate. (As matters developed, the khan submitted. If there had been contingency plans to use Armenians to overthrow the khan, no such action was in fact taken.)

The deep impression that the conquest of Ganjeh, and later, Qarābāgh made on the east Caucasian Muslims can be seen by the readiness of Muslims in various khanates to believe that Russia planned to inflict a similar fate upon them. For example, when Major-General Zavalishin attempted to force the khan of Baku to submit in the summer of 1805, there was a mass exodus of terrified Muslims from the city. They fled again in September 1806, when Russian troops approached once more. Shortly before that time, the inhabitants of Derbent had been persuaded to overthrow their khan and surrender to the Russians by deliberately planted rumors of the terrible fate that awaited them unless they surrendered. In Qarābāgh, rumors that the Russians planned to exterminate the Muslim inhabitants found wide acceptance in 1806 and 1810. By Tsitsianov's own admission, the reason of the khan of Shakki refused to send 500 cavalry soldiers to assist the Russians was not disloyalty but fear of a Russian attack (which was not in fact contemplated at that time).[39] The general did not pursue this line of thought or question whether his tactic of intimidation, which inspired such mistrust, made it more difficult to obtain the khan's cooperation.

Of the remaining khanates, only Shirvān was taken without conquest. Mostafā, the khan, thought he might derive an advantage over his rivals by siding with Russia, but Tsitsianov's usual unwillingness to moderate his demands stiffened the khan's resistance. It took an invasion by Russian troops to frighten the khan into signing a treaty in 1805.[40] All the other khanates that were added to the Russian Empire were taken by force: Qarābāgh, Shakki, Baku, Qobbeh, and Derbent in 1806; Tālesh in 1813; and Yerevan and Nakhjavān in 1827. However, other factors influenced the stages of the annexation process before the violent resolution. One of the most important of these factors was the traditional pattern of domestic and external power rivalries. Thus, even when rulers volunteered to become Russian vassals, they were not motivated by the admiration for Russian civilization that Russian authorities ascribed to them. The khans of

Baku, Shirvān, and Derbent-Qobbeh all offered to submit to Russia in return for Russian support for their territorial ambitions and their struggles with rivals for power. Hosein Qoli Khān of Baku sought Russian backing against the revived strength of Derbent-Qobbeh. Mostafā Khān hoped Russia would recognize his authority over a Shirvān enlarged to the dimensions of the bygone domain of the Shirvānshāhs. When Mostafā objected to Tsitsianov's terms, the general contemplated replacing him with the khan's younger brother, who was very enthusiastic about the idea. Tsitsianov lost all interest in the plan once Mostafā submitted. Sheikh 'Ali Khān of Derbent-Qobbeh wanted an ally to defeat the coalition between his younger brother and Dāghestāni opponents, which had almost succeeded in overthrowing him, and also wanted Russia to support his reconquest of Sāleyān, then under Shirvāni control. Since Tsitsianov lacked the means to compel Sheikh 'Ali and Hosein Qoli to submit when they balked at his demands, no agreement was concluded. After Tsitsianov's death, Hosein Qoli and Sheikh 'Ali fled as new Russian forces approached their khanates. Baku and Qobbeh were annexed outright; in Derbent, all real power was in Russia's hands, although there was a figurehead khan.[41]

Whatever punishment the Russians would have liked to inflict on Hosein Qoli, they never captured him. Alexander Tormasov's plan to kill Sheikh 'Ali, who continued to fight the Russians for several years after the loss of his domains, came to nought. After Javād, the only khan killed by the Russians was Ebrāhim Khalil of Qarābāgh. There was no plan to eliminate rule by khan there, and the vitriolic Tsitsianov had died five months before the conquest of the khanate. Ebrāhim Khalil's death was the product of his own weak position and the Russians'. In 1804 and 1805, the khan took a pro-Russian stance and signed a treaty of submission in May of 1805. However, Russia's military weakness, especially after the death of Tsitsianov, left Qarābāgh vulnerable to repeated, devastating raids by Iranian troops and by the son he had sent to be the shah's hostage in 1798. It was clear that his subjects were disgruntled with the khan's anti-Iranian stance. In June of 1806, he again submitted to the shah, who sent troops to expel the Russians from Qarābāgh. The Russian officers were angry and bitter over the military embarrassments they had not anticipated, as well as over the killing of their chief. Among those whose morale was particularly affected was the commandant in Shushā, Major D. T. Lisanevich, whom Tsitsianov had made a scapegoat for the Russian forces' poor showing in Qarābāgh in 1805. Lisanevich was a brave and arrogant man who did not bear the abuse lightly. When he became suspicious of Ebrāhim Khalil's activities, he sought information about the khan's loyalty from the khan's second son and a grandson, both of whom were eager to take power and accused the khan of treason. Lisanevich then attacked the khan's camp at night, killing the khan, one of his wives, a young son, and most of his entourage. Even Gudovich thought the killings improper and held an inquiry. Lisanevich defended his actions on the grounds that Ebrāhim Khalil was a traitor. The major was exonerated and continued to serve with distinction in the Caucasus until 1825, when he was killed by a Caucasian he had insulted. Ebrāhim Khalil's second son was made khan of Qarābāgh on Gudovich's orders.[42]

Shakki was the only khanate in which a long-standing struggle for power worked to Russia's advantage, if only briefly. For years there had been an often violent rivalry between the khan and a younger brother, with the occasional intervention of Shirvān and, in 1795, Iran. After Āqā Mohammad's death, the khan of Shirvān intervened in Shakki to restore the previous ruler. Therefore, in 1804, Salim tried to use the Russians as he had the Iranians, accusing his brother of anti-Russian actions, offering to pay an immense sum in tribute, and generally promoting Russia's interests. While Salim was out of power, Tsitsianov had nothing good to say about him, but when an attempted conquest by Shirvān created unrest and Salim seized power, Tsitsianov welcomed him as a Russian vassal.[43]

This symbiotic relationship might have continued had it not been for the harshness of Russia's treatment of Caucasian Muslim rulers, specifically, the murder in 1806 of Ebrāhim Khalil and his wife, who was Salim's sister. This needless act of violence was doubly horrifying to Salim. If one khan who had submitted to Russia could be killed in a surprise nighttime attack, no vassal khan was safe. Whether Salim, who did not flinch from killing his eldest brother's seven children after seizing power in 1795, felt any sorrow over his sister's fate for her sake cannot be proven. However, his complaint that the Russians killed her even though they knew she was his sister showed that he interpreted her murder as a sign of contempt for him. As he explained to the Russians:

After this occurrence where will your trustworthiness be accepted? I dishonored and sullied myself in all Mohammedan places by submitting to Russia . . . . [Salim described his battles against Russia's enemies] but finally, in reward for my services, they [the Russians] captured my sister alive and killed her even though they recognized her, from which I saw your trustworthiness and learned.[44]

Having become disenchanted with the Russians, Salim expelled the garrison from Shakki in the summer of 1806. In October of that year, Major-General Nebol'sin, the commander of Russian troops in Qarā-bāgh, invaded the khanate and stormed its capital. Salim, who escaped to the mountains, soon regretted his clash with Russia and asked for an imperial pardon, but Gudovich, once more in charge of Caucasian affairs, considered Salim irredeemably treacherous and was determined that neither Salim nor any member of his family should ever rule Shakki again. In December of 1806, Alexander, acting on Gudovich's advice, proclaimed Ja'far Qoli Khān Domboli, the anti-Qājār rebel and former governor of Khoi, to be the new khan of Shakki.[45]

The last three khanates Russia acquired were all taken in conjunction with operations directed against Iran—Tālesh in the first war, Yerevan and Nakhjavān in the second. The khan of Tālesh had never sighed a formal treaty of submission to Russia but did ask for, and sometimes received, Russian military protection. (This khanate was so peripheral to Russia's main concerns that Russia did not wish to establish a permanent garrison there.) After Tsitsianov's death, the khan took the expedient of submitting to Iran as well but sought to rely on Russian assistance.[46] Some of the Iranian attacks in the later years of the war did considerable damage, and an ever-increasing number of the khan's subjects rejected his authority and sided with Iran. In August 1812, Tālesh was conquered by an elite British-trained corps of the Iranian army; but, in the following December and January, after the outcome of the war had already been decided, the khanate was conquered by Russian troops in extremely bloody fighting in which both sides suffered an appalling number of casualties.[47] The khans of Yerevan and Nakhjavān were both removed in 1805 by the shah on the grounds of disloyalty. The government of Nakhjavān was entrusted to a cousin of the former khan. The new khan of Yerevan, Hosein Qoli, was one of the most able men in Fath 'Ali's government and ruled Yerevan from 1807 until its conquest by the Russians in 1827. At that time, Yerevani troops suffered a decisive loss at Russian hands; the inhabitants then revolted and submitted to the Russians. Nakhjavān had been taken a few months earlier without serious opposition.

During the first three decades of the nineteenth century, Russia fulfilled its territorial objectives in the eastern Caucasus, although it did so at great cost to all concerned. Russia's officials never learned the lessons of 1796. They underestimated the natural obstacles—difficulty of communication, unfamiliar climate and diet, food shortages—but, more important, they failed to learn that khans and their subjects might have a different notion of their best interests than the ones the Russians expected them to have. To the Muslims of the eastern Caucasus, Russia was, at best, a potentially useful ally against traditional rivals, as long as it did not attempt to exert too great a control over a khanate's affairs. At worst, it was the arch-enemy of the existing order, intent on destroying every aspect of Muslim civilization. Russia's tactics of intimidation encouraged those fears, but the Russians never questioned the desirability of using such tactics, in part because their preconceptions blinded them to the nature of the problem and in part because there was virtually no review of official conduct in the disputed provinces. St. Petersburg set only the broadest policy guidelines and left great leeway to officials on the scene, who took even more leeway than their superiors had intended. As long as the local officials produced results, and even sometimes when they did not, St. Petersburg would not cavil over the means by which the goals were pursued. This broad latitude could not solve some of the officials' most serious problems. Even the submission of many khanates to Russia did not mean that the inhabitants accepted Russian rule. Thus, the fighting between them and the Russians persisted, while, at the same time, Russia became involved in wars with Iran and the Ottoman Empire. The Russians were dismayed by a situation they did not understand and, therefore, reacted with indignation at the outrageous behavior of their Muslim opponents. Outrageous behavior deserved stern punishment, so the spiral of mutual suspicion and conflict continued until sheer force gave the victory to Russia.

VI

The Origins of
the First Russo-Iranian War

The war between Russia and Iran was not caused by Iran's sending 20,000 men to attack Tsitsianov in 1804, as Foreign Minister Adam Czartoryski directed Russia's ambassador in Constantinople to tell the Turks.[1] Still less was it the result of British manipulation of Iran for the purpose of expelling Russia from the Caucasus, or Russia's need to block British or French imperialist expansion in the region or Russia's need to prevent the Iranian "feudal elite" from seizing control there, as some Soviet writers have alleged.[2] The first explanation reflects the characteristic inability of Russian officials to understand that people might perceive their own interests as different from those of Russia. The other explanations have more to do with Cold War propaganda than with history. The French and the British did not become involved in the conflict between Russia and Iran until after the fighting had begun. Russia sought and occasionally received the support of local rulers and tribal chiefs whom Soviet writers usually describe as the "feudal elite." One Soviet author went so far as to fabricate evidence to support his charge that British economic imperialism provoked Russia into fighting a defensive war. He claimed that consul Skibinevskii alerted his superiors to the fact that an 1801 treaty between Iran and Britain gave Britain permission to build ships in Lankarān and monopolize the purchase of Gilāni silk.[3] Neither the commercial nor the political treaty of 1801 contained such provisions, nor did Skibinevskii's report on Anglo-Iranian relations mention those nonexistent details.[4]

91

The real causes of the First Russo-Iranian War lay in what the recently established Qājār dynasty perceived as a Russian military threat to its hegemony and in the need of that dynasty to enhance its legitimacy by asserting its sovereignty over the northwestern border provinces. These reasons were not entirely the same as the ones for which the war was continued for nine years. Once the fighting began both sides had to reconsider their attitudes in light of unexpected difficulties. At the same time, the conviction that royal honor demanded pursuit of the thwarted goals made the war itself a reason for continuing to fight. The Napoleonic wars also affected the war in the Caucasus, since Russia participated directly in those grueling contests while France and Britain tried to manipulate Iran, at times to keep Russia distracted by Caucasian problems, at times to end the distraction. However, none of these concerns applied to the start of the war.

The symbolic importance of the eastern Caucasus to the Qājār dynasty becomes clear when viewed in the context of the political instability from which Iran had suffered since the breakup of the Safavi empire. In the violent power struggles that gripped Iran for the rest of the eighteenth century, ambitious men looked for any possible asset that might help them defeat their rivals. Military strength was indispensable but might not have been sufficient in itself. One of the most important ways to enhance a claim to power was to appropriate in some way the mantle of the Safavis. In narrowly legalistic terms, no such claim was credible to a Shii Iranian, for whom the only legitimate rulers could be the divinely chosen leader of the faithful, the twelfth *imam* (the last in a series of descendants of 'Ali, Mohammad's son-in-law), or the Safavis (who claimed descent from the seventh *imam*). However, the devout, as well as the more secular, occasionally made pragmatic adaptations. The theocratic element of Safavi kingship began to decline during the reign of the first shah of the dynasty, Ismail (who ruled from 1501 to 1524), in the wake of his humiliating defeat by the Ottomans in 1514 and his administrative reforms, which separated religious and secular administrative jurisdictions. By the time Ismail's son inherited the throne, the tribal confederation (the Qizilbash) that formed the core of Safavi support "no longer held the person of the shah in any special respect, whatever the official myth might be."[5] The succession to the throne was often contested during the Safavi era, but the competition was based on secular factional rivalries without concern for the messianism of the dynasty's official ideology.

Although the charismatic aspect of Safavi prestige was gone, the might of Safavi kingship remained a potent image. This was proven dramatically by the fate of Shāh Tahmāsb II. By the 1730s, Tahmāsb's armies, led by the future Nāder Shāh, had reconquered most of Iran including the northwestern territory up to the Aras River. Further operations beyond that line were interpreted by renewed difficulties with the Afghans. Therefore, Shāh Tahmāsb tried to complete the conquest of the northwest while his general campaigned in the northeast. However, Tahmāsb was defeated resoundingly and had to cede the territory Nāder had conquered. This defeat gave Nāder a chance to rally opposition to the shah by denouncing the territorial loss as "contrary to the will of Heaven."[6] Nāder then deposed Tahmāsb and eventually claimed the throne for himself. After the breakup of Nāder's empire, many contenders for power used a puppet Safavi to provide symbolic legitimacy.[7]

The Qājārs were in a particularly good position to appropriate Safavi prestige since they had been members of the Qizilbash confederation. Therefore, the main ideological justification for the new dynasty's pretentions was that the Qājārs, as loyal defenders of the Safavis, had reunited the provinces that had once comprised the fallen empire and had simultaneously restored the power of Shii Islam (which Nāder Shāh, as a Sunni, had opposed). Therefore, the struggle for control of the northwestern marches was a pillar of the ideological justification for Qājār rule. Āqā Mohammad's demand that Erekle submit addressed the issue clearly:

The late Shāh Ismail Safavi, may his grave be fragrant, in the period of conquering the kingdoms of Iran had sovereignty over Georgia. . . . By the grace of God, we have solidified our claim to the throne. That realm [Georgia] ought to be an appendage of the kingdom of Iran once more, in accordance with ancient law.[8]

Āqā Mohammad did not claim the title of shah until after his 1795 Caucasian campaign, which, from his point of view, secured the submission of Georgia and other neighboring principalities. He was crowned shah in March of the following year. At that time, he put on the sacred sword from the shrine of Sheikh Safi od-Din, the ancestor of the Safavi shahs. He then proclaimed his intention to subdue all of Khorāsān next and campaigned there later in the year. The city of Herāt, then under Afghan control, was one of his main objectives. Keeping to his theme of restoring the empire to its Safavi dimensions, he claimed the city on the grounds that it had been part of Safavi Iran.[9] (As matters developed, he never reached Herāt. The Russian operations in the Caucasus forced him to cut short the Khorāsān campaign.)

The Qājār dynasty survived a critical test when the supreme authority passed from Āqā Mohammad to his chosen heir, Fath 'Ali. The new shah obtained the endorsement of one of the most influential Shii *mojtaheds* (especially venerated religious scholars). The *mojtahed* named Fath 'Ali his deputy and "permitted" the new shah to take the throne.[10] There were a number of challenges to the central government from one of Fath 'Ali's brothers, (whose power was based on the western Iranian plateau), a scion of the Zand family in the vicinity of Esfahān, the Shaqaqi and Domboli Kurds and Afshar Turcomans in Azerbaijan, a grandson of Nāder Shāh, as well as Afghan tribesmen in Khorāsān. All of these opponents had been defeated by 1803. As early as 1800, it was clear that the anti-Qājār forces in Khorāsān were on the wane. Only in the northwestern marches did Fath 'Ali continue to encounter serious difficulties.

Fath 'Ali shared his predecessor's opinion on the status of Georgia. In 1800, when Kovalenskii wrote the shah demanding that he drop all claims to Georgia, return the people captured during the 1795 attack, and pay reparations for the damage done at that time, the enraged shah had his chief vizier, Hāji Ebrāhim, explain the basis for his claim to the eastern Caucasus. The tone of the letter, althought forceful in setting forth the shah's argument, was not insulting as was the Kovalenskii message. In fact, Hāji Ebrāhim referred flatteringly to Paul and expressed the desire for cordial relations with Russia. However, with regard to the Russian claim to Georgia, Hāji Ebrāhim minced no words. Georgia had always been part of Iran, he wrote. Erekle's treaty with Catherine was illegal and treasonous:

Since the time when the globe divided into four parts, Georgia, Kakheti [a Georgian province] and Teflis [Tbilisi] were included in the Iranian state and in the time of previous Iranian shahs the inhabitants always adhered by service and obedience to their [the shahs'] decrees but were never part of the Russian realm, except on that occasion when King Erekle, ... contemporary of .... Āqā Mohammad Khān, had the notion to cast off the rule of his customary sovereign [and] embark upon a path of hostility against Iran. ... What trust do the agreements of King Erekle deserve? What value can his signature have? For example, if one of the peoples located on Russia's borders gave itself over utterly capriciously to Iranian sovereignty [and] initiated a treaty and other agreements with it [the Iranian government] would such a deal have force? In no way could it place itself under Iranian suzerainty. ... Now, thank God, the authority of the Iranian throne is fully affirmed, for all khans, rulers, and commanders bow their necks before it. .... [11]

The letter closed with an announcement of the shah's intention to send 60,000 soldiers to the eastern Caucasus. According to Hāji Ebrāhim, this was intended not for the conquest of foreign territory but for the establishment of law and order within a part of the empire and the maintenance of the Russo-Iranian border (as it stood before the recent Russian expansion).[12] This theme of reestablishing Iranian control over the country's northwestern borderlands was echoed in a number of proclamations from Fath 'Ali Shāh to various Christian and Muslim Caucasians.

Another point raised in several proclamations to inhabitants of the disputed provinces illustrates the way in which Russia's heavy-handed treatment of Georgia strengthened the Qājār argument. When Russia abolished the rule of the Bagrations, Fath 'Ali Shāh was able to style himself the defender of Bagration legitimacy by recognizing the princes Alexander (Erekle's son) and T'eimuraz (Giorgi's son) as the *vālis* of Georgia and sending troops to restore their kingdom to them. The shah also tried to win over Prince P'arnaoz, Prince Alexander's younger brother.[13]

While the Qājārs' desire to reestablish Iranian hegemony over the eastern Caucasus was vital to their own prestige, that was not the specific cause of the war with Russia, even though it increased the ill will between the prospective combatants. Fath 'Ali had threatened to drive the Russians from the Caucasus, but the war did not begin in earnest until there was a direct Russian military threat to the Qājār government. This threat had two aspects. The first was the way Fath 'Ali perceived Russia's involvement in the Caucasus as being directed against his authority. The other was the way Russia deliberately took the offensive against Iran and tried to intimidate the shah.

Although Russia's official policy was to extend its border only to the Aras and Kura rivers, there was little reason for Fath 'Ali to feel sure that there would be no attack on the territory farther south, especially since Russian ambitions occasionally ranged beyond that line. St. Petersburg readily agreed to Tsitsianov's proposals to take control of Tabriz (the capital of Azerbaijan) and Khoi (located on the Turkish border), even though both were south of the proposed border, and, once the war had begun, accepted his plan to invade Gilān as well.

Even if the Russians had not advocated such measures, there would have been good reason for the shah to suspect Russia of hostile intent. Catherine made several attempts, albeit unsuccessful ones, to establish Mortezā Qoli, Aqā Mohammad's rebel brother, as the ruler of the south Caspian coast, and her 1796 proclamation to the Iranians and Caucasians announced her intention to liberate Iran from Aqā Mohammad's tyranny. Fath 'Ali's government interpreted these actions as proof of Catherine's desire to conquer Iran.[14] In writing about the 1796 campaign, one chronicler compared it to the dismemberment of Iran in the 1720s.[15] Given this frame of reference, Russia's annexation of Georgia and the establishment of a Russian garrison there would certainly appear ominous to the Qājār court. Most alarming were Tsitsianov's attacks on neighboring Muslim-ruled areas. As another chronicler expressed it, the Russians, having taken Georgia, decided to take the surrounding territory.[16] In other words, Russia was encroaching on Iran. The process began with Tsitsianov's ill-fated attempt to crush the Lesghis of Jaruteleh. To officials in Tehran, this was an attack on Iranian vassals.[17] The official's alarm increased greatly when they learned of the conquest of Ganjeh. Javād Khān recognized Fath 'Ali Shāh as his suzerain, was expected to fight for the shah against the Russians, and was considered under the shah's military protection. Of particular importance was the fact that the conquest of this vassal principality was a sudden move not preceded by any explanation or declaration from Tsitsianov to the shah.[18] Presumably, the silence made such a great impression on the Tehran court because it implied contempt for the shah and set a precedent for attacks without warning on other parts of his realm.

If 'Abbās Mirzā's army had reached Ganjeh before the storming of its citadel on January 3, 1804, the Russo-Iranian War would have begun there rather than at the Armenian monastery of Echmiadzin in Yerevan the following June. As it was, the Iranian army arrived too late, and, since winter was not usually a time for campaigning in the area, the army returned to territory south of the Aras. It is highly probable that the shah would have preferred to avoid war. Instead of ordering a counterattack immediately, he had his new chief vizier, Mirzā Shafi', send Tsitsianov a stern warning, giving the general a chance to back down and avoid war. The tone of the letter was self-assertive to the point of offensiveness. No doubt the desire to appear resolute and intimidating was a contributing factor in the choice of wording, but so too was the outrage over Russian harshness in Jaruteleh and Ganjeh and the feeling that those actions were directed against Iran. These themes emerged in Shafi''s references to "the destruction by you [Tsitsianov] of promises of friendship" and his charge that "prolonging your stay in Tbilisi on the pretext of conducting trade, you now extend the hand of oppression to the borders of Ganjeh and Dāghestān." The letter closed with a warning to Tsitsianov to leave Iranian territory immediately in order to avoid war.[19]

Tsitsianov enjoyed using such language in addressing others but could not stand to be insulted in the same way. Therefore, Mirzā Shafi''s letter, instead of producing the desired result, played into the general's hands by encouraging his eagerness for war with Iran. Tsit-sianov's reply was a virtual declaration of war. He characterized Sha-fi''s reference to him as a merchant as a gross insult to the Russian Empire that required punishment by the sword. The only way to avoid war was for Iran to turn over the Bagration princes Alexander and T'eimuraz, which would have diminished greatly the shah's ability to enforce his own suzerainty or restore Bagration rule in Georgia. The letter contained a direct threat to Iranian security:

If you, desiring the good fortune of Persia, will come to your senses and reflect that neither the empty, grandiose threat nor the Persian army numerous as the sands of the sea and who fight with feathers, not swords, are frightening to those who are accustomed to conquer in all parts of the world. . . . [20]

In fact, Russian authorities were rather eager for war with Iran. The most eager was Tsitsianov, but, as in the case of his dealings with Caucasian khans, his extreme measures were warmly received by his superiors. All these advocates of war greatly underestimated the difficulties and saw it as a way to achieve expansionist goals speedily, asserting Russian superiority over "Persians." Tsitsianov viewed his command of the war against Iran as he viewed all aspects of his Caucasian service, namely, as the opportunity to create dramatic confrontations and, in winning, impress the tsar. Tuchkov noted that Tsitsianov was extremely pleased when the Iranian choice for Catholicos of Echmiadzin imprisoned his Russian-backed rival, because that act provided grounds for war with Iran.[21] In any event, the general had virtually guaranteed the outbreak of war by his efforts to conquer various khanates and his letter to Mirzā Shafi'. He also did his best to belittle the shah in St. Petersburg's eyes, as when he wrote to Tsar Alexander that Javād Khān had received a proclamation "from the Iranian sovereign—a name which is sometimes given to Bābā Khān in Persia."[22] Similarly, once the war began, he proclaimed the triumph of Russian arms over the cowardly Iranians.[23] Contempt for Iranian military prowess was widespread among the officers serving in the Caucasus and, through their influence, among St. Petersburg officials as well. Even after the setbacks suffered by Russian arms during the summer of 1804, a young officer, Michael Vorontsov, son of the ambassador to London and nephew of the chancellor of the empire, wrote to his father that Fath 'Ali was known to be an ineffectual coward who dared not spend much time away from Tehran for fear of rebellion.[24]

One of the clearest indications of Tsitsianov's desire for war with Iran was his vigorous effort to make certain that St. Petersburg did not negotiate a settlement with the shah in 1805. Authorities in the capital were willing to consider negotiation, provided the terms were highly favorable to Russia, once they heard rumors that the shah had been intimidated by the putative Russian victories of 1804. St. Petersburg's willingness to make peace was soon intensified by the need to concentrate all of Russia's energies on the war against Napoleon. However, Tsitsianov opposed such ideas and persuaded his superiors that the war against Iran could not be stopped without undermining completely Russia's position in the Caucasus and, by inference, Russia's honor. At first, he argued that it was necessary to inflict "painful punishment" on Iran for all the trouble it had caused in 1804. Later, he emphasized that the shah would never accept the loss of the Caucasus to Russia and would try to take it back.[25]

Despite its preoccupation with other matters, St. Petersburg approved Tsitsianov's conduct of the war, including his plan to strike nearer the heart of Qājār power by a campaign inland from Gilān. As Czartoryski observed after the first battles, the victories that he believed Tsitsianov had won demonstrated the superiority of the courage and leadership of the Russian military.[26]

The shah's efforts to enforce his claim to the Caucasus in 1800 and 1802 were comparatively small-scale and eneffective. There were no major battles; the Iranians did not carry out their plans to attack Georgia, nor did they seek a confrontation with Russian troops. Troubles with the Afghans in the northeast diverted troops that the shah might otherwise have sent to the Caucasus, but by 1802 the emergency had passed. Military concerns did not keep the shah from staging a more ambitious campaign in the Caucasus in 1802, yet he chose not to do so. Only in 1804, after the attack on Ganjeh, the unconstructive exchange of letters with Tsitsianov, and the receipt of intelligence that other vassals—the khans of Yerevan, Nakhjavān, and Khoi—were conducting treasonous negotiations with the Russians, did Fath 'Ali Shāh make a greater commitment to war in the Caucasus.[27] Not until that time did he lead an army to the region, although he had taken the field personally in the Khorāsān campaign of 1799, 1800, and 1802.

The potential for conflict was considerable, given that Russian rulers and Iranian rulers especially believed that control over the eastern Caucasus was vital to royal prestige. The immediate cause of the war was Russia's threat to the security of the Qājār realm.

VII

The War, 1804 – 1813

The first war between Russia and Iran lasted for nine years, from the unsuccessful Russian campaign against Yerevan in 1804 to the disastrous Iranian losses at Aslānduz and Lankarān in 1812 and 1813. Russia's victory was not a foregone conclusion. Each side had a number of advantages, as well as some serious disadvantages. Russia did not win the war so much as manage not to lose it. The Caucasian theater was for Russia secondary to the European. However, for Iran, the war was overwhelmingly important. This was modern Iran's first extensive contact with European Christian powers—not only with Russia but also with Britain and France. While fighting the war, Iran made its first westernizing reforms, specifically in the military. In contrast, the Second Russo-Iranian War (1826-1828) raised no new issues but was essentially a brief recapitulation of the earlier conflict.

At first glance, it seems as though the Russians' confidence in an easy victory over Iran was well justified. Russia was an immense country with prodigious resources. By 1805, it had an army of well over half a million men (and more than doubled that number over the next seven years). Even though these men were not at all battle-ready, the number of men under arms was prodigious compared to traditional eighteenth-century professional armies. During the late eighteenth century, the army had proven that it could be a match for Europe's best. Field Marshall Suvorov dazzled Europe by leading an Austro-Russian army across the Alps to resounding victories in Italy in 1799. Russia also had a Caspian navy to maintain communi-

99

cations with the troops in the Caucasus and threaten the coastal provinces under the shah's control. Modest though this fleet was, the Iranians had nothing to match it.

Quite a few of the officers who served in the eastern Caucasus were well-trained soldiers of considerable personal courage. There were men such as Major-General Peter Nesvetaev, an infantry officer who had distinguished himself in Catherine's second war with the Ottoman Empire and then in Poland before being sent to the Caucasus in 1804. There his achievements included the conquest of Shakki. Another able commander was Colonel Kariagin, who in June of 1805 was trapped with his 400 men in a small fort in Qarābāgh by an Iranian force of 10,000 to 20,000. The Russians held out for a week of bitter fighting during which Kariagin, his subordinate (Major Kotliarevskii), and more than a hundred of his men were wounded. Many others were killed and at least 57 surrendered. When he ran low on food, water, and ammunition, and had only 150 soldiers fit for combat, he agreed to surrender. During the truce he had requested on the pretext of obtaining his superior's permission to surrender, he led his men in a nighttime escape into the nearby mountains, where Armenians gave him food and shelter.[1] Kotliarevskii went on to become an even better known hero of the war in the Caucasus. He fought in many of the important battles of the era, from the storming of Ganjeh—during which he was gravely wounded—to the final battles of Aslānduz and Lankarān, in which he commanded the victorious Russian troops. At Lankarān, he preferred, as usual, to be in the thick of things rather than command from a safe distance and, as a result, suffered a serious head wound that left him incapacitated for the remaining thirty-eight years of his life. The Russian army was also supplemented by contingents formed by new subjects, such as the Qarābāghis, who fought alongside the Russians in 1805, and the Georgians, who participated in Tsitsianov's sieges of Yerevan and Baku.

However, Russia's advantages were more apparent than real. Every one of its strengths counted for less than expected, and a host of unforseen problems complicated matters still further.

The most obvious problem was that Russia could not devote its full attention to the war against Iran because Russia was also at war with France (1805-1807 and 1812-1815), the Ottoman Empire (1806-1812), and, briefly, Sweden (1808-1809). (Russia was also officially at war with Britain from 1807 until 1812, but there were no military clashes between the two states. The disruption of trade with Russia's principal commercial partner was the most serious repercussion of that war.) Although the Ottoman Empire claimed suzerainty over the western Caucasus and consequently opposed Russia's claim to the Georgian principalities there, the causes of the war between these two empires were related solely to European affairs. Napoleon and Alexander each sought to strengthen his own influence in the Balkans, and each had a measure of success. While France's diplomatic influence increased in Constantinople and its military position in Dalmatia grew stronger, Russia became more aggressive about strengthening its position in parts of the Balkans, especially in Moldavia and Wallachia. In December 1806, the Ottoman Empire formally declared war. Russia soon had cause to regret involvement in this war. In the first year, it tied down 40,000 Russian soldiers; the fighting dragged on for six years.

These developments had direct repercussions on the Russo-Iranian War. First, the troops sent to the Caucasus to fight Iran had also to be used against the Ottoman positions in the western Caucasus. The gains there were small in comparison with the drain on Russia's resources. In a single unsuccessful attack on an Ottoman border province in 1807, Russia lost 900 men it could hardly spare from its small contingent in the Caucasus.[2] The Treaty of Bucharest, which ended the war, restored to the Ottoman Empire most of the territory Russia had conquered, including the coastal fort of P'ot'i (the most important strategic position in the western Caucasus), as well as Moldavia and Wallachia in the Balkans.

Russia's preoccupation with France and the Ottoman Empire led Alexander to try to end the war with Iran on several occasions between 1806 and 1808.[3] Russian authorities, who did not understand the seriousness of Iranian claims to the disputed territories, blamed France for the collapse of the peace talks. In 1807, shortly before the Franco-Russian peace, France had signed a treaty of alliance with Iran, the Treaty of Finkenstein, in which France promised to help Iran regain Georgia. However, the chief obstacle to peace was the Russian insistence that Iran formally cede all the territory north of the Aras and Tālesh, even though Yerevan was still effectively in Iranian hands and other parts of the region were under no more than nominal Russian authority. Alexander was unrelenting, and he maintained, "I certainly will not make any concessions, their [the Iranians'] claims are mad."[4] He also insisted that Russia had to have the river border it wanted because "this barrier is necessary to prevent the incursions of barbarian peoples who inhabit the land."[5] The war against Iran was resumed with another costly and unsuccessful attempt to conquer Yerevan.

The Russians also had other enemies to fight in the Caucasus. Raids by Lesghis from the high mountains on Georgia's northeastern border were a recurrent problem. They sometimes acted in concert with one of the Bagration pretenders or other mountain tribes and sometimes on their own initiative. Since their aim was to raid, not to conquer, they preferred to avoid pitched battles with the Russians but caused considerable disruption nonetheless, as in 1805, when some 20,000 of them swept past the 150 Russians guarding the northeastern border and raided Georgia. Other mountain tribes periodically battled the Russians. Among the most dangerous were the Ossetes and Chechens, who lived in the area where the narrow road linking Georgia and the Caucasian Line crossed the high mountains. In 1804 and on several later occasions, they completely cut the road or raided travelers on it, thus blocking communications. Some of the western Georgians also opposed the expansion of Russian power in the Caucasus. The foremost of these opponents was King Solomon of Imeretia, who had been forced into nominal submission in 1804 but who repeatedly fought the Russians until they conquered his principality in 1809. The principality of Mingrelia had been on hostile terms with Imeretia and therefore chose to make common cause with Russia in 1803. Abkhazia submitted in 1809, but a civil war in which one side was anti-Russian complicated the takeover. Guria did not submit until 1811.

Even the east Caucasian principalities that formally submitted to Russia could not be considered securely in the Russian camp. The khanates of Qarābāgh, Shakki, and Derbent-Qobbeh were all the scenes of armed struggle against the Russians. The Georgians, many of whom had looked to Russia to protect them from external and internal strife, were disenchanted by the termination of Bagration rule, heavy-handed Russian administration, and the privations caused by famine, plague, and prolonged warfare (from which the Russians had failed to protect Georgia). This led to the defection of Georgian nobles (to Imeretia, the high mountains, and Iran) and rebellions in which all levels of society participated. There was a serious rebellion in the north in 1804, some minor disturbances in 1806 and 1810, and a massive explosion in the north and east in 1812 that involved Georgian peasants and mountain tribesmen. The road across the mountains was cut, a Russian garrison of 214 was massacred, and Russians elsewhere were under siege or in retreat. The rebellion in Georgia was put down by the summer, but fighting in the high mountains lasted into the spring of 1813.

The natural environment provided as many obstacles as the human one. Ironically, for all of Russia's insistence that the Aras and Kura rivers constituted the only secure border with Iran, for most of the years the Aras could be forded at so many places that the Russians could not have hoped to patrol them all. Throughout the war, Iranian troops crossed and recrossed the Aras without difficulty. The geographical difficulties that had plagued the 1796 expedition remained a problem. Even when the road between Georgia and the Caucasian Line was not under attack, it posed many hazards. Attempts were made to improve it, but it was still extremely narrow (in some places ten to twelve feet wide) and vulnerable to avalanches, floods, and blizzards. Artillery and large carts could not travel along this route, and fatal accidents occurred regularly. The mountainous terrain of most of the war zone and the many thick forests prevented Russia from maximizing its clearest military advantage, its artillery, which was difficult to transport or use effectively in the narrow confines within which the fighting often took place.[6]

Contrary to the Russians' expectations, they were not able to use their naval supremacy on the Caspian to compensate adequately for the difficulties they encountered on land, either in supplying troops in the Caucasus or in attacking enemy coastal positions. Not only was there a serious climatic problem, in that severe storms and icebergs made sailing the Caspian perilous during the winter, but the Russian navy was unequal to the task. Many naval vessels were in disrepair, and the quality of their weapons was as often substandard. For example, when the navy attempted to bombard Baku into submission in 1805, it only had two suitable guns and both broke after five days' use. At this time, the Caspian fleet had only eleven seaworthy vessels and, therefore, had to be supplemented by rented merchant boats for the transportation of supplies. Renting provided a limited solution for the problem since the cost was high and the budget small.[7]

Service in the Caucasus in the early nineteenth century was made still more hazardous by a variety of health problems. Russians, as newcomers to the area, were especially susceptible to illness from unfamiliar foods and water, scorching summer heat, and diseases to which natives had acquired immunity. Baku, Qobbeh, Ganjeh, and the land along the Aras were considered particularly unhealthy areas. In addition, repeated epidemics swept through the Caucasus. Plague reappeared in the region in 1803. There are no statistics on the overall casualties, but in Tbilisi, where the mortality rate was particularly high, 500 people died of plague in a single month. Every year during the next decade, an outbreak of the disease occurred somewhere in the Caucasus, the period from 1808 to 1812 being especially bad.[8] In addition to all the other problems caused by the plague, communications—including the transportation of supplies and reinforcements—were interrupted by periodic quarantines.

The ravages of war and disease, and the simple fact that there was a Russian military presence in the Caucasus, disrupted the region's economy. The economic problems not only added to the troubles of the native inhabitants but also made it impossible for the Russians to fulfill the expansionists' optimistic prediction that a large part of the cost of taking and governing the eastern Caucasus could be financed by local revenues. The sudden increase in Russian spending connected with the administration of Georgia and military needs produced rapid inflation in the cost of food and other essentials but not a rise in incomes. In addition, Russia's currency was in a disadvantageous position. Through Russian purchases, the silver rubles passed into general circulation, where the exchange rate with local coinage was about one-sixth below what Russian authorities had expected. Much of the coinage passed out of circulation altogether through trade between local and foreign merchants and melting down for use by local silversmiths. At the same time, the various natural and war-related disasters produced a sharp decline in the region's economy. Taxes (from areas under direct rule) and tribute (from vassal states) fell into arrears. Since Russia was at war in other quarters from 1805 on, the government was unwilling to increase the allocation of funds for the Caucasus. As a result, the Russian commanders-in-chief in the Caucasus had to reduce the scale of their operations to keep within the limits of their revenues. An important part of the revenue was in kind, primarily foodstuffs, rather than in cash, and had been expected to fill the Russians' needs for provisions. However, food was scarce for most of the war era, and there was a serious famine in 1811. Many of the rubles that were supposed to pay for the war against Iran and the administration of the newly conquered provinces went instead to buy food and rent ox carts to transport it.[9]

Even apart from the shortages of essential supplies, the quality of the Russian army in the Caucasus was substandard. Although daring and ambitious men were able to win recognition for their deeds in this theater of war, the whole mountain region was generally regarded as one of the less prestigious places in which to serve. Assignment to the Caucasus was commonly used as punishment for some major disgrace, such as dueling, or for generally inadequate performance. The Caucasus long remained a dumping ground for those out of favor (for example, the Decembrists in the 1820s and, in the 1830s, the poet Lermontov, who had angered Tsar Nicholas by criticizing Pushkin's enemies). Ever since the annexation of Georgia, service in the Caucasus had had a bad reputation. The high cost of living and the absence of familiar amenities greatly lowered the morale of those who served there. Unethical conduct of all sorts was widespread. Corruption was common in a variety of forms, from looting the subject population to gift giving by officers to their superiors. Drunkenness, gambling, and, to the outrage of Commander-in-Chief Paulucci, living openly with mistresses were typical of the Russian life-style in the Caucasus. Men who served in the Caucasus were rarely promoted to positions elsewhere, especially since they were perceived as men who were not good enough to obtain more prestigious appointments in the first place.[10]

Besides their poor reputation, the soldiers assigned to the eastern Caucasus were not an impressive fighting force. In fact, many of them had never seen battle before. This group included Lieutenant-General Rtishchev, the commander-in-chief from 1812 to 1816, who was sent to the Caucasus even though he did not wish it after thirty years of honest but undistinguished service. Major-General Zavalishin, who commanded the ill-fated Caspian campaign of 1805, was also a newcomer to combat duty. When reinforcements could be spared for service in this area, they were usually raw recruits who not only were untested in battle but were unfamiliar with the use of their weapons.[11]

Others had more experience but were not particularly able or successful. Tsitsianov was a case in point, as was his successor, Gudovich. By the time Gudovich returned for his third tour of duty in the Caucasus, he was about seventy, more irascible than ever, and aware that he was not equal to the demands of his office. Things went badly from the start. His vanity was wounded by Lieutenant-General Glazenap, who, in the interval between Tsitsianov's death and Gudovich's arrival, launched an expedition from the Caucasian Line to take Derbent and Baku. Therefore, Gudovich stopped the expedition after it had conquered Derbent and gave the command to one of his cronies. Glazenap retired from active service. Gudovich then picked a senseless fight with Major-General Nesvetaev, whom he accused of cowardice and incompetence for preparing to conquer Shakki and Yerevan. Nesvetaev was allowed to proceed in Shakki, but the attack on Yerevan was canceled so that some of Nesvetaev's troops could be sent to Baku, where they were not needed. Before long, Gudovich had lost the confidence of most of his subordinates. His most ambitious and least successful undertaking was his Yerevan campaign of 1808. He began the siege of Yerevan with about 3,500 men in October, traditionally considered too late in the season to begin a campaign. At the start of the siege, he predicted a speedy victory and was especially confident that his artillery would breach the walls of the citadel. Only after he failed did he try to put the blame on the lack of artillery and manpower. In fact, the operation had just been poorly planned. (Even the ladders for climbing the citadel walls were too short.) After a six-week siege, he attempted to storm the citadel, having ordered the massacre of all enemy combatants. Instead, the Iranians put up an effective defense and repulsed the attack, killing nearly 300 Russians and wounding nearly 600 more. Gudovich indignantly remarked that the Iranians used defensive measures they had not used before and blamed French interference. After two more weeks of waiting for the Iranians to surrender, he lifted the siege and began an arduous journey back to Georgia through snow-covered mountains, and many more soldiers died. Alexander was appalled by the poor preparation for the campaign, and Gudovich resigned.[12] No more major operations against Iran were undertaken until 1812.

Desertion was a serious problem in the Russian army as a whole and especially in the Caucasus. This is not surprising considering that the rank and file was composed of peasant draftees forced to serve for a twenty-five-year term and that morale in the Caucasus was particularly low. By the latter years of the war, starvation had driven increasing numbers to desert. It was fairly easy for a soldier to escape from his unit since Russian authority was confined to a few garrisons in strategic locations and villagers often helped soldiers make good their escape. The exact number of deserters is not at all clear since Russian authorities were usually reticent on the subject and many deserters who settled in Iran were treated much the same as prisoners of war. A French visitor to Iran during the 1830s claimed that at one point there had been 6,000 Russian deserters there, although most had subsequently returned to Russia. There are a few Russian reports of desertion by groups of from 20 to 90 men. There were a few officers among the deserters, including a lieutenant who was with Kariagin when Kariagin was nearly defeated by the Iranians in 1805 and a lieutenant-colonel who had been commandant at Elizavetpol' (Ganjeh) for several years before his defection in 1808. Deserters and prisoners of war received various treatment in Iran. Some endured poverty and neglect or occasional harassment. However, 'Abbās Mirzā often provided better treatment since he found the Russians useful as military advisers. His army included a Russian unit of about 200 men who fought valiantly on the Iranian side in the battle of Aslānduz in 1812 and another of 400 men who did a poor job in the fighting in Tālesh in 1813. Other Russian deserters and prisoners formed honor guards at the courts of the shah and several of his sons. A few converted to Islam, but others who did not were nonetheless allowed to marry and begin a new life in Iran. Some were made officers in the Iranian army.[13]

The biggest problem with the Russian soldiers in the Caucasus, whether they were stalwart veterans or disgruntled cannon fodder, was that there were not nearly enough of them. Troops were allocated to the Caucasus as a whole, rather than to specific areas of acute need. This meant that there could be more than 40,000 men in the region as a whole but far fewer than 10,000 of them in the eastern Caucasus. The overwhelming majority of the troops were stationed at the Caucasian Line to prevent tribes from the high mountains from attacking the Russian agricultural settlements north of the mountains. After 1805 St. Petersburg would not spare reinforcements and in 1811 recalled two regiments of infantry and two of cavalry for service on other fronts. Russia's effective military strength in the eastern Caucasus was less than the allocations, often by 2,000 or more, because of the high rate of death, illness, and desertion. By 1811, there were fewer than 3,000 soldiers to garrison the eastern Caucasus and fight Iran.[14] Not only were the Russians few in number, they were also predominantly infantry, by a ratio of about 2 to 1. Therefore, they lacked the maneuverability as well as the numbers to deal with the Iranian army. Their maneuverability was further impeded by a dearth of horses for the cavalry and of pack animals for transporting military supplies.

The strengths of the Iranians were virtually the mirror image of the Russians'. Even though the war brought the introduction of new military principles, the traditional army was not without its good points. First of all, it was many times larger than the Russian opposition. It seems to have numbered approximately 50,000 men for most of the war era, although some estimates range well over 100,000, including emergency levies. The shah also had an elite guard of several thousand. The army was mostly cavalry, with each tribe expected to contribute a certain number in proportion to its size. The Afshar tribesman from from the Lake Urumiyeh region in western Azerbaijan were apparently the best. Levies from the sedentary population made up the infantry. Soldiers had to provide all of their own equipment. Except for the highest ranks, the pay was very low, which made the taking of booty essential. Although the Iranian army bore little resemblance to the tightly organized Western armies of the day, European soldiers repeatedly commented on the Iranian soldiers' martial skills. Russians involved in the 1804 Yerevan campaign were surprised by how well the Iranians fought. Several British and French visitors were struck by the courage and capacity to endure hardship of the Iranian soldiers. The cavalry was noted for its expert horsemanship. Riders could gallop over rough terrain and then stop abruptly without being thrown. This meant that the Iranian cavalry was far better suited to operating in the rough Caucasian terrain than was the Russian infantry. Iranian sabers were often of high-quality steel and were used with deadly skill by the soldiers. Firearms, whether hand guns or artillery, were of very poor quality, but the cavalry soldiers were superior marksmen nonetheless. Their skills included being able to fire accurately over their shoulders while galloping away from the enemy, a tactic that the Russians found disconcerting.[15] (The Iranians also used the lance and the bow and arrow.)

The quality of the military leadership varied greatly. Although Fath 'Ali sometimes brought his troops into the war zone, more immediate direction of the Iranian effort was entrusted to the heir presumptive, 'Abbās Mirzā, who in 1804 was fifteen years old. At first, the real commander was Soleiman Khān, a cousin of Āqā Mohammad, who had a reputation for drunkenness. As 'Abbās grew older, he took charge, immersing himself in military affairs, displaying his courage by risking his life in battle, and punishing officers for cowardice. At least two of the Iranian generals were men of notable bravery and dedication. Hosein Qoli Khān, son of Mohammad Khān of Yerevan, had played a crucial role in defeating Fath 'Ali's enemies in the struggle for the throne and was made governor of Yerevan in 1807. He was allowed virtually complete autonomy and distinguished himself as a general and an administrator for the next twenty years. Even the Russians respected him as a soldier. The other outstanding leader was Sādeq Khān Qājār, who was made the general of an elite corps of European-style infantry and, with the help of two British artillery officers, conquered Tālesh in 1812. The British officers were withdrawn soon after because of the Russo-British alliance against Napoleon, but Sādeq showed that he could continue zealously without the British. In January 1813, Sādeq, the ten generals under his command, and 2,500 other soldiers valiantly defended Lankarān against an attack by Kotliarevskii. The Iranians kept fighting through five days of heavy bombardment, but Sādeq Khān and half his troops were killed when the Russians stormed the fortress.[16]

The Iranians employed several customary tactics against the Russians with considerable success. The tribal habit of raiding for booty harmonized with the tactical necessity of avoiding the formal battles in which Russian strengths would have been best utilized. Until the deployment of European-style units late in the war, the Iranians relied primarily on guerilla raids, picking off small, isolated detachments, burning crops in the fields, and carrying off people and herds of animals. (Sieges were used only in dire emergencies, as in the Russian blockade of Yerevan in 1804.) 'Abbās Mirzā often repeated a saying of Āqā Mohammad's, "Never come within reach of the Russian guns, and never, by the celerity of the cavalry, allow a Russian villager to sleep in peace."[17] Both sides employed the tactic of relocating, sometimes forcibly, inhabitants of the disputed provinces, but the Iranians did so to a far greater extent than the Russians. Many Ganjevis were removed, apparently with their consent, to areas under Iranian control. Perhaps as many as several thousand Qarābāghis, as well as several hundred Turcomans from the southern border districts of Georgia, were also moved, although the latter group eventually returned to their homes.[18]

Iran also supported Caucasian opponents of Russian expansion with messages of encouragement, promises for money, and, rarely, plans for coordinated military action. Sheikh 'Ali had such contacts with the Iranians but relied primarily on his own resources. Several Bagration princes, especially Alexander (Erekle's eldest surviving son), relied heavily on support from every possible source—Georgians, tribes from the high mountains, Prince Solomon of Imeretia, and, most of all, Iran. Sheikh 'Ali's years of guerrilla raiding exasperated the Russians greatly. In 1809, Commander-in-Chief Tormasov, in essence, admitted his inability to defeat Sheikh 'Ali by conventional military means when he came up with a scheme to stop the khan by finding someone to turn him in or assassinate him or, if that failed, by restoring him to power in Qobbeh. (No suitable assassin was found, and the plan was dropped.) Sheikh 'Ali's local success could not by itself have driven the Russians from the Caucasus. Prince Alexander's success was also local and, in addition, episodic. He blamed his failures on inadequate Iranian support but to the end of the war kept asking for more help.[19] The reverse situation, in which Russia tried to win over Iranian subjects, also existed. Apart from the khans of the disputed provinces, several prominent individuals who lived in territory controlled by Iran also had contacts with the Russians. Sometimes the aim was to test whether Russia would offer more than Iran, as was the case with the governor of Tabriz and the leaders of the Shāhsavan tribe. Sometimes the individual had broken with the shah before seeking Russian favor, as was the case with Ja'far Qoli Khān of the Domboli Kurds. He was unusual in that he and a band of followers migrated to Russian territory. Armenians, especially from the Tehran area, did likewise. However, most of those who looked to the Russians became disappointed by their weak showing in the war and in some cases were brought under tighter Iranian control.[20]

Morale among the Iranian troops seems to have been fairly good. Even though the pay was poor, the opportunity to take booty was a considerable attraction. In fact, the tribal levies expected the shah to provide them with some campaign each year. (If the government had not been strong, the tribes might well have raided within Iran.) Herds of animals and a wide variety of objects were carried off, but the most valuable and prestigious type of loot was slaves, particularly Georgian women who were highly valued as concubines. There was also a slave trade conducted by merchants, but the war provided opportunities for Iranian soldiers to kidnap slaves themselves. In 1810, an incentive of another sort was provided by the declaration of a holy war against the Russians. Several *mojtaheds* agreed to the government's arguments that a holy war was incumbent upon pious Muslims because the Russians had invaded Iran and oppressed Muslims.[21] Reports of Napoleon's invasion of Russia, to which a rumor of Alexander's surrender had been added, buoyed the Iranians' hopes for a time.

While some of the characteristics of Iran's traditional army gave it an advantage over the Russians, others had the opposite effect. The most obvious problem for both tactics and morale was the woeful inadequacy of Iran's artillery. Until the French-assisted military reforms, there was no functional heavy artillery at all, only a few cannon left over from the Safavi era or captured from the Russians. One of the Russian cannons was fired on ceremonial occasions at the shah's palace in Tehran, but the rest were broken beyond repair. The only kind of artillery used in battle was the *zamburak* ("little wasp"), a small, short-range piece similar to the European falconet. *Zamburaks* were mounted on camels for great mobility and usually fired in group volleys to compensate for the fact that they were not carefully aimed (or designed for accuracy). The *zamburaks* and projectiles were made of copper, (which was very expensive) or lead (which was too soft and heavy). The projectiles were often flawed; this caused them to break easily or, worse, explode upon firing. The clamor of battle and their frequent injuries caused many of the camels to run amok during a battle, doing at least as much damage to the Iranians as to the enemy. Many of the infantry's guns were also extremely poor, especially the type that had so long a barrel it required a two-foot-high crutch to support the front. However, this mattered little since the infantry was not considered important.[22] The artillery's shortcomings created a further problem—Iranian soldiers, who were unfamiliar with heavy artillery, were easily frightened by Russian artillery. Even the ferocious Āqā Mohammad was intimidated by it. His determination to avoid pitched battles with the Russians was a recognition of his army's weakness as well as its superior maneuverability. He remarked to his grand vizier, Hāji Ebrāhim, on the subject of how to oppose the Russian campaign of 1796: "Can a man of your wisdom believe I will ever run my head against their walls of steel, or expose my irregular army to be destroyed by their cannon, and disciplined troops?"[23] When pitched battles did occur, Iranian troops sometimes scattered in panic when faced with Russian artillery, as did some Kurdish units during the fighting in Yerevan in 1800.[24]

Many of Iran's problems in the war stemmed less from its technological inferiority to the Russians than from its fundamentally different concept about how armies should be run and wars fought. By European standards, the Iranian army was disorganized and undisciplined. Each Iranian cavalry regiment was composed of the members of a single tribe, whose strongest loyalties were usually to their fellow tribesmen. As a result, the regiments did not coordinate their efforts and were quick to mutiny when an affront to tribal honor was perceived. Their movements resembled a tribal migration, with random groups traveling toward a general objective at widely varying rates and arriving as long as several weeks apart. Wherever they went, they lived off the land, which meant that to many villagers on the Iranian side of the border as well as the Russian that the cavalry was just the latest band of marauders to plunder the sedentary population. Battle was conceived of as the traditional tribal raid in which large numbers of cavalry swept down on an outnumbered opponent. Instead of taking part in a coordinated attack, each soldier used the battle as an opportunity to display his individual prowess and take booty. These achievements, not the total defeat of the enemy, were the goals of a battle. As a result of the Iranian practice of stopping to loot before the battle was over, troops repeatedly allowed the Russians to escape or even regroup and counterattack. On some occasions, the Iranians were so weighted down with plunder that their slow departure from enemy territory made them vulnerable to attack.[25]

Although the traditional system produced some excellent commanders, it more often rewarded court favorites without regard to their ability. Like many of the armies of early modern Europe, there was no clear-cut distinction between military and civilian service by the elite, and the best positions often went to court favorites, who were not necessarily competent. Commanders were usually allowed to appoints their own subordinates, and they usually chose relatives or members of their personal entourage. These people were loyal to their benefactors, not the army or the state. The organization of the army, especially the practice of giving a commander the money and food intended for distribution to his men, minimized accountability and maximized the opportunity for embezzlement. As in other armies, there were a number of important-sounding sinecures, most notably the command of the heavy artillery. (*topchibāshi*) in an army that had none. The commander of the army (*lashkarbāshi*) in the late war years was Mehrāb Khān, who had no qualifications for his office and used it for its opportunities to collect graft. One of his techniques was to threaten to punish officers for misconduct and then extract from them payment for his leniency. There were some striking examples of inept leadership by commanders who actually took the field. 'Ali Khān commanded the garrison of a fortified village controlling the mountain pass that the Russians would have to cross into Tālesh. When Kotliarevskii approached, 'Ali fled without putting up a fight. At first, Fath 'Ali was enraged and planned to execute the cowardly officer. Instead, he commuted the sentence to a fine and eventually restored 'Ali to his former office of chief groom (*shāter bāshi*). There are other instances of commanders being disgraced briefly and then returned to favor.[26]

The Iranians did not take several precautions against the Russians because they had not been needed against traditional foes. Iranians did not fight at night and did not expect the Russians to do so either. As a result, there were never more than a small number of sentries posted around an Iranian camp at night. Camps were set up without organization, except that the commander's tent was always at the center, with his highest-ranking subordinates around him. This meant that ammunition and artillery were not stored where they were readily accessible, even after the westernizing reforms. There were no predetermined rallying points in case of attack, so soldiers scattered instead. At least some tents were made of white fabric, which made them visible from a considerable distance in the moonlight. No particular importance was placed upon tight secrecy either. Plans for a forthcoming battle were bruited about the whole camp and enemy spies picked them up. These security problems caused the Iranians problems on many occasions, most important at Aslānduz in October 1812. 'Abbās Mirzā led a force of about 5,000 European-style infantry to the south bank of the Aras with the intention of crossing into

Qarābāgh and defeating Kotliarevskii, who was just north of the river with 2,000 soldiers. Kotliarevskii found out and attacked first. Although difficulties in fording the Aras prevented him from reaching the Iranian camp during the night, lax security was still in effect when he arrived in the early morning. Kotliarevskii's men were about 300 yards from the camp before they were discovered by the Iranians who fled in disorder (although they later regrouped in a fort), leaving some of their artillery, most of their ammunition, and virtually everything else behind. During that day's fighting and the next, roughly 40 percent of the Iranian contingent was killed.[27]

While Iran was at war on its northwestern frontier, it was also involved in smaller conflicts elsewhere. Fighting broke out between the Iranians and the Afghans in 1805 and 1811. In 1811, Iran also sent troops against the Wahhābis (a sect that advocated a return to its concept of the pure faith of Mohammad) in Arabia. The Iranians suffered heavy casualties, but Iran's security was not jeopardized. Relations with the Ottoman Empire were a more serious problem. In addition to the long-standing rivalry between the neighboring empires, there were specific points of friction that nearly caused a war between them during this era. In 1811, Kurds from the Ottoman province of Byazid staged a devastating raid deep into Azerbaijan, destroying at least fifteen villages. Iran responded by sending the governor of one of the affected districts to attack the Kurds, whose leader was killed in the reprisal. About the same time, the pasha of Baghdad, who was on good terms with Iran, was replaced by someone who was distinctly hostile. The shah's eldest son Mohammad 'Ali, the governor of the western province of Kermānshāh, argued that the Kurdish raid and developments in Baghdad were grounds for war with the Ottomans. Yet Iran was so desirous of assistance against the Russians that it had endeavored since 1803 to obtain Ottoman cooperation in the war. Talks on this subject were resumed in 1809 and after two years of negotiation led to an agreement to stage a joint attack on Russia's Caucasian forces. However, the plan came to nought because the Ottoman general sent to work out the details with the Iranians was assassinated by an agent of his political rival. Instead of cooperating with the Ottomans, Mohammad 'Ali's army of around 30,000 fought to oust the pasha of Baghdad. Finally, in 1812, Fath 'Ali's concern over the war with Russia and the sultan's willingness to take conciliatory measures in the Baghdad dispute ended the fighting between Iran and the Ottoman Empire. However, there was no renewed cooperation in the Caucasian war, and the Ottoman Empire made a separate peace with Russia.[28]

Some of Iran's most serious difficulties in the war with Russia were by-products of its domestic problems. Fath 'Ali Shāh's position was much stronger than the Russians thought, but it was not nearly as strong as he would have wished. There is little solid evidence from which to draw a portrait of the shah's character. Iranian chroniclers could only describe the shah or anyone in his favor in laudatory clichés. European visitors were not necessarily more reliable, since they saw what they wanted to see, which in turn hinged primarily on what they wanted from Iran. One thing that was clear was that Fath 'Ali was very different from Āqā Mohammad. The second Qājār shah was less harsh and probably less dynamic as well. He did not show any signs of the shrewd pragmatism that had enabled his uncle to see through comforting illusions. After the execution in 1801 of Hāji Ebrāhim, the sage chief vizier the shah had inherited from the previous reign, Fath 'Ali was not particularly well advised. His chief vizier, Mirzā Shafi', was a man of mediocre talents who spent most of his time maneuvering against the more able 'Abdol-Vahhāb, head of the chancellery. Fath 'Ali's manners were polished, and he was well educated in the Iranian cultural tradition, including writing poetry. He enjoyed a life of luxury; he took great care of his appearance, especially his magnificent beard, which extended to his waist, and dressed splendidly. Harford Jones, British ambassador to Iran from 1807 to 1811, saw the shah riding out of camp wearing a purple velvet coat covered by a diamond-studded mesh, a gold cumberbund studded with pearls and a jewel encrusted dagger tucked in it, a scimitar in a diamond-and-ruby-covered scabbard, and a steel helmet topped by a large diamond. The shah enjoyed the pleasures of a large harem and fathered some 300 children. John Malcolm, who went on missions to Iran in 1800, 1808, and 1810, considered Fath 'Ali "humane and accomplished" but "timid, weak" and "avaricious."[29] The shah never led his troops in battle in the Caucasus the way his uncle had. Every year during the war, Fath 'Ali journeyed to the northwest, marshalled some of his troops, and sent some of them into battle. However, he assigned primary responsibility for the conduct of the war to his son 'Abbās. There are several possible explanations for why he limited his role in the conduct of the war, but there is no solid evidence to support any of them. According to one chronicle, he planned to take charge of the 1804 campaign and leave 'Abbās as governor of Tehran. Only after repeated entreaties did he grant 'Abbās's wish to lead the campaign and thereafter left him in charge of the war. However, this explanation does not jibe with either the shah's mistrust of his sons—in light of which, putting the heir presumptive in charge of the capital meant inviting a coup—or his administrative policy, which included reviving the Safavi practice of making his sons provincial governors, with Azerbaijan reserved for the heir to the throne. Whatever the reasons, Fath 'Ali's role in the fighting was undistinguished.[30]

The shah had no problems with local rebellions during the war years, but he could never be sure of his sons. He faced the age-old problem of hereditary monarchy—a prince's ambitions hinged on taking his father's throne and nature did not always bring the transition quickly enough. Most of the later Safavis lived in fear of rebellions by their sons. More recently, Nāder Shāh had ordered his eldest son blinded when a coup was suspected. Fath 'Ali feared several of his sons but the eldest, Mohammad 'Ali, most of all. Mohammad 'Ali was born in 1789 to a Georgian slave who was one of Fath 'Ali's concubines. While illegitimacy did not carry a social stigma, it did mean that this prince would not be his father's chosen heir. Āqā Mohammad had made other arrangements for the succession by having his nephew marry a woman from a rival branch of the Qājārs, the Davahlu, to heal the rift between the two factions and produce a son who would become the third shah of the dynasty. This was 'Abbās, who was about seven months the junior of Mohammad 'Ali and was formally designated nā'eb os-saltaneh (viceroy-crown prince) in Āqā Mohammad's will.[31]

The half-brothers were strikingly different people who became enemies in childhood and sustained the animosity until Mohammad 'Ali's death in 1821. The elder brother was robust, articulate, and assertive from childhood. Even those who disliked him were impressed by his intelligence and imposing demeanor. He reveled in war and was noted for his fearlessness, although his detractors considered him reckless as well. His temperment was exceedingly volatile and imperious. He insisted on having his way in all things, whether it be that the Portuguese discovered the New World (a subject about which he was surprisingly well informed except for that particular) or his demand that his father allow him to attack Baghdad in 1811. (He threatened to stab himself if he were denied.) He was angry and bitter at having been excluded from the succession. There was a story told about him that may or may not be literally true but is certainly illustrative of his character. One day, when Mohammad 'Ali and 'Abbās were children, the two boys were brought to a place where they were told to wait for Āqā Mohammad. Food was set before them; 'Abbās would not eat until his granduncle arrived, but Mohammad 'Ali began to eat voraciously. At that point, Āqā Mohammad entered and berated the impatient child. There was an argument, ending with Mohammad 'Ali's promise to kill 'Abbās whenever the opportunity arose.[32]

'Abbās was not a natural warrior. A sickly youth, he had to work hard to develop the physical skills at which his older brother excelled naturally. He suffered recurring bouts of ill health throughout his life—hepatitis, venereal disease, dropsy—and by the time he reached his twenties, he had begun to age prematurely. He was a man of considerable charm and dignity whose large, expressive eyes, flashing smile, and attentive listening won the affections of the European emissaries, at least until the war ended and they decided that he had failed to reform Azerbaijan along western lines. Having charge of the war against Russia could have enhanced his reputation, but it might also have damaged it if he were defeated. That would have strengthened Mohammad 'Ali's hand in the expected battle for the throne. Therefore, it is possible, as some Europeans charged, that 'Abbās's interest in reforms was superficial, that he viewed reforms—especially westernizing ones—as a panacea, and that his court was filled with sycophants who encouraged this illusion. What the proponents of this view do not mention is that he had good reason to be disenchanted with reforms. The shah encouraged him but would not give him adequate support, while the French and British dropped him when they no longer needed him. Whatever his motives, he invested no small energy in reforms. His direct contact was primarily with military reforms, which he gave his vigorous support in a host of ways. Civilian reforms were left primarily in the capable hands of his chief vizier, Mirzā Bozorg, who had grown up in Shirāz and had had more extensive contact with European traders. Mirzā Bozorg gained his earliest administrative experience under Karim Khān Zand and later rose to prominence in the service of Āqā Mohammad. He impressed quite a few European visitors with his probity and concern for the public good. By the later war years, Azerbaijan was considered one of the most prosperous, best governed provinces of the empire.[33] Pierre Jaubert, who was sent to Iran by Napoleon in 1805, expressed the prevailing European admiration for 'Abbās when he wrote:

This prince possesses enough instruction to feel the need to acquire more. . . . No one among the Persians esteems the sciences and arts of Europe more than he. . . . In sum everything predicts that if he mounts the throne of Persia someday he would display qualities which would make him be counted in the number of the greatest sovereigns who have reigned over this vast empire.[34]

Mohammad 'Ali was jealous of 'Abbās's position as heir presumptive and leader of the war against Russia. He belittled 'Abbās's accomplishments in battle and claimed he could do better if given the chance. 'Abbās supported military westernization and was the object of great attention by French and British emissaries. Therefore, Mohammad 'Ali proclaimed his dedication to the traditional style of warfare. He repeatedly criticized Europeans and their ways as inimical to Islam. However, he also wanted to be included in the dealings with those same European emissaries and had a few French and Italians train a contingent of his soldiers in the European manner. According to rumor, his traditional army exceeded by several thousand the size allowed by the shah. The purpose of his army, supposedly, was to make ready for his seizure of power. He pressed the shah to allow him to join in the war against Russia and finally obtained permission in 1809. The resulting campaign did nothing to advance the Iranian cause. All that was accomplished was that Mohammad 'Ali and his troops plundered Muslim tribes along the Georgian border and then returned heavily laden. Since the attack he was supposed to make on the Russians never occurred, the Russians were able to concentrate their efforts on fighting 'Abbās's army in Ganjeh. 'Abbās and his men narrowly escaped the encircling Russians. Mohammad 'Ali repeatedly pressured the shah for permission to campaign elsewhere. So strong was the assumption that he planned to seize power that, when he campaigned in Baghdad in 1811, rumors spread that he intended to use his large army to take the throne on his return. In fact, no such attempt was made.[35]

Although the shah feared a coup by one of his sons, it was precisely that fear that kept him from strengthening 'Abbās's position or curbing the ambitions of other sons. He occasionally compared 'Abbās favorably to the others, citing in particular 'Abbās's avoidance of luxury and his dedication to winning the war. After the 1809 debacle, he even gave 'Abbās temporary jurisdiction over the military affairs of Kermānshāh as a reproof to Mohammad 'Ali. He also tried to distract his volatile eldest son with a large harem but to no avail. Yet he was reluctant to emphasize 'Abbās's status as heir by making a formal declaration or by making 'Abbās a cosignatory to a treaty of alliance with Britain. The shah believed he had to encourage the ambitions of each son to prevent their rebellion. With several sons, military success was touted to be the key to advancement. There is a possibility that Fath 'Ali withheld some of the assistance he might otherwise have given 'Abbās for fear of making this son too strong."[36]

Fath 'Ali's adult sons also played a role in Iran's economic troubles, which in turn hampered the country's war effort. The shah had to

meet the expenses of the government and the royal family with inadequate revenues. Nearly a century of turmoil had greatly disrupted
Iran's economy. Several epidemics of plague and cholera, as well as
droughts and earthquakes, had compounded Iran's troubles during
the war years. In addition to internal weaknesses, Iran suffered from
an unfavorable balance of trade. Its principal trading partners were
Russia and India. Trade with Russia was favorable to Iran and continued during the war years, albeit at a modest level subject to periodic interruptions, as when the Russians burned Anzali after an unsuccessful attack in 1805. However, the profits from this trade at its
most prosperous could not have compensated for the unfavorable
balance of trade with India. During the latter years of the war, the
deficit amounted to more than a quarter of a million pounds annually,
according to a very rough estimate. Karim Khān Zand reportedly left
a nearly empty treasury at his death in 1779, even though he was an
unusually beneficent ruler whose reign was noted for its comparative
security and prosperity. Āqā Mohammad managed to leave his nephew
a considerable treasury reserve, but that was not enough to solve the
country's financial problems. Fath 'Ali's revenues came from a variety
of sources, notably the harvest tax paid by peasants on crown lands
and the annual contributions by provincial governors, tribal chiefs,
and government officials. However, most of the shah's revenues and
assets were in kind—cereals, animals, and jewels—and so were not
readily negotiable for financing the war or other governmental expenses. Moreover, the amount of revenue derived from the provinces
was reduced because of the administrative system, according to
which provincial governorships were given to the shah's favored sons.
Except for their annual gifts to the shah, the sons sent no tax monies
to the central government. Instead, they used their revenues to pay
for the armies with which they might one day seize the throne and
to maintain lavish courts symbolic of the dignity to which they aspired. For example, 'Ali Mirzā, the governor of the southwestern
province of Fārs, spent approximately 75,000 pounds a year on the
upkeep of his court. All of these economic problems meant that the
revenue of the central government was not large enough to support
extremely expensive undertakings. The amount of the average annual
revenue can only be guessed at, considering the government's arcane
system of bookkeeping and the tenuousness of European estimates,
which ranged from 1½ million pounds to 3 million, the former being
more plausible. Several British emissaries to Iran complained that the
government's expenditures were limited not only by the paucity of
revenues but also by Fath 'Ali's extreme avarice. However, this judg-

ment may have been colored by the fact that those critics felt that the shah was not spending enough on the war against Russia. The charge is not implausible, but neither is it provable. The shah might also have limited his contribution to the war because he was concerned about the government's solvency or because he feared making 'Abbās too strong. If he was a miser, he nonetheless gave British representatives expensive ceremonial presents, such as gold coins and gold brocade robes.[37]

Whatever his motives, Fath 'Ali did not assume primary financial responsibility for the war. That burden was to be borne instead by the government of Azerbaijan. The province had some important economic assets, especially its good pasture and farm lands around Khoi in the northwest and Ardabil in the northeast and its location on the trade routes to the Caucasus and Anatolia. 'Abbās and Mirzā Bozorg tried to stimulate the provincial economy by curbing the depredations of local officials and developing newly discovered mineral resources. Despite the province's relative prosperity, there were districts, especially around Miyāneh in the south, which were extremely poor. Early in the war, there was an outbreak of plague in Yerevan (then considered a part of Azerbaijan) in which many Iranian soldiers and an unknown number of civilians died. Moreover, when Fath 'Ali made Hosein Qoli Khān the governor of Yerevan in 1807, he separated that area from the Azerbaijani administration, giving Hosein Qoli control of all of Yerevan's revenue. In some ways, this change made excellent sense—Yerevan prospered under Hosein Qoli's rule and the khanate's army was successful in opposing the Russians. However, it weakened the war effort in other ways. The rivalry between 'Abbās and Hosein Qoli impeded their cooperation against the common enemy. The loss of Yerevan's revenue worsened 'Abbās economic position at a time when he was trying to strengthen his army by having French officers organize European-style infantry and artillery units, among other changes.[38]

The resources of Azerbaijan were not equal to the demands put on them. According to Mirzā Bozorg, the provincial government taxed as heavily as it dared but occasionally operated at a deficit. In the years during which Fath 'Ali sent his own troops into battle, his treasury covered the expenses, but he sometimes refused to send 'Abbās money on the grounds that Azerbaijan's revenues were sufficient. The enlargement of Azerbaijan by the inclusion of some territory further south could not alleviate the serious financial problem. After 1810, the British paid Iran an annual subsidy of 150,000 pounds that went primarily to defray the expenses of 'Abbās's European-style regiments. However, since the cost of training, equipping, and paying these soldiers greatly increased the cost of the war it is not certain that his financial problems were alleviated by the British subsidy.[39]

The sum of all the strengths and weaknesses was that each side had some victories but neither side was able to translate its strengths into decisive supremacy. It is not true that Iran was defeated in all the battles, as a modern writer has recently claimed.[40] In fact, the opening campaign of the war, the Yerevan campaign of 1804, and several that followed it went very well for the Iranians.

Late in June 1804, Tsitsianov led fewer than 3,000 Russian, Georgian, and Armenian soldiers across the Yerevani border. His first objective was the Armenian religious center at Echmiadzin, where he encountered 'Abbās's army of 18,000. While the Russian artillery inflicted heavy damage, the Iranians showed that they were effective soldiers in their own way. The battle was an Iranian victory in that the Russians failed to take the monastery and had to withdraw. This initial success was nearly undone by serious blunders during the next few days. In keeping with their traditional concept of warfare, the Iranians allowed the enemy to escape instead of pressing home the advantage. A few days later, the Russians returned to Echmiadzin and collected the provisions they had sought there. Next, an Iranian detachment was surprised by the Russian soldiers marching toward Yerevan and was routed. Although the survivors were driven from the field in disorder, they were able to regroup and participate in the fighting at Yerevan. The Iranians displayed similarly impressive recuperative powers many times during the war. Russians, used to the European distinction between a retreat in good order (which meant that the army was still capable of giving battle) and retreat in disorder, often mistook seemingly chaotic Iranian withdrawals for a complete breakdown of the army only to find soon after that the Iranians were ready to fight again.

The next major event of the campaign was the siege of Yerevan, which lasted from July until September, and was a more clear-cut victory for the Iranians. It was, in reality, a double siege. Mohammad Khān, some of the city's inhabitants, and 6,000 to 7,000 troops (including reinforcements from 'Abbās) held out in the citadel. Tsitsianov's men occupied the rest of the city and its immediate environs but were, in turn, surrounded by 'Abbas's much larger force supplemented by some of the shah's troops. Once again the Russian artillery was an effective weapon, but the Iranians were able nonetheless to inflict heavy casualties and prevent a Russian advance. They

burned the wheat fields and cut all communication between Tsitsianov and Georgia. The 200-man contingent sent to fetch supplies
from Georgia was surrounded by 6,000 Iranians and most were
killed (of the few survivors, most were enslaved). Finally, with a large
proportion of the Russians dead wounded, another thousand ill, and
the rest weakened by five weeks of living and fighting on half-rations,
the Russians retreated. Their troubles were not over. They were still
short of food and water; so many of their pack animals had died that
the beleaguered soldiers had to haul the baggage themselves; and
Iranian raiders harried the retreat, picking off stragglers and setting
fire to the parched fields. Not even Tsitsianov tried to claim this as a
victory. (An indication of the extent of the Russian losses is the absence of an official report of their own battle casualties for the siege
or the campaign as a whole.)[41]

There were few other large-scale undertakings until the closing
months of the war. The 1805 Russian campaign to take Anzali and
cross Gilān to Qazvin forced the Iranian government to curtail its activities on the Caucasian front in order to concentrate on Gilān. The
precaution turned out to be unnecessary, since the Russians became
bogged down in the Gilāni swamps after leaving Anzali and were
soon defeated by the provincial army. After Gudovich's failure at
Yerevan three years later, both sides limited themselves to the strategy
that suited them best: the Iranians raided enemy territory while
avoiding pitched battles; the Russians concentrated on defending
populated areas from those raids. Each side enjoyed occasional success. Raids frequently ended with a retreat hastened by the arrival of
Russian reinforcements. However, such retreats did not affect the
Iranians' capacity to stage more raids. For example, a Qarābāghi fort
located on the route used by the Iranians in many of their raids was
the scene of some of the most intense fighting in the summer of 1810.
A regiment led by Kotliarevskii took the fort from an Iranian garrison by storm. Once in possession of the fort, the Russians could not
prevent the Iranians from raiding the surrounding countryside or removing the inhabitants to the south bank of the Aras. Although the
Iranians suffered heavy losses when they attempted to retake the
fort, they were able to continue raiding as late as November and carried off several score inhabitants and thousands of animals.[42]

As the war dragged on, there seemed to be no end in sight. Some
of the principals on both sides realized this. In the spring of 1812,
Fath 'Ali remarked to the British ambassador, Gore Ouseley, that,
since the Russian position in the Caucasus was defensive, it would
not be burdensome for the Iranians to sustain the current level of

warfare for years. The shah had an ulterior motive for raising this point in that he was arguing for increased British assistance so that Iran could increase its war effort, but the argument was well grounded nonetheless. Commander-in-Chief Tormasov had reached the same conclusion in 1809, when he told St. Petersburg that Russia lacked the means to take the offensive and win the war. He argued that Russia needed an interval of peace with Iran during which Russia could strengthen its position on other Caucasian fronts and then take the offensive against Iran.[43] (Given the image of the Iranian army that had developed in St. Petersburg over a generation, Tormasov's argument carried little weight.) However, the war between Russia and Iran did not last for half a century, as did the conquest of the high Caucasus. The most important factor in upsetting the balance between the opposing sides was the intervention first of France, then of Britain, which are discussed in the next chapter.

VIII

France and Britain in Iran

The Qājārs's initial exposure to the British and the French was limited, but positive, and led Fath 'Ali to seek Western assistance in his war against Russia. Anglo-Iranian contacts centered on the growing trade with the East India Company and the stationing of a company "resident" in the Persian Gulf port of Bushehr (Bushire). In 1799, Richard Wellesley, the governor-general of India, became concerned over the threats posed by the Durrāni Afghans, who had raided Lahore, and by the French, whose troops were in Egypt, from where they might attack India. Therefore, Wellesley sent his resident in Bushehr and, soon after, Captain John Malcolm (an East India Company soldier with experience in civilian administration) to obtain Fath 'Ali's cooperation in opposing these two threats. Malcolm's efforts produced the Anglo-Iranian political and commercial treaties of 1801. The most significant provisions of the political treaty were the Iranian commitment to bar the French or the Afghans.[1] Relations between Iran and the company remained amicable for the next few years, even though the Afghan and the French dangers subsided and the Iranian ambassador to India was killed in a scuffle in 1802. (The company paid the ambassador's son a generous pension.)

As relations between Russia and Iran deteriorated, Fath 'Ali looked for British support, either military or diplomatic, to help him expel the Russians from the eastern Caucasus. He was encouraged in this by a highly questionable interpretation of the 1801 political treaty, which, he argued, had committed Britain to aid Iran if it were at-

123

tacked by *any* third party. In addition, Samuel Manesty (the company resident at Basra, near the mouth of the Tigris) became alarmed over a threat to India that he believed would result from a Russian victory in the Caucasus. The territorial dispute provided what he believed to be a golden opportunity to increase British influence in Iran. Chance gave him the means to establish contact with the shah. The company resident at Bushehr fell ill and could not deliver the governor-general's official condolences on the death of the Iranian ambassador to India, so the job fell to Manesty. In 1804, he journeyed to Iran, where he led the government to believe that his country would provide aid, and received a letter from Fath 'Ali to King George III. For the next two years, Iran sent repeated pleas for assistance to the company, all without avail. Officials of the company and the British government viewed the problem very differently than did the shah or Manesty, who was rebuked. First, British authorities considered the 1801 treaty nonbinding on themselves since it was never formally ratified. France was no longer a danger in Egypt or the Levant, while the Afghans were absorbed in internecine conflict. Second, the British did consider the treaty binding to the extent that Iran was prohibited from obtaining French assistance. Third, Britain and Russia were partners in the Third Coalition against Napoleon (1805-1807); therefore, neither London nor the company would condone hostilities against a valuable ally. In fact, British officials looked with favor on Russian expansion in the Caucasus, an important point to keep in mind in light of later russophobia.[2] John Warren, the ambassador to Constantinople, viewed the Russian takeover of Ganjeh as a suitable measure for the protection of Georgia and approved further expansion to a natural river border, while he deplored "a most insolent Letter" from the shah, demanding that the Russians leave the disputed territories.[3] Lord Leveson Gower, the ambassador to St. Petersburg, lamented the "perfidious" murder of the highly esteemed Tsitsianov.[4] British officials rarely showed an interest in Russo-Iranian relations, but, when they did, they sided with Russia.

For two years, from 1805 to 1807, the Iranians negotiated with the French while voicing a preference for aid from the British, if only the latter would provide it. Finally, the Iranian government concluded a treaty of alliance with France. The French had been trying to make an alliance with the Qājārs since 1795, when two French agents had been sent to propose a joint attack on the Ottoman Empire and the use of several thousand Iranian soldiers to aid Tipu Sultan of Mysore in his war against the British. However,

Āqā Mohammad was not impressed by the humble appearance of the two emissaries, who had traveled without an entourage, disguised as botanists to allay Ottoman suspicions. In any event, he was preoccupied with affairs in the Caucasus and Khorāsān. Therefore, his response was polite, but evasive, stressing the desirability of increased trade. The Iranians first showed an interest in a military alliance with France in 1802 or 1803, but this coincided with the uneasy peace that followed the Treaty of Amiens, a time when Bonaparte was preoccupied with diplomatic maneuverings within Europe. Therefore, France did not reply to the Iranian overtures. Then, in 1804, matters took a new turn as rumors of Napoleon's victories reached Iran. The French consul general at Baghdad, Jean-François Rousseau, who had once lived in Iran, began to correspond with some of the prominent Iranians whom he had met. Fath 'Ali responded late in 1804 by asking for French assistance in military technology. A series of French agents were sent to encourage the shah over the next two years, while the British continued to reject his requests for help and word reached Iran of Napoleon's impressive victories in central Europe. Finally, an Iranian ambassador (Mirzā Mohammad Rezā, vizier to Mohammad 'Ali Mirzā) departed late in 1806 to meet with Talleyrand and negotiate a treaty of alliance. The following May, the two diplomats signed an agreement, the Treaty of Finkenstein, directed against Britain and Russia. France recognized Georgia as part of Iran and agreed to "direct every effort to the ouster of the Russians from that province." Toward the end, France was to sell Iran artillery and rifles and also send French officers to "strengthen his [Fath 'Ali's] fortresses and to organize Persian artillery and infantry in accordance with principles of European military art." Iran was obliged to declare war on Britain, invade India, and encourage the Afghans to do the same. Iran was also to facilitate the French navy's use of Persian Gulf ports and allow the French army to go to India via Iran. Fath 'Ali did not intend his promise to join France in the conquest of India to amount to anything in the forseeable future. While voicing enthusiasm for the Indian campaign, he demanded that the restoration of the Caucasian provinces be settled first.[5]

In accordance with the terms of the treaty, Napoleon sent Iran an embassy headed by Count Claude Gardane (sometimes also spelled Gardanne), a cavalry officer whose courage under fire won him a promotion to brigadier general in 1799. His embassy—which included a number of infantry, artillery, and engineering instructors—was involved in the first significant effort to reform the Iranian army along

Western lines. Before the arrival of the French, some Russian deserters had been employed to train Iranian soldiers, but this tentative effort had had a minimal impact. Early French-directed reforms accomplished little more. Several of Napoleon's emissaries to Iran during
the years between 1805 and 1807 encouraged 'Abbās's interest in
Western military techniques. These men translated a few French military treatises and began to drill a very small number of 'Abbās's infantry and artillery soldiers. Fath 'Ali wished to expand the scale of
the French efforts and asked that more instructors be sent with the
new ambassador. The shah regarded military Westernization as one
of the major benefits of the new alliance with France and a key to
victory. He may have been influenced by the Ottoman military reforms begun by Sultan Selim in the 1790s, although the cautious
shah would not have been reassured by the sometimes violent opposition of traditionalist groups, especially the Janissaries, and the occasional disturbances caused by some of the new-style troops. The
factor that seems to have impressed the shah most was the long
series of victories European states had inflicted on the armies of
Islam over the past several generations. As he wrote to Napoleon:

French troops, better drilled than those of the Orient in the handling of arms,
are more accustomed to maneuver and are more coordinated in their movements; for this reason the soldiers of the West always have the advantage over
Oriental irregulars; and the latter ultimately succumb in their wars against the
former; in accordance with the union which now reigns between our two empires....Your Majesty will without doubt find it in his generosity to send
Iran some skilled instructors, who will teach our subjects the new maneuvers
so suited to assure the palm of vengeance over our enemies.[6]

Gardane's men trained between 2,500 and 4,000 infantrymen
and artillerymen. In some ways, the *sarbāz*, as the new infantry was
called, was a hybrid of European and Iranian ideas. Uniforms had
vaguely French-style jackets with traditional sheepskin hats and
baggy trousers. The soldiers learned the rudiments of Western drill,
a radical and rather befuddling departure from their tradition. One
chronicler observed in amazement the French-trained infantry as
they stood at attention: "Not one of all those soldiers could move
without his [the instructor, Captain Verdier's] permission."[7] An
artillery officer working in Esfahān managed, despite equipment
and manpower shortages as well as the hostility of several local officials, to deliver 20 cannon to the shah. France also agreed to sell
Iran 20,000 muskets. The engineers taught a few soldiers the basics

of fortification, made some improvements on existing structures (most notably at Yerevan), and drew up plans for the construction of new forts, such as 'Abbāsābād, near the border with Qarābāgh. Fath 'Ali was pleased with developments and asked France to send another 30 officers and a host of artisans, including painters, printers, potters, jewelers, mining engineers, and armaments makers. (The purchased weapons were not delivered, the officers and artisans not sent, because of the Franco-Russian rapprochement and the subsequent deterioration of Franco-Iranian relations.)[8]

The French, and later the British, also trained Western-style cavalry units, but the new ideas made little headway against deeply entrenched ideas about how this most prestigious branch of the military ought to function. In particular, Iranians objected to European ideas about how to use the lance. Some European borrowings were made without regard to their practicality in the Iranian setting. Spurs, for example, were of doubtful use to these already expert horsemen and were a menace to the soldiers, who were accustomed to sitting on their heels.[9]

Whatever the potential for these reforms to have improved Iran's martial capabilities, the efforts faced so many obstacles that little was accomplished. Foremost among the obstacles was the shah's disillusionment with French promises to end the war in the Caucasus and his expulsion of the French in the spring of 1809. Moreover, 'Abbās's financial problems kept him from maintaining all his *sarbāz* as a standing army (although he tried to circumvent this problem by occasionally granting land as payment in lieu of cash). As a result, the *sarbāz* received episodic training. The whole undertaking was so recently begun that *sarbāz* were not ready for battle by the time the French departed. In any case, the French officers would not have been able to lead the *sarbāz* in battle against the Russians because of the Franco-Russian alliance. Some of the new cannon were poorly cast and were liable to explode. The fortifications also suffered from structural flaws, largely as a result of design modifications in keeping with Iranian practices, such as placing the heavier stones in the upper parts of the walls (making them likely to collapse) and adding structures to the outer reaches of the fort (permitting the enemy a clear line of fire into the center of the fort from the outworks). And the frequent earthquakes in Azerbaijan damaged many fortifications.

Many of the problems were inherent to the process of change, rather than to the specific conditions of the French activities, and so persisted when the British took over. The reforms were unpopular with some of the soldiers serving in the new units and also with religious leaders. Although the new uniforms preserved a few elements of traditional dress, the overall appearance was European—and therefore vaguely Russian. The new drill was similarly tainted. Some Iranians argued that to dress in this manner and submit to this discipline was a betrayal of Islam. 'Abbās responded by wearing the new-style uniform and learning the drill himself. In the early stages of the reform, he also had the new units train where they could not be seen so as to avoid provoking opposition. The shah openly demonstrated his support for the reforms by having members of his own court wear the new uniforms and ordering the prince-governor of Shirāz to do likewise. Some of the 'ulama (Islamic religious leaders) as well as 'Abbās's political rivals, argued that the presence of infidels in Iran was injurious and the adaptation of infidel fighting methods contradicted the example set by Mohammad. Mirzā Bozorg counterattacked by obtaining the endorsement of other 'ulama and circulating Koranic references to the armies of the Prophet fighting in dense groups (the implication being that this was like the European carré). The government rationale was that it was reviving the practice of early Islam, which Christians had learned but the faithful had forgotten. 'Abbās used the distribution of British-made flags to the new infantry, cavalry, and artillery corps as an occasion to propagandize for the reforms. In separate ceremonies for each of the three branches, he had a prominent member of the 'ulama bless the flags and tell the troops that they should regard the flags as they would the banner of the Prophet; they should choose death over the loss of their flags.

Discipline was another major problem. The Western-style army was composed of men from various Azerbaijani tribes, but each tribe had to be kept separate. (For example, under British tutelage, there were separate regiments of Shaqaqis, Kangerlus, and Shāhsavans.) 'Abbās's repeated attempts to reorganize the army along nontribal lines failed; the soldiers' tribal solidarity was often stronger than their military discipline. Not surprisingly, officers from the traditional army also opposed the innovations. Given the vested opposition to the reforms and the novelty and stringency of the new regimen, discipline was hard to maintain. 'Abbās tried to improve the attitude of the soldiers in the new army through rewards—higher pay for the rank and file, land grants, and gold and silver medals. He put himself under the command of his foreign officers when he participated in the infantry and artillery training and recognized those officers' complete authority in disciplining the troops. During the period of British influence, a soldier who appealed to 'Abbās about the punishment meted out by a foreign officer was liable to have his punishment doubled. Despite all these measures, the problem was never fully resolved.

For all the reforms' shortcomings, Fath 'Ali and 'Abbās still believed that the adaptation of Western military techniques could break the deadlock in the war with Russia. 'Abbās continued to drill his *sarbāz* according to the new regimen even after the French left. (He preserved these units, which he valued for their experience, when the British organized another Western-style army.)[10]

In the early stages of the Franco-Iranian alliance, Napoleon thought that encouraging Iran to keep fighting for all the disputed Caucasian provinces would be a useful drain on Russia's military strength in Europe. Therefore, he advised the shah, "For your part, attack with vigor the enemies [the Russians] that my victories deliver to you weakened and demoralized. Retake from them Georgia and all the provinces which had been [part of] your empire and close the Caspian ports to them."[11] His attitude soon reversed itself. One month after the Treaty of Finkenstein was signed, Napoleon inflicted a devasting blow to the Russian army at Friedland. At the end of June, he and Alexander concluded an alliance by the Treaty of Tilsit. No attention was given to the Russo-Iranian dispute. This could be justified formally by the fact that the Treaty of Finkenstein had not yet been formally ratified. However, the basic issue was that Iranian affairs had been reduced to a minor issue in French eyes. The shah might still be a useful ally in some conjectural invasion of India, but his cooperation could not be purchased at the cost of antagonizing Russia. Moreover, the Spanish uprising, which began in 1808, tied down some 300,000 French troops and forced Napoleon to postpone any plans for Asian campaigns.

Even before Gardane reached Iran, his instructions had been changed. Instead of helping Iran fight Russia, he was to mediate an end to the war as quickly as possible. By coincidence, the moment was a propitious one because the combatants had of their own accord begun to discuss the possibility of negotiating a settlement. St. Petersburg had wished to open negotiations as early as 1805, but Tsitsianov ensured the defeat of that idea. In 1806, with Tsitsianov dead and the central government alarmed over the outbreak of war with the Ottoman Empire, the tsar recommended negotiations with the Iranians if they were at all possible. Russia was even willing to waive, at least temporarily, its unenforced claims to Yerevan and Nakhjavān. Gudovich, who would not have dared to exceed orders the way Tsitsianov did, was further encouraged to pursue negotiations by a letter he received from Mirzā Musā, the governor of Gilān and the court astrologer. There is some ambiguity about the terms Mirzā Musā proposed, an important point since the Russians believed that the shah waived his claim to Georgia. The original has not survived, and the only direct reference to it comes in a letter from Gudovich to one of his generals, which means that the likelihood of misinterpretation is great. (There is indirect evidence that Mirzā Musā did write to Gudovich on the subject. Later correspondence between Gudovich and Iranian officials contains a few references to that letter without eliciting an Iranian disclaimer of its authenticity.) The Iranian peace proposal seems to have been motivated by the hope that, with Tsitsianov gone, the Russians might be more willing to compromise. The tone of the letter, according to Gudovich's summary, put the blame for the war on Tsitsianov, specifically that he devastated lands subject to Iran: Yerevan, Ganjeh, and Dāghestān (Derbent, Qobbeh, and the eastern high Caucasus). Gudovich believed this meant that Iran admitted that Georgia was not one of its vassals. However, Qarābāgh was excluded from the list although the shah certainly considered that part of his domains. When the shah had sought help from Britain and France to enforce his claims in the Caucasus, he had repeatedly specified Georgia as an objective. Moreover, by 1806, he was dealing from an apparent position of strength. France was promising assistance, and Russia's Caucasian forces were in disarray. It is improbable that Fath 'Ali would have reduced his demands under such circumstances, but the Russians, believing that he had, were outraged later in the negotiations by unambiguous demands for the cession of Georgia. Although they lacked a common understanding of the terms, the Russians and the Iranians began to correspond on the subject of peace. There was no fighting, apart from a few raids along the border, during 1807 and most of 1808.[12]

Gardane was in Iran during that period and worked assiduously to mediate a peace agreement. He hated being in Iran; the living conditions did not meet his standards, and the climate aggravated a painful war injury. He begged to be released from his assignment, even having his wife intercede on his behalf with the Empress. However, while he was there, he was wholly committed to accomplishing something impressive for France by guaranteeing the supremacy of its influence in Iran and excluding the British. To that end, he promised the shah everything at a time when neither his own country nor Russia would permit the fulfillment of such promises. He declared in writing that the settlement would involve Russia's cession to Iran of all the disputed territories, including Georgia. He assured the shah that Napoleon had great influence over Alexander and would make the tsar agree to all these demands. He also proposed, as a way of cementing Iran's ties to

France, that the peace talks between the Iranian and the Russian ambassadors be held in Paris, with Napoleon's mediation. As a result,
the shah, 'Abbās, and their favored officials were encouraged to maxi-
mize their demands on Russia while relying on Gardane and France
to deliver complete victory. There was never an opportunity to test
whether the Iranians might have been willing to yield on some points
in the process of serious negotiations because they confronted only
nonnegotiable demands.[13]

Russia's position was as intransigent as Iran's but even less tenable
because it was so remarkably ill-conceived. St. Petersburg's brief initial
willingness to allow some leeway on the status of Yerevan and Nakhjavān was quickly replaced by a renewed claim to the two khanates,
even though they were still under Iranian control. From Gudovich's
first letter to the Iranian government to the collapse of the negotiations, Russia demanded that Iran waive any claims to all the territory
north of the Aras and the Kura on the grounds that the claims were
tenuous and the area of little value. (Alexander, in his discussions with
Ambassador Caulaincourt, carried the matter further by claiming that
Russia already controlled the territory in question, including Yerevan
and Nakhjavān. Caulaincourt and his superiors in Paris took the tsar at
his word.) The Iranian government replied—with more aplomb than it
was usually given credit for by Europeans—that, if the area was worth
so little, there was no good reason for Russia to want it and furthermore that, if large rivers were necessary for secure borders, Russia
should stick to its established river boundary in the northern Caucasus.
(Gudovich misinterpreted this last remark as an Iranian claim to all
the land up to the northern Caucasus.) If the French were not to be
trusted, as the Russians argued, then surely the greater danger would
be to Russia (which had until recently been France's enemy) than to
Iran (which had had only peaceful relations with France). The Russians tried lying in ways they could easily be caught, like telling the
Iranian government that Napoleon could not help because he was dy-
ing of some illness at a time when he was writing the shah of his victories in eastern Europe. Gudovich was under the illusion that Iran
was in dire straits, that the shah could never make an alliance with
France because he feared a French invasion, and that he and Hosein
Qoli Khān of Yerevan were willing to give up that khanate and Nakhjavān because of the excessive defense costs. The commander-in-chief
believed that there was a rebellion in Khorāsān in 1808, which was
not the case. He also mistook John Malcolm's unsuccessful attempt to
persuade the shah to revert to a British alliance for a successful invasion of the province of Fārs. The Russian Ministry of Foreign Affairs

(specifically, S. M. Bronevskii, the Asia expert and veteran of the 1796 campaign) drew up a lengthy argument designed to persuade the Iranian government of the advantages of making peace on Russian terms. In addition to pressing the claim that the disputed territories had all rebelled against Iran, Gudovich was to tell the shah that, if he (Fath 'Ali) yielded to all of Russia's demands, Russia would recognize him as shah and thus give him a secure claim to his throne that he could not achieve by himself. Similarly, 'Abbās was to be told that he would be strengthened in his rivalry with his elder brother by giving up the war against Russia. The peace talks broke down when Russia became impatient with Iran's refusal to yield. Therefore, Gudovich decided to frighten the Iranians into concessions by conquering Yerevan late in the year after the Iranian army had disbanded for the winter. The result contradicted his expectations in every way.[14]

The failure of the peace negotiations marked the defeat of Gardane's efforts and drove Iran from the French camp to the British. Part of the fault was Gardane's personally. He promised too much. The last straw was the attack on Yerevan that made a mockery of his assurances that Russia would not dare threaten that khanate as long as France mediated in the negotiations. While Fath 'Ali was considering whether to receive another British mission, this one under Sir Harford Jones, Gardane lost his opportunity to continue diplomatic maneuvers by demanding that Fath 'Ali expel Jones on pain of the departure of the French embassy. The shah, unimpressed, gave Gardane his leave. The French ambassador then compounded his problems by requesting to leave via Russia. His intention was to try to salvage French interests by negotiating a peace settlement along the way, but, influenced by the recent disappointments, the Iranians interpreted his request as a sign of his pro-Russian bias.

Even if Gardane had been a shrewder diplomat, there would have been little he could have done to change the course of events. Ambassador Caulaincourt was quickly rebuffed when he offered Alexander French mediation at peace talks to be held in Paris. The tsar made the cutting reply that France had no more business involving itself in Russia's Caucasian affairs than Russia did involving itself in France's Spanish affairs. In response to Russian wishes, Caulaincourt ordered Gardane to help France's ally by ridding it of the war with Iran. Gardane's job was to ensure that Iran agreed to Russia's terms. The Iranian government did not know about these exchanges, but it did perceive French coldness in other ways. The commercial treaty negotiated in 1808 was not ratified by France. Iran's ambassador in Paris was snubbed and prevented from communicating with his government for a year. In sum, France's involvement in Iran initially bolstered Iranian hopes. When this alliance proved counterproductive, the shah did not abandon the principle but rather looked for a different ally — Britain.[15]

Since the British and then the French had courted the shah, it was not surprising that he thought he had some leeway to play the one against the other and thus obtain the greatest assistance against Russia. The British reaction under these circumstances was poorly coordinated. The first British action regarding Iran since the Manesty fiasco was taken by Lord Minto, the governor-general of the East India Company's holdings in India. He reacted to the Franco-Iranian alliance by sending John Malcolm back to Iran. Part of Malcom's problems stemmed from the fact that he reached Iran in the summer of 1808 at at time when Fath 'Ali still hoped that the French would obtain a favorable peace agreement. However, another important cause of his failure was his hectoring tone. He scolded the Iranians for failing to comply with the anti-French provisions of the 1801 treaty and implied that the shah would face Britain's wrath unless the French were expelled immediately. Malcolm was indignant that the Iranians were preoccupied by their own self-interest and did not comply with his demand regarding the Gardane mission. Even Lord Minto faulted Malcolm's contemptuous treatment of the Iranians. The shah considered Britain to have violated the treaty by not aiding him against Russia and would allow Malcolm no more than to negotiate with the governor of Fārs, perhaps with the intention of using this as a way of pressuring Gardane. Malcolm, of course, refused the terms and withdrew. In any case, he seems to have been more interested in using this incident as a justification for seizing an island in the Persian Gulf for use as a commercial center and military base than in negotiating.[16]

London was also concerned about developments in Iran, and in 1807 had appointed Harford Jones as the king's envoy to Fath 'Ali. Jones was a longtime company servant, resident at Basra from 1786 to 1794 and at Baghdad around the turn of the century. During those years, he visited southern Iran several times and befriended a number of prominent individuals, among them Mirzā Bozorg, who had been a vizier in the Zand government. Unlike Malcolm, Jones seems to have felt genuine admiration for a number of Iranians and tried to understand their views. Although appointed before Malcolm, he reached India shortly after Malcolm's departure for Iran. He then waited for the outcome of that mission and did not arrive in Iran until the close of 1808. Unlike his predecessor, Jones emphasized the desirability of improving Anglo-Iranian relations. Fath 'Ali was more inclined to listen after the breakdown of the peace talks and summoned Jones to

Tehran, where a preliminary treaty of alliance was agreed upon. In addition to a provision that obligated Iran to deny any European army passage to India or the Persian Gulf, Britain agreed to a provision requiring that it would assist Iran against any attack by a European power, including one begun prior to the treaty. The assistance could take the form of direct military action, subsidies, or mediation.[17]

Britain's position in Iran was not yet secured. The shah still wished to keep his options open and so did not break completely with the French. Although Gardane had left in April, two members of his embassy remained in Azerbaijan until the end of the year. As Fath 'Ali explained to a member of the Jones mission, Britain wanted him to break with France, which was not his enemy and was helping him in the war with Russia. Britain professed friendship but had as yet provided no help. The shah used this occasion to pressure Britain into giving large-scale assistance: 30,000 soldiers and 20,000 guns, or 200,000 tomāns (about £150,000). At the same time, Lord Minto, in a fit of pique that Jones and London had succeeded where he and Malcolm had failed, did his best to sabotage the Jones mission. In 1809, he ceased to honor Jones's bills, thus raising doubts in Tehran whether Jones was a legitimate representative of his government empowered to negotiate a treaty.

The following year Minto went further, firing Jones (which he lacked the authority to do) and sending Malcolm to replace him. Minto was jealous of his authority and wanted Malcolm to remain in Iran even if London confirmed Jones's mission. As a result, the shah then had three options: he could recall the French, who still corresponded with him and sent secret emissaries to Iran; he could accept the 1809 preliminary treaty, in which the exact terms of assistance had not been specified; or he could try to obtain even more favorable terms from Malcolm, which seemed promising in light of Malcolm's extravagant gift giving on his first mission to Iran. The French were clearly in the weaker position, although they kept trying to recoup their losses and the shah's government occasionally sent friendly letters. Malcolm was initially well received, and various officials wrote of their preference for dealing with him over Jones. That was not surprising since Jones and Mirzā Shafi' had clashed over the size of the proposed subsidy. However, Mirzā Bozorg favored Jones and had considerable influence over the shah. Eventually, London thwarted Minto's power play by confirming Jones as the official British representative in Iran. Malcolm had to withdraw, but Jones was also removed. In his place, London sent Sir Gore Ouseley, a former company employee with a reputation as a Persian scholar. The new emissary negotiated another treaty, much like the preliminary one except for added details about the nature of British assistance, 'Abbās's endorsement of the treaty, and his recognition as heir apparent.[18] Ouseley remained in Iran through the end of the war with Russia and had considerable influence on its outcome.

Fath 'Ali would not have consented to renewing his alliance with Britain unless that country promised to aid him in the war against Russia. This meant Britain, or more precisely the company, was committed by treaty to provide officers and weapons for a Western-style army and a subsidy to pay for it. One of the few points on which Jones, Malcolm, and Ouseley agreed was that the assistance was not a good idea. They felt that the Iranian soldiers could be very effective using their traditional cavalry methods while members of a Western style army would need a long period of training before they could be ready for active duty. However, they all reconciled themselves to the project, which the shah and 'Abbās believed indispensible.[19]

The two main differences between the military reforms directed by the French and the British were that the efforts of the British were on a larger scale and produced troops who played an important role in the last battles of the war. The subsidy from the governor-general was a major asset. This paid the salaries of the new army's officers and men and of the fifty or so British instructors and artisans. It also paid for a large quantity of weapons and related military supplies. By the close of the war, Iran had received some 16,000 muskets and 20 cannon, as well as 1,000 sabers sent as a gift from Malcolm to 'Abbās. In addition, the British manufactured gunpowder, gun carriages, and other items in the Tabriz citadel. The advisers also built or reinforced a number of fortifications. The appearance of the new army was changed. The infantry uniform closely resembled the hybrid style of the French-trained soldiers, except for a change in color, but the artillery was clothed in the British style. (In the process, the British hoped to do their own business interests a service by having the new army clothe its soldiers in British woolens.) The soldiers were required to be clean shaven, an unpopular symbolic break with Iranian preference that even 'Abbās opposed until he witnessed an accident in which a soldier's beard was ignited by a spark from a gun. The British also trained a fife corps, which became quite adept at playing English dances, much to the shah's delight.

Not everything went smoothly. In addition to the basic problems that the French had also confronted, the British also faced some problems peculiar to their circumstances in Iran. First of all, the French-trained units were still in existence and bitterly resented the

British presence. An attempt to put the French-trained Shaqaqi infantry under British command produced considerable friction. Given the current ascendancy of the British in Iran, the French-trained *sarbāz* could not hope to be the most-favored units in the new army, and their hostility complicated the task of military reform. Financial problems, mostly related to British expenditures in Iran, were another important source of trouble. Apparently, some Iranian officers in the new army embezzled or postponed payment of subsidy monies destined for the troops under their jurisdiction. Since the British officers made a strenuous effort to end looting, the ordinary soldier was left with an inadequate wage and barred from the usual method of supplementing his income. Ouseley claimed that the shah compounded the financial problems by diverting a large part of the subsidy for his private purposes. However, there is no solid evidence on this issue. The ambassador's contention was that, before his arrival, none of the shah's officials had dared explain that the subsidy was other than a personal gift for the shah to use however he wished. That specific argument is contradicted by Jones's account of his discussions with the shah when the subsidy was first arranged. At that time, Jones explained the precise meaning of the subsidy. Since he spoke in Persian directly to the shah, there is no possibility of distortion by some intermediary. Ouseley derived his ideas about the shah from Malcolm, who stressed the shah's avarice, so it is hard to judge whether Ouseley's accusation was based on fact or a presumption of corruption. However, there is no doubt that money problems harmed the morale of the British officers serving in Iran, expecially Captain Charles Christie (in charge of the new infantry), Lieutenant Henry Lindesay (in charge of the artillery), and Ensign William Monteith (the engineer in charge of fortifications). All were promised bonuses (from their own government or the company) for their service in Iran but received none and in fact went into debt. All were eager to leave Iran. Ironically, Christie and Lindesay were 'Abbās's favorites and stayed with him after the rest of the British were withdrawn in the autumn of 1812 because of the Anglo-Russian alliance.[20]

Despite all the problems, by 1812 'Abbās had a European-trained army of about 13,000 infantry, cavalry, and artillery (of which most were infantry). He and the shah were pleased with the results and optimistic that victory was at last within reach. The fledgling units had begun to see action in 1810 and experienced some modest successes and failures. Their most important victories came early in 1812 in Tālesh and Qarābāgh. In Tālesh, the principal opposition came from the khanate's tribal cavalry, with only a small number of Russians involved. However, in Qarābāgh, about 2,300 European-style troops defeated nearly 900 Russians at Soltānbud, within fifty miles of Shushā. Christie and Lindesay led the infantry's advance on the Russian position, while Major D'Arcy (the commander-in-chief of the new army) directed the artillery, which made the most important contribution by blowing up the Russian magazine. Christie and Lindesay won the Iranians' admiration by putting themselves in the thick of the fighting, thus proving that they would not shrink from fighting their fellow Christians. The Russians lost more than 300 killed, including their commandant and 12 other officers, and suffered about an equal number wounded. (The Iranians lost 140 killed, including 2 British sergeants.) After a day of battle, the surviving Russians surrendered. The Iranians raided the surrounding area and returned to a position south of the Aras with their prisoners and booty.

Although the new army's victory was as heartening to the Iranians as it was humiliating to the Russians, there were clear signs that the new army had serious flaws. There were as yet no Iranians with sufficient training to lead the troops. Furthermore, centuries of military tradition could not be unlearned in a few years. The new army had made undeniable progress, but it was still in an unsatisfactory transitional stage between two methods of warfare. A striking example of this is the way the new infantry performed satisfactorily in the first wave of attack on the Russian position at Soltānbud and then broke ranks when victory was imminent in order to plunder. This enabled The Russians to regroup and drive off the attackers. At the time, no one guessed that the inexperienced new army would soon face a critical test.[21]

The year of 1812 ought to have been a good one for the Iranian war effort in light of the early victories, the anti-Russian uprising in the Caucasus, and the French invasion of Russia, but instead it became a time of disaster. The invasion began in June, when Napoleon sent more than 600,000 soldiers to force Russia into submission. As Russia marshalled its military resources for the defense of the nation, it also strengthened its international position by concluding an alliance with Britain in August. In October, when Ouseley finally learned of the Anglo-Russian rapprochement, he realized that the anti-Napoleonic cause required that Russia be freed of its Caucasian distraction. Therefore, he recalled the British officers from the Iranian army. Fath 'Ali and 'Abbās were extremely upset and after much pleading persuaded Ouseley to let Christie, Lindesay, Dr. Cormick (the prince's physician), and 13 drill sergeants remain with the prince's army in the event of any fighting with the Russians. Raids following the well-established pattern continued during the autumn, when 'Abbās sent his cavalry to lead a hoped-for uprising. Commander-in-chief Rtisch-chev was convinced that he lacked the means to stage a major offensive against the Iranians, so he concentrated instead on strengthening border defenses against the recurrent raids. In keeping with that policy, he sent Kotliarevskii to take charge of the Qarābāghi frontier. At the same time, 'Abbās made his camp as he often did just south of the border at Aslānduz, where it was comparatively easy to ford the Aras forty miles west of its confluence with the Kura.

Kotliarevskii exceeded his order to follow a purely defensive course of action and decided to make a preemptive attack on the prince's camp. The battle began at the end of October as Kotliarevskii caught the Iranians unprepared. The Iranians had the larger force—some 5,000 men, including several hundred *sarbāz* as well as the shah's elite infantry—but the 2,000 Russians had the advantage of surprise. The camp was overrun, and the Iranians retreated in poor order, leaving most of their supplies behind. Lindesay and the artillerymen were not even at the camp at the time, having been sent to prepare for 'Abbās's planned hunting excursion. They returned when they heard the sounds of battle and only with difficulty managed to save the cannon and a small quantity of ammunition. Lindesay and Christie both wanted to make a last-ditch stand at the camp, but 'Abbās insisted on a retreat to a small fort on a nearby hill. After a few hours' fighting, the Russian assault was contained. Many Iranians crowded into the fort designed to hold a small fraction of their number. Two infantry companies led by Christie blocked the Russians' path to the hill, while the artillerymen under Lindesay's command did the best they could until the ammunition ran out. There were also many desertions. That night a despondent 'Abbās tried to decide what to do next. He eventually resolved to stay and fight, despite the British officers' advice that he retreat beyond the Russians' range of attack. As usual, there were no guards posted around the camp. Before dawn, Christie finally obtained 'Abbās's permission to guard the most likely attack route. By the time these soldiers moved into position, the Russian attack had begun. What followed was less a battle than a slaughter. Many Iranians fled in disorder, while those who remained put up little resistance. Eleven of the thirteen artillery pieces were lost after they became stuck in the uneven terrain as 'Abbās had them moved from the fort to the base of the hill. The Russians advanced on the heels of the fleeing Iranians, with the result that many of the Iranians were caught in the crossfire as their fellow countrymen tried to stave off the attack. The thatched roofs of the fort caught fire and

300 of those inside were killed. In all, about 2,000 Iranians were killed and more than 500 were captured. Christie and one of the drill sergeants were also killed. According to some reports, Christie survived the battle but was killed as he lay wounded because the Russians were angry that any British continued to aid Iran. The Russians lost only 28 killed and 99 wounded.[22]

Iranian morale was shaken badly. Some of the disappointment was expressed as criticism of Britain for betraying Iran to Russia. Then at the start of the new year came the Lankarān disaster. The Russians took no prisoners "because on account of the obstinance of the Persians in defending that fort and the arrogance with which the proposal to surrender was rejected no one was shown mercy by the soldiers."[23] In two months, Iran lost about 5,000 soldiers of its new army. Yet Fath 'Ali, 'Abbās, and Hosein Qoli Khān of Yerevan were not ready to admit defeat. Border raids continued into the summer of 1813. Despite the losses suffered at Aslānduz and Lankarān, the Iranian government perceived encouraging signs. Although Napoleon had left Moscow by the time of Aslānduz, the slowness of communications meant that Iran was still receiving word of French triumphs well into 1813. Even when news of the French retreat finally arrived, rumor had it that Napoleon had merely regrouped his forces in Poland to prepare for a new invasion of Russia. Therefore, the Iranians kept expecting Russia to recall its troops from the Caucasus for service in Europe. They also hoped for renewed uprisings in Georgia. Moreover, the shah still counted on ample support from Britain. A few British officers and some 12,000 arms that had been ordered a long time before arrived in Iran after Aslānduz. The shah also ordered thousands more weapons, while British soldiers in Tabriz drilled infantry recruits and manufactured cannon. By the spring of 1813, Iran's new army had recovered to near its pre-Aslānduz strength. When Fath 'Ali reviewed the new army that summer, it looked impressive and encouraged his hopes of military success. In addition, the shah knew he was entitled to receive the British subsidy for the duration of the war, so he was less worried about the cost of continuing to fight. However, Britain was determined to end a war that no longer served its national interests. Therefore, the British ambassador compelled Iran to make peace.[24]

The British had been involved twice in unsuccessful attempts to negotiate peace since the restoration of their diplomatic influence in Iran. In 1810, the shah was concerned about rumors that France had obtained a Russo-Turkish peace, which would permit the transfer of more Russian troops to the east Caucasian front. He was even more concerned about the behavior of his British ally, which was slow to give the promised aid and, when Minto tried to remove Jones, gave the impression of being disorganized and unreliable. Therefore, it was in the shah's interests to prolong the negotiations with Russia until the ambiguities were cleared. By contrast, two years later, Iran initiated preliminary negotiations when it was in a strong position, having won the symbolically important victory at Soltānbud and knowing that the Russians were hard pressed by the rebellion in Georgia and the high mountains. On this occasion, the Iranians reduced their demands, asking for the cession of all the Muslim-ruled khanates and one Turcoman district of Georgia but dropping the claim to Georgia as a whole.

In both years' negotiations, the Russians believed that their own military problems made peace with Iran highly desirable, yet they offered no meaningful concessions. The only modification was the temporary dropping of Russia's claim to Yerevan and Nakhjavān, but that had little practical effect since it controlled neither. In 1810, St. Petersburg recommended using the Afghans against Iran rather than making the slightest concession. Even the reduced insult value of waiving the claim to Yerevan and Nakhjavān was balanced by a more vigorous insistence that Iran surrender Tālesh, whose khan had submitted to both Iran and Russia and where Russian protection had been extremely ineffective. Commander-in-chief Rtischchev tried to persuade St. Petersburg that Tālesh was not worth the manpower it would cost Russia or the damage Russia's claim to that khanate would do the peace negotiations. However, Chancellor Rumiantsev insisted that Russia had a claim based on the khan's desire for Russian protection for the past twenty years. All Rumiantsev would concede was the possibility of an independent Tālesh with no Iranian involvement. The biggest inducement Russia offered Iran was the recognition of Fath 'Ali as shah (Russian officials deliberately called him Bābā Khān, his precoronation name) and the promise of Russian protection. Not surprisingly, both sets of peace talks were miserable failures. The Russians, who had never understood Iran's point of view or even that there could be a rationally considered Iranian point of view that differed from Russia's, blamed the British for the failure of the negotiations in 1810.

Jones was quite eager to claim responsibility since he regarded the prolongation of the war as one of his primary objectives, especially since it would help the Ottoman Empire in its war with Russia, something the British desired greatly. Of course, the Iranians told Jones what he wanted to hear about the collapse of the peace talks and coincidentally emphasized Iran's devotion to Britain's interests at a time when Iran was counting on British assistance. In fact, the Iranian attitude was influenced by the suspicion that Russia would use an armistice or a peace agreement to consolidate its position and prepare for a new wave of conquest. The eventual clarification of Jones's official position also bolstered the Iranians' resistance.

The situation in 1812 was different. Ouseley sincerely hoped for an end to the Russo-Iranian War. He sought to expedite the negotiations by urging 'Abbās, who was extremely dissatisfied with the Russian proposals, not to abandon peace efforts. He also sent Rtishchev advice about the kinds of terms to offer. Ouseley was right when he said that the Iranians would not accept Russia's terms, but he displayed peculiar judgment when he suggested that peace could be made on the basis of Russia keeping all the territory it claimed but then ceding some unspecified areas to Iran. When Russia rejected this, James Morier, Ouseley's representative at the talks, proposed an armistice, the provisional cession of some territory, and the initiation of new peace talks in St. Petersburg. The Russians rejected this idea as well, and the peace efforts collapsed in September.[25]

After Aslānduz, relations between Ouseley and the Iranian government chilled considerably. Ouseley believed that the Iranians had acted in bad faith when they rejected his peace proposals in 1812, and they made a similar charge against him with regard to the withdrawal of the British officers. However, the ambassador played his trump card—he briefly withheld subsidy payments, thus forcing the shah to heed to his advice. The ambassador saw nothing wrong with his peace plan and was determined to put it into effect in 1813. His first priority was "to assist our good friends and Allies the Russians, even in this remote quarter."[26] He proposed a one-year armistice for the negotiation of a preliminary peace treaty. During the armistice, each side would retain the territory currently under its control. He further advised the Russians to cede a small portion of the conquered territory as a sop to Iranian pride. Ouseley genuinely believed that Russia would see the advantages of relinquishing Muslim-ruled areas and even Georgia, which he considered an unnecessary burden. Russia's interests would be served better, he thought, by turning Georgia into an independent state or at least a protectorate. He confidently predicted that the trade opportunities resulting from such a change would prove beneficial to Russia. If Russia were reluctant, the East India Company could pay it to return Georgia to Iran. He expected the price to be modest, the equivalent of two years' subsidy. When confronted by Russian opposition, he rationalized that such obstructionism was localized in the Caucasus and that the tsar was more benevolent. In the event that Russia were unwilling to cede any territory to Iran, Ouseley felt that Iran ought to be satisfied by the restoration of traditional local rulers in the disputed provinces. He did not explain why he felt Iran should be pleased by that. Iran's lack of enthusiasm for the plan he ascribed to three factors: the shah's insatiable greed, which made him unwilling to make peace and give up the subsidy; Mirzā Bozorg's ambition for himself and 'Abbās, which made him see the continuation of the war as the only way to perpetuate his importance; and, finally, the Iranians' boorish self-absorption. As he explained to Castlereagh:

There is a very perverse trait in the Persian character, which renders them insensible of and ungrateful for, all favors conferred upon them; for, being the most selfish egotists in the world, they judge everyone by themselves, and invariably impute some latent ignoble or even inimical motive to actions and propositions the most candid and ostensibly kind and disinterested.[27]

Only two years later, after the war was over, did he admit that Fath 'Ali doubted that Russia would yield any territory, regardless of promises, and objected to ending a long war without any gains. When faced by Iranian resistance, Ouseley threatened to end the subsidy unless his peace plan was accepted. Furthermore, he compelled the Iranians to make him supervisor of the Iranian part in any negotiations with Russia and the judge of whether Russia's best offer was acceptable. The purpose of this was to ensure that Iran did not hold out for excessive demands and in the process force Britain to keep paying the subsidy.

Russia did not like Ouseley's plan any better than the Iranians did. Rtishchev vetoed the one-year armistice since he thought it was just a trick to buy time during which Iran would prepare for a new campaign against Russia. Instead, he demanded a fifty-day armistice during which the preliminary peace treaty would be signed on the basis of the terms proposed by Russia. No territorial concessions would be made in that treaty. Not until later would an Iranian ambassador be allowed to go to St. Petersburg to ask the tsar to cede some territory. Rtishchev thought that Alexander, as a compassionate man, would probably accede to the Iranian request. He even agreed to sign an agreement to that effect, although it had to be separate from the treaty. However, it is doubtful that by the time he signed the article he believed that any territorial concession would be made since he had learned that Rumiantsev was unhappy about the whole idea and especially about Ouseley's role in this matter. There was little reason for Rtishchev to feel inclined to make concessions. Even more than the victories at Aslānduz and Lankarān, early news of Napoleon's expulsion from Russia filled him with patriotic fervor. He hoped that the news would impress the Iranians. In fact, that was not the case.

Ouseley persuaded himself and the shah that Iran would gain territory after the provisional treaty. As a further reassurance, Ouseley promised the shah that, if Russia did not make adequate territorial concessions, the subsidy payments would continue. Ouseley foresaw no difficulty since he would be the judge of what was adequate. That hope and Ouseley's threat to cut off the subsidy led Fath 'Ali to agree to end the war.[28]

Peace talks were held at Golestān, a village in northern Qarābāgh. Rtishchev represented the Russian government. Iran was represented by Mirzā Abu'l-Hasan, a nephew of the late grand vizier Hāji Ebrāhim. After his uncle's execution, the mirzā spent two years in India, where he learned something of British ways. He later returned to favor in Iran and served in the administration while receiving a regular stipend from the East India Company. He had been sent as ambassador to Britain for the ratification of the preliminary treaty of 1809. Then Ouseley secured his appointment as Iranian representative at the peace talks to ensure British influence on the outcome. The mirzā made a favorable impression on Rtishchev, causing Rtishchev to be somewhat more conciliatory than he or his colleagues had been in other negotiations—for example, when he consented to wait while the mirzā sent the separate article about territorial concessions to Tehran for approval, instead of demanding immediate acquiescence. There were no substantial negotiations in the drafting of the treaty. Rtishchev essentially dictated the terms but yielded in part to Abu'l-Hasan's requests for modification of certain points that were peripheral to Russia's interests. Thus, Russia's intention to state its formal recognition of Fath 'Ali as shah was discarded in response to the mirzā's objection that it was demeaning—Fath 'Ali was the acknowledged shah and did not need Russia's endorsement. It was sufficient that the treaty referred to the shah by his proper name and title. Another proposal to include Russian support for 'Abbās's succession was also rejected on the grounds that Fath 'Ali did not want to provoke his other sons by an open reference to 'Abbās as the heir designate. Therefore, the article was revised to state Russia's support for the shah's chosen successor without mentioning 'Abbās's name. The border between Russia and Iran was based on the current disposition of each side's forces, although the precise manner in which the border was described in the treaty was a source of dispute. Eventually, Rtishchev resolved the matter by leaving the Tālesh border to be decided later by a binational commission and giving the geographical markers of the rest of the border. In essence, Iran ceded Tālesh and all of the khanates north of the Aras and the Kura, except Yerevan and Nakhjavān, to Russia. Since the border coincided with the *status quo ad presentem*, Russia acknowledged Iranian control of Moqri, a Qarābāghi border district that the Russians had abandoned as unhealthful and virtually inaccessible from the rest of Qarābāgh. Moreover, Iran recognized Russia's sovereignty over all of the rest of the Caucasus from the west Georgian principalities to the high mountains, thus denying any Ottoman claim to those lands. There were also provisions aimed at improving Russo-Iranian trade and one that guaranteed the voluntary repatriation of those who had been captured or migrated from one side of the border to the other. The treaty included a stipulation that only Russian naval vessels might sail the Caspian, but there had been no Iranian naval activity there at any point during the war.[29]

Rtishchev and Mirzā Abu'l-Hasan signed the treaty on October 24, 1813. According to the treaty, both sovereigns had to ratify it within three months. Fath 'Ali signed the treaty at the end of the year. The following summer, Ouseley traveled home via Russia, where he expected to persuade the tsar to make some territorial concessions. He was received warmly in St. Petersburg but did not achieve his goal. For the next twenty years, he waited to be rewarded with a peerage that never was granted. The Treaty of Golestān, which he helped to bring about, satisfied neither signatory. The war was over, but the underlying grievances remained unresolved.

IX

The Consequences
of the Struggle
for the Eastern Caucasus

There were two obvious results of the military confrontation of Russians, east Caucasians, and Iranians. The first was that Russia acquired most of the disputed territory. This inevitably changed the social, economic, and political structure of the affected principalities. Modern studies have been done on the changes that occurred in Georgia, but little attention has been given to the impact of the Russian takeover on the inhabitants of the khanates. The second result was widespread dissatisfaction with conditions as they stood in 1813. Many Muslims were not reconciled to being part of the Russian Empire. Empire builders were displeased that some of the land north of the Aras remained in Iranian hands and that the British seemed to have so much influence over the Iranian government. Members of that government were disheartened by the costly, humiliating defeat. These various problems led to a second war during the late 1820s. The brief second war was in many ways a recapitulation of the first, with the difference that the Russian victory was more decisive. It ended Iranian hopes of regaining any of the land north of the boundary Russia had attained after a generation of struggle and also led to the increase of Russian influence over Iran's internal affairs.

The fact that some khans or would-be khans signed treaties of vassalage with Russian authorities meant that aspects of the traditional power structure continued to exist in some khanates—for example, Qarābāgh, Shirvān, Tālesh, and Shakki. The other khanates were administered directly by Russia after the flight or death of their khans.

145

Yet the dichotomy was not complete. Where Russia ruled directly, it employed local notables and kept some traditional practices. Where khans ruled, their authority even in internal matters was subject to limits imposed by the Russian authorities. Moreover, rule by khans was gradually supplanted by direct rule. When khans remained in power, they did so as functionaries of the Russian government, with Russian titles and modest salaries. An example was Mahdi Qoli Khān of Qarābāgh, who was named a major-general and given the salary appropriate to that rank. The salaries must have been important to the khans, considering the loss of revenue because of war-related disruptions. The khans' financial ties to Russia were both a symptom of and a reaction to the extent of Russian involvement in the khanates' internal affairs, as for example in Shirvān, where the lucrative fishing concession was transferred from the jurisdiction of the khan to that of the Russian treasury. In at least one case, Russian authorities intervened to reorganize taxation of the peasantry. This occurred in Qarābāgh, which had fallen into arrears in its tribute payment. The Russians attributed this to the insufficient loyalty of the ruling family and other notable landlords and sent an official to draw up the new tax rolls. Although the traditional legal system continued to function, Russian authorities barred the khans from imposing the death penalty or downgrading a notable's social status since these powers conflicted with Russian law. Of course, the Russian military presence was a constant reminder that the khans retained their autonomy on Russian sufferance. In any event, indirect rule ceased to exist by the 1820s. In Shakki, the khan's son had been allowed to succeed to power after his father's death, but, when the son died in 1819, the khanate was brought under direct rule. In the other two cases, annexation was a reaction to the khans' flight to Iran (Mostafā of Shirvān fled in 1820; Mahdi Qoli of Qarābāgh, in 1822.) Russian officials later acknowledged that Mahdi Qoli had been driven out by the machinations of the commandant, General Madatov, but the khan was not reinstated. Both fugitives obtained Russian permission to return during the early 1830s, and they received government pensions. (In Tālesh, local autonomy was ended during the second war.)[1]

Russian direct rule was a variable mixture of local and Russian traditions that were not systematized until the 1840s. All the former khanates—except Ganjeh (Elizavetpol'), which was turned into a district of Georgia—were converted to provinces; and all were governed by military officers who had broad executive powers. Many local notables were appointed to fill a wide variety of subordinate positions from executive counselor to district or village chief. The commandants were supposed to enforce the law, but there was considerable uncertainty about what the law was. In theory, the commandants were expected to decide matters in accordance with local common law, but, since they had at best a tenuous notion of what that was, the basis for their decisions was ambiguous and consequently a source of dissatisfaction. Commander-in-Chief Paulucci tried to resolve the problem in two provinces (Qobbeh-Derbent and Baku) by setting up judicial-administrative panels that were composed of the local commandant and representatives of the inhabitants and whose proceedings were carried out in the local language. He also tried to clarify the bases of the law: existing common law was to be used when it was fitting; Russian law was to be used in all other cases. There was a tendency to enlarge the sphere of Russian law, expecially since all political offenses were tried by courts-martial. (Elizavetpol' was in a different position, being subject first to Russian law, then Georgian.)[2]

The financial system, too, was a mixture of local and Russian practice. Basically, the Russians continued to levy the same kinds of taxes and sell the same kinds of concessions as the khans had, although not necessarily to the same concessionaires. In general, the sources of revenue were less productive than they had been before the Russian takeover because of the accompanying warfare and emigration. Whatever revenue was collected went to the Georgian rather than the imperial treasury. The quest for increased revenue led Russian authorities to seek new concession agreements that promised higher profits. The rationale for invalidating existing agreements was that any contract with a deposed khan was no longer binding. In some cases, the Russians created new concessions and taxes. For example, new taxes were imposed on silk, gardens, and the use of water for irrigation, while concessions were created for the making of pottery and wine and the use of the farmland that had formerly belonged to the khan. These innovations were very unpopular with the local inhabitants, and the land concession was abolished in 1811. Although the specific concessionaires changed in a number of cases, no group lost or gained. Russians and Armenians (some of whom lived in Russia) held the great majority of concessions before and after the Russian takeover. The tax-farming concessions were eliminated, and collection was reassigned to regular state officials. Similarly, tariff concessions on intraregional and foreign trade were abolished, and tariff collection was transferred to state officials. A few minor taxes were eliminated (such as the ones on butter and salt), which produced little revenue but were burdensome to the inhabitants. The most important kind of change was the partial, episodic substitution of payments in cash for payments in kind (especially the share of the flocks). There was not nearly enough Russian money in circulation to allow the government to demand payment in rubles, although the government preferred that taxes be paid in that form when possible. Most ordinary peasants and pastoralists had difficulty acquiring enough of the local currency to pay the taxes, and the cash equivalents set for natural goods, especially sheep, were excessively high.[3]

Except for the apex of the social structure—the khans, whose positions were eliminated for political reasons—the social structure in the new provinces was changed only slightly during the first generation of Russian rule. Direct Russian rule was accompanied by the confiscation of the khans' land holdings and other property, but some of the relatives of the dispossessed khans made their peace with the new regime and received pensions or had successful careers in Russian service. Sons or other relatives of several khans entered the Russian army or judiciary and achieved positions of high rank and trust. One of the sons of Mostafā Khān of Shirvān (who had fled to Iran with his father) returned home after the Second Russo-Iranian War, served in the Russian army in the war to subdue the high Caucasus, and was promoted to colonel. A grandnephew of Ebrāhim Khalil Khān of Qarā-bāgh was decorated for his role in the siege of Sevastopol in the Crimean War. Many notables also found it worthwhile to cooperate with their new masters. Of course, the Russians needed them to carry out most of the administrative duties, which meant that the political change at the top did not necessarily alter their standing. Since the Russians had confiscated lands belonging to political opponents, one of the most common rewards for cooperative *begs* was the grant of land (either the income from land or possession conditional upon service). *Begs* who participated in the widespread anti-Russian activities were punished by loss of status and lands. The new government also raised some local supporters to the status of *beg* and gave them land grants as well. However, many of the inhabitants regarded this group of people with contempt. At least in Elizavetpol' and perhaps elsewhere, the Russians were more likely to favor Christian supporters than Muslim supporters. The violent circumstances of the Russian takeover greatly impeded a variety of economic activities in a host of ways, from the destruction of artisans' workshops to the flight of agricultural laborers, and consequently reduced the profits of many merchants. However, Russia's policy was not deliberately hostile toward local merchants. Caucasian Armenian merchants were among those who competed successfully for the purchase of concessions, and some of the more successful local merchants received various rewards, including honorific appointments as military officers. The peasantry certainly did not gain as a result of Russian policy and seem to have become worse off in many cases. Before the conquest, the *ra'yats*, the larger category of peasants, were in a better position than Russian peasants in that the *ra'yats* were not bound to the land and owned their own homes and other property. However, Russian authorities brought practices in the conquered territory closer to what existed in the heart of the empire by converting local peasants into the equivalent of state peasants who were bound to the land but not to a landlord, or, with the widespread distribution of land grants to *begs*, into serfs of the grants' recipients.[4]

The early years of the nineteenth century were a time of important demographic changes in the eastern Caucasus. Apart from the death in battle of combatants and civilians (probably fewer than 3,000), tens of thousands of the region's inhabitants migrated away from their home districts. They were motivated by the dangers of war and famine as well as by political discontent. Still others were relocated by force. Some migrated to more remote parts of their own khanates and away from government control, most notably in Qobbeh and Qarābāgh, but more often they left their khanates altogether. Sometimes they moved to another part of the region, like the Qarābāghis who moved to Shirvān or the Shirvānis who moved to Tālesh. While these areas remained under the separate authority of their khans, the population shifts, with the consequent changes in the tax base, were cause for bitter disputes among the khans. Even more people left the area subject to Russia and settled in districts under Iranian control. In Qarābāgh, Ganjeh, Yerevan, and the Muslim border districts of Georgia, people often emigrated in large groups, for example when members of a tribe or inhabitants of a particular village were led across the border by their chief or local administrator. Some emigration was involuntary, especially in the case of Qarābāghi Armenians captured by raiding Iranian soldiers. There was also a certain amount of reverse migration. Even during the wars, some notables and their followers reached an understanding with the Russians and returned to their former homes. After the treaties of Golestān and Torkmānchāi still more people returned. However, the total number of Muslims who emigrated exceeded by far the number who returned. The situation with the Armenians was strikingly different. There was a noticeable influx of Armenians into the area under Russian control, at first primarily to Tbilisi. These immigrants came from various Muslim-ruled places, including Yerevan, where Armenians were subject to harassment for their pro-Russian sympathies. Later, after Yerevan was made part of the Russian Empire, that province became the focus of large-scale Armenian immigration. With these important exceptions, most parts of the eastern Caucasus had far fewer inhabitants at the end of the Russian takeover than at the start.[5]

Russia's acquisition of the eastern Caucasus weakened Islamic religious institutions, although incidents of deliberate persecution were few. However, Russian policy showed many of the region's Muslims that their religion was in danger. Not surprisingly, the status of Islam was lowest in Elizavetpol' and Georgia. The Muslim community in Tbilisi was small, perhaps consisting of forty households. These people were allotted one mosque but prohibited from having others, and the land grants (*vaqfs*) used to fund mosques and other pious institutions were confiscated. Similar confiscations occurred in Elizavetpol', with financial hardship for the '*ulama* a result. Moreover, the sharia was replaced by Russian (later Georgian) law and the '*ulama* were barred from their customary legal functions, except for domestic law, for which services Russian authorities allowed them to charge only minor fees. Within a year, the '*ulama* were reduced to penury. Tsitsianov responded by arranging for a limited number to be paid salaries by the state. These '*ulama* had to have the approval of the Russian government and were expected to promote loyalty to Russia. A number of symbolic acts reflected the degraded state of Islam throughout the region. A number of mosques and theological colleges were converted to secular purposes by the Russians. In Elizavetpol', the main mosque was turned into a church. In Baku, the city's finest mosque, a Safavi building, was turned into an arsenal and another into a Russian Orthodox church. Several of the religious structures in New Shemākhi, the capital of Shirvān, were also made into arsenals. The requirement that Georgian and Armenian women abandon the veil, which had become as customary among them as among their Muslim neighbors, may have seemed to Caucasian Muslims an ominous portent of further violations of their standard of decency. Whatever the new government's intentions, Muslims were prepared to believe that full-scale persecution was planned; periodic alarms to that effect cropped up on several occasions. Yet the practice of Islam was not wholly fettered. A visitor to Derbent during the 1840s found that the city's main mosque still received an income from land grants. The Muslim women he saw still went completely veiled in accordance with tradition. While he was in Derbent the ten-day-long public Moharram rites, an emotion-charged commemoration of the martyrdom of the Prophet's grandson Husein were allowed to take place unimpeded.[6]

The economy of the eastern Caucasus performed unevenly in the first generation of Russian rule. Of course, there were obvious negative factors stemming from the competition for political hegemony, but there were a variety of other problems as well. The overall volume of trade increased but not impressively. Russia's Caspian trade and its overland trade via Tbilisi, intended to be a center for dealings with western Asia, both showed a substantial excess of imports over exports. Tariff policy was part of the problem. Russian authorities kept most of the tariffs on trade among the east Caucasian provinces and with European Russia to provide sorely needed revenue, despite the complaints of merchants. These tariffs were not eliminated until the 1830s. While tariffs on trade with Iran do not seem to have been a problem in general, the brief experiment with taxing the export of petroleum products from Baku brought a sharp decline in purchases by Iranians and led to the repeal of that tax. However, there was no reconsideration of the increased price charged for the oil, which led to a slump in exports to Iran. Periodic bans on trade between Baku and Iran during the first war also seem to have done lasting damage to the city's commercial contacts. Baku long gave the impression of being a lesser commercial center, actively involved in trade but not especially prosperous. In the earliest years of Russian rule, foreign merchants were required to pay their customs duties in Tbilisi because the only customs office was located. This was a considerable inconvenience for many merchants. Even after a few more customs posts were established along the Caspian coast, problems continued to exist. Also, as long as parts of the region were ruled by khans, tariffs were not standardized since khans generally imposed smaller duties than the Russian authorities. Finally, the Treaty of Torkmān-chāi (1828) set the rate at 5 percent for the entire region. Russian authorities knew that smuggling was widespread, but they lacked the means to prevent it.

Difficulties in transportation compounded the region's economic problems. Even though there were large quantities of fish to be caught in the Sāleyān fisheries and a strong demand for fish in the markets of European Russia, the transportation cost of fishing in Sāleyān from a base of operations in Astrakhan pushed the market price uncompetitively high, with the result that the much sought after fishing concession ran at a loss for years. Tbilisi's commerce suffered from similar problems, despite the high hopes of selling Russian products, above all textiles, to Iran and the Ottoman Empire via Tbilisi. The difficulties of communication between Russia and the Georgian capital were much the same as they had been before the Russian takeover.

The road across the high mountains, though improved, long remained inadequate for the transportation of large quantities of goods. The political situation there was not stabilized until the middle of the century. There was some travel between Astrakhan and Baku but very little between Baku and Tbilisi. Russia could not even begin to develop a route linking Tbilisi with Russia via the Black Sea until the Ottoman Empire gave up its claim to the west Caucasian coast in 1829. As a result, it cost less for an Iranian merchant to buy goods from Russia via Ottoman markets than from Tbilisi. That city enjoyed a temporary boom during the early 1820s while Iran and the Ottoman Empire were at war, but after 1823 trade reverted to the usual routes and the boom ended.

In agriculture, the picture seems to have been fairly bright, although not in Elizavetpol' or Qarābāgh, which suffered the greatest war damage. Elsewhere agricultural production increased substantially after 1813, although still within the context of traditional methods of production and parameters of good harvests. Russian authorities made a few efforts to introduce new crops (such as sugar cane in Tālesh) and new technology (such as improving silk-spinning machines in Shirvān), but these did not progress beyond the experimental stage in the first few decades of Russian rule.[7]

In the years after 1813, some members of the Iranian government became increasingly distressed about the ramifications of the Russian gains embodied in the Treaty of Golestān. One ominous symptom of the damage to the shah's prestige was the rebellion of the governor of Astarābād in 1813. That particular problem was resolved speedily, but there were other challenges to the authority of the central government over the next few years. Moreover, the government found that its dealings with Britain and Russia produced fewer advantages than expected. 'Abbās Mirzā was especially concerned that the loss to Russia would jeopardize his chance of succeeding to the throne. At the same time, various British and Russian officials were dissatisfied with the state of affairs in Iran.

Fath 'Ali Shāh had been encouraged by Ouseley and Rtishchev to hope that the humiliating territorial concessions in the Treaty of Golestān would not be permanent, that Russia would restore some of the territory to which the shah had formally waived all claims. Such was not to be the case. When Mirzā Abu'l-Hasan was sent on an embassy to St. Petersburg in 1814 to mark the establishment of peace between Iran and Russia, the Russian government did not use the occasion to make any territorial concessions. For the next dozen years, there were attempts to negotiate a mutually acceptable definition of the border, but the two sides could not agree on a number of small details, let alone the transfer of a larger area from Russian to Iranian suzerainty.

The best opportunity for a conciliatory border settlement occurred when Alexander sent General Ermolov to Iran in 1817. The tsar was willing to make some token concessions. His basic premise was that his role in the reconstruction of Europe after the Napoleonic wars was far too important for Russia to be distracted by additional costly warfare in the Caucasus just so that Russia could extend the westernmost part of its border with Iran as far south as the Aras. In keeping with this train of thought, he also felt that some minor territorial concessions would be a reasonable price to pay for improved relations with Iran. When he thought of concessions, he had in mind nothing as substantial as giving up a province. Rather, he was willing to yield the small Qarābāghi border district of Moqri. It was cut off from the heart of the province by mountains and had a climate that the Russians found lethal. By the end of the first war, they had given up defending it and the Iranians had taken it (so that according to the peace on the basis of the *status quo ad presentem* it was Iranian territory anyway). Alexander also was willing, as he had been in 1812, to allow Tālesh to be an independent principality rather than insisting on its inclusion into Russia. Once again Alexander allowed a "hard liner" to alter the direction of Russian policy. Ermolov was convinced that the security of Russia's Caucasian possessions demanded that Russia retain all the territory it currently held and that it conquer Yerevan and Nakhjavān as soon as possible in order to reach the Aras. He looked forward to the next opportunity for war against Iran.

Ermolov's mission to Iran was extremely unfortunate from the point of view of people in either country who desired improved relations. Obviously, his refusal to yield an iota on the territorial issue produced consternation in the Iranian government. Moreover, his conduct compounded the insult. He refused to observe the custom of removing his boots and putting on special footgear when entering a notable's quarters. Since the Iranians used their carpets for eating, sitting, and so on, they found it distasteful to have someone track in the outside dirt on his boots, but Ermolov believed that any concession to foreign ways was demeaning. Ermolov also was cool to 'Abbās but sought out Mohammad 'Ali. When Ermolov reached the shah, he not only refused to relinquish any territory but also proposed an alliance against the Ottoman Empire, offered to provide soldiers to train the Iranian army, and asked that Russian troops be given free passage through northeastern Iran to attack Khiva. He was refused on all points and returned to Tbilisi to take command of Russia's Caucasian provinces. In 1825, he grew impatient with the unsuccessful attempts to define the border and sent troops to occupy the north shore of Lake Gokcha (now called Lake Sevan), which had great strtegic value as a route of march into Yerevan. 'Abbās viewed this as an act of aggression, but Ermolov would not yield. Both men looked to war as the solution.[8]

Iran's relations with Britain were only slightly better than its relations with Russia. Even though the "great game" (the Anglo-Russian rivalry over Iran, Central Asia, Afghanistan, Tibet, and India in the late nineteenth and early twentieth centuries) had its roots in this era, many important British policy makers did not share their successors' alarm over the growth of Russian influence in Iran. Some British officials in India and western Asia were concerned about this, but they were unable to bring British policy into line with their views. Even Lord Moira, who succeeded Lord Minto as governor-general in 1813, was far less concerned about Russian expansion toward India than about the danger that Iran, having received military assistance from Britain, would direct its army against the East India Company's holdings. British diplomats in St. Petersburg considered Russia's involvement in the Iranian marches to be of so little consequence to British interests that they rarely mentioned it in their reports. When they did report some development in that quarter, they did so in terms which were neutral or even rather sympathetic to the Russian endeavor.[9]

Most important, the cabinet in London demonstrated its lack of interest in using Iran as a buffer between Russia and India by consistently limiting the scale of British involvement in Iranian affairs from the end of the first war to the end of the second. The Foreign Office was displeased with Ouseley for having committed Britain to give Iran more aid than London thought necessary, especially with regard to the subsidy. When he left Iran in 1814, no regular ambassador was sent to replace him. There was instead an interim arrangement by which his subordinate James Morier and Henry Ellis, who was sent on a specific assignment from London, took charge of relations with Iran. Their task was to renegotiate the definitive treaty in order to reduce the scope of the subsidy obligations. While most of the provisions remained the same, Morier and Ellis made several significant changes. They added a new article (the third) that specified that the mutual assistance pact was exclusively defensive, that is, that aid would be given only in the event of a foreign invasion of Iran. There followed a stipulation that was not strictly related to the rest of the article but showed what concerns lay behind this emphasis on the defensive nature of the pact: Britain as well as Iran and Russia would decide what the Russo-Iranian border was to be. In other words, London wanted to ensure that it would not be maneuvered into supporting an Iranian attempt to drive the Russians from the eastern Caucasus. In the next article, which dealt with the specifics of assistance, that same problem was addressed even more directly. Britain would not assist Iran in any war it started. There was also a provision that reflected London's fundamental uneasiness about paying a subsidy under any circumstances. It specified that any subsidy payments were to be used exclusively to gather and discipline (that is, train in the Western style) an army and that British authorities would make sure the money was put to no other use. London was so unworried about the involvement of other European countries in Iran that the treaty even included British assent to Iran's hiring military instructors from any European country not at war with Britain.[10]

Britain had already begun to extricate itself from the unwelcome burden of the subsidy even before the treaty revision. In theory, Ouseley had committed Britain to continue the payments until the restoration of peace—which could be interpreted as meaning until Russia returned some of its Caucasian conquests. However, the subsidy no longer suited London's needs since Russia had become an ally in the war against Napoleon. Britain paid the subsidy in 1814 but cut costs substantially by deducting from the subsidy the cost of armaments and other wares that had been sent as gifts. After that, Britain stopped paying the subsidy for several years, although it allowed a few officers to remain to drill 'Abbās's army. Morier and Ellis left Iran in 1815 after completing their assignment, and the status of the British mission to Iran was further downgraded. Matters were left in the hands of a chargé d'affaires, Major Henry Willock, Ouseley's aide-de-camp, while London laid the groundwork for putting relations with Iran under the jurisdiction of the governor-general in Bengal, a change accomplished in 1824. Subsidy arrears were paid at this time as a way of inducing the shah to accept an ambassador from the East India Company instead of London. The transition was rough nonetheless, and it was not until 1826 that the governor-general allowed his ambassador to journey to Iran. As the border dispute between Iran and Russia intensified, the company's ambassador, John Macdonald (Kinneir), tried without success to mediate. British diplomats in Iran disagreed on whether the Russian occupation of the north shore of Lake Gokcha constituted an invasion, but London was certain that it did not. In 1826, when Iranian troops attacked

Russian positions in Qarābāgh, Elizavetpol', and elsewhere, Britain decided that this was exactly the kind of irredentist war it should not assist. Therefore, no subsidy was paid during the second war.[11]

Whatever Fath 'Ali's feelings about the growth of Russian power on the border of his realm, he did not display great concern, not even after the difficulties about Lake Gokcha. His motives are not directly known. Court chronicles are uninformative. British diplomats, who had a low opinion of the shah as a leader, attributed his lack of action to miserliness and weakness. In any case, his options would have been limited because of the economic slump that followed the cholera epidemic of the early 1820s and because he also had to worry about the defense of his other borders, in the northeast against the Turcomans and in the west against the Ottomans. Changes in key administrative positions may also have influenced the disposition of the central government. Mirzā Shafi' died in 1819 and his replacement was not forceful. This enabled two other officials, Mirzā 'Abd ol-Vahhāb, the chancellor, and Mirzā Abu'l-Hasan, the de facto head of foreign affairs, to expand their already considerable influence. Both these powerful men wanted to avoid war with Russia. The prowar faction had lost its most effective spokesman when Mirzā Bozorg died in 1822. After some delay, his son, Mirzā Abu'l-Qāsem, succeeded as 'Abbās's chief vizier, but for several years he lacked his father's influence with either the prince or the shah and was involved in a fierce rivalry with the two dominant officials in Tehran.[12]

In any event, it was 'Abbās, not his father, who played the key role in Iran's relations with Russia. His motives were not obscure. He felt the defeat in the first war acutely and looked for ways to compensate for the personal humiliation. He used a minor border incident as an excuse for war with the Ottoman Empire (1821-1823), as a result of which Iran gained some concessions, mostly with regards to the security of Iranian merchants and pilgrims traveling in the Ottoman Empire. The most noteworthy event of the war was the death (from cholera) of Mohammad 'Ali. However, the elimination of the most likely rival for the throne did not mean that 'Abbās would be assured of a clear succession. There was always the danger that some other brother might profit from any troubles that befell 'Abbās. (This indeed happened briefly after 'Abbās suffered repeated defeats in the second war and the shah displayed special favor toward his other sons—Mohammad Hosein, the governor of Kermānshāh, and Hasan 'Ali, governor of Khorāsān.)

'Abbās's prime hope of strengthening his position was to refight the war with Russia with better results than the previous time. The court chronicles downplayed the prince's role in starting the second war, not a surprising decision since the war ended so badly for Iran. Ironically, the possibility of Russian aggression in the Lake Gokcha incident was not mentioned. Rather the chroniclers cited the machinations of refugee khans (of Baku, Shirvān, and Qarābāgh) and the declaration of a holy war against Russia by some of the most prestigious Shia leaders, who acted in response to stories of Russian offenses against Muslims. However, these factors were able to influence Iran's decision because 'Abbās already wanted war. He made it possible for the refugee khans to encourage anti-Russian activities in their former domains because he stationed those men in districts close to the border for that very purpose. Similarly, the prince encouraged rumors of Russian outrages and hoped to obtain a declaration of holy war from Shia leaders as a way of pressuring his father into war and mobilizing popular support as well. Even after the reduction in British aid in 1815, 'Abbās kept up his Western-style army (including Russian deserter units) as best he could. The task was not easy. A cholera epidemic during the early 1820s took a heavy toll on his army and the population of Azerbaijan as a whole. The biggest problem was financial in that he had to pay the new army's expenses with the revenues of Azerbaijan alone; the subsidy was cut off and the shah refused to contribute. This meant that the arsenal was neglected and the troops were underpaid and were only called up for training sporadically. Despite everything, 'Abbās was confident that his new army would bring him victory. He was also encouraged by the intensity of anti-Russian sentiment among inhabitants of the lost provinces. In conversations with British officials, he was quite open about his eagerness for war. Then in 1826 came news of Alexander's death the preceding year and the attempted coup by the Decembrists. The rumors did not make clear that this loosely organized group of reform-minded nobles had already been defeated by January 1826. This seemed to be the ideal time to strike at a weakened foe. At last Fath 'Ali consented to authorize a war.[13]

The second war exhibited many of the same characteristics as the first. The most striking difference was that the second was much shorter, lasting a mere fifteen months. The Russian army suffered again from insufficient manpower and uneven leadership, especially in the early stages. The Iranian army was weakened by rivalries among tribes, between the traditional and Western-style armies (both 'Abbās's and some of the shah's infantry), and between 'Abbās and Hosein Qoli Khān of Yerevan. Most of the burden of financing the war fell on Azerbaijan, the inhabitants of which became increasingly resentful of the heavy taxes. Plundering during battle still interfered with the Iranians' ability to press home an early advantage and was widespread even among the Western-style army because of their inadequate pay. Yet the Iranian effort was not an unmitigated disaster from the start. Local uprisings inflicted serious defeats on Russian troops even before the Iranians attacked. There was little of the wavering in choosing sides that occurred during the first war. Inhabitants of Elizavetpol', Qarābāgh, Shirvān, Shakki, Tālesh, and the Muslim border districts of Georgia battled fiercely with the Russians, killing whole garrisons in several places, especially Elizavetpol', and expelling the Russians elsewhere. The Iranian invasion began in July with attacks across a broad front from Georgia to Tālesh and Baku. The invaders won several battles and besieged the Russian garrisons of Shushā and Baku. However, neither fortress was captured, and by September the advance was stopped, most significantly by the rout of 'Abbās's army in Elizavetpol'. There was a lull in the fighting during the winter. At that time, Ermolov was recalled and Paskevich given command. Fighting resumed in the spring. The Russian advance faced some serious opposition, especially in Yerevan, but ultimately Paskevich and his subordinates were victorious. While 'Abbās concentrated his efforts on the area around Khoi, the Russians took Nakhjavān, Yerevan, and 'Abbāsābād. The road to Tabriz lay open before them. The city's terrified inhabitants were convinced that resistance would provoke drastic reprisals. The local garrison did not inspire confidence and in fact did not attempt a defense. A few of the city's notables arranged a peaceful surrender to the Russians in mid-October.[14]

When this happened, the shah realized that the cause was lost and agreed to open negotiations. As in the talks that ended the first war, Russia dictated the terms. Russia demanded Yerevan and Nakjavān and set out the terms for the transfer of populations across the new border. Several demands had significant implications for Russian influence in Iranian affairs. Russia recognized the shah's designate as heir to the throne, as it had done in the previous treaty. This reflected Russia's desire to increase its influence over 'Abbās but also meant that Russia would have grounds to intervene in the succession. A separate commercial treaty compelled Iran to allow the establishment of Russian consulates anywhere in Iran and guaranteed extraterritorial privileges, a sharp contrast with the shah's previous objection even to the revival of the Russian consulate at Anzali. The most obviously disagreeable provision from Iran's point of view was the one by which the government was compelled to pay reparations to Russia for the costs incurred in fighting the war and the losses suffered by Russian subjects. It would also have the effect of binding Iran to Russia through indebtedness. The sum was later set at 20 million rubles (about £3 million), which Fath 'Ali refused to pay for several months. A brief attempt by 'Abbās to resume the war at the start of 1828 was a total failure and resulted in the occupation of more of Azerbaijan by Russian troops. Further resistance was hopeless. Ambassador Macdonald encouraged 'Abbās to comply with Russia's demands by offering to contribute 250,000 tomāns toward the reparations if 'Abbās agreed to cancel the subsidy provisions of the 1814 treaty with Britain. The prince accepted the proposal (although he only received 200,000 tomāns). He and Paskevich signed the treaty at Torkmānchāi, a village south of Tabriz, in February 1828. Most of the reparation charges were paid off within the year, but to accomplish this 'Abbās had to empty his treasury and give up most of his valuables, in addition to yielding to British demands in order to obtain the additional 200,000 tomāns. Fath 'Ali did not contribute to these payments. The outstanding debt gave Russia the means to ensure the cooperativeness of the Iranian government. The latest version of the Anglo-Iranian treaty, shorn of its subsidy provisions, remained in effect until the 1850s; the Treaty of Torkmānchāi governed Russo-Iranian relations until the fall of the Russian monarchy.[15]

The whole generation of increased contact with European nations, be it through war or the nonviolent encounters resulting directly from war, had the odd effect of both stimulating and discouraging the acceptance of Western influence. 'Abbās maintained at least a remnant of his European-style army until his death in 1833, and the Russian deserter brigade lasted several years beyond that. However, this kind of reform had lost its original attraction as a panacea for all of Iran's problems. The same was true of other kinds of Western influence. Beginning at the time of the Jones mission, a handful of young Iranians had been sent to Britain for training in a variety of subjects primarily related to military technology. A few people were also sent on diplomatic missions. Some of these men held prominent positions after their return as diplomats, military officers, and spokesmen for change (for example, as a producer of European-style firearms and a publisher of Iran's first newspaper). But these men were few in number, and the obstacles they faced were many. There was little hope of reform by a government that showed increasing lethargy in the wake of demoralization and financial strain. Moreover, the public reaction to European influence was emphatically negative after the disasters of the second war with Russia. Trends that would eventually produce change were set in motion, but the results would not be noticeable for many years to come.[16]

The most conspicuous results of the years of struggle for the Caucasus were the decline of the Qājār government and the simultaneous increase in foreign (that is, Russian and British) intervention in Iranian affairs. Fath 'Ali became less and less concerned with the affairs of state during the remaining six years of his life. His own ineffectiveness and the loss to Russia stimulated a number of provincial rebellions, as well as a general increase in provincial disregard for the authority of the central government. 'Abbās, who as a young man hoped to become a great ruler (either in the traditional Islamic sense of the strong warrior who is solicitous of his subjects' well-being or in the mold of Peter the Great, with whose role as a reformer he was acquainted) found his military reputation tarnished, the task of reform far more difficult that expected, and his very succession to the throne imperiled. In the years after 1828, he sought new, less formidable targets for his military operations, first provincial rebels and then the Salor Turcomans, who conducted frequent, devastating raids across Iran's northeastern border. He was on his way to attempting the conquest of Herāt when he died in 1833. A very reluctant Fath 'Ali was eventually persuaded by Russia and Britain to name 'Abbās's eldest son, Mohammad, as heir to the throne. Mohammad, having been raised in Tabriz, where he had contact with Russian agents and their Iranian supporters, was generally perceived as being under Russian influence. Such influence at 'Abbās's court and in northern Iran generally increased greatly in the years after 1828. The popular anti-Russian feeling that was demonstrated grimly in the murder of Ambassador Griboedov and members of his entourage in 1829 did not influence the attitude of the elite. Russia was important because of its guarantee of the succession, the reparations issue, and the strenuous activities of its diplomatic agents and because it had demonstrated its military superiority over Iran. Russia's position was enhanced by another victory over the Ottoman Empire in 1829. Then there was no countervailing force to rely upon since Britain continued to limit the scale of its involvement in that quarter. The only factor that prevented Russia from exerting even greater influence for the next generation was its preoccupation with more urgent matters elsewhere: the war in the high Caucasus and the growing rivalry in the Ottoman Empire which culminated in the Crimean war. When Fath 'Ali died in 1834, Mohammad was not prepared to enforce his claim to the throne and had to face the rival claim of his uncle, Hosein 'Ali, who had earlier tried to profit from 'Abbās's discomfiture in the second war with Russia. The Russian and British ambassadors orchestrated Mohammad's ascent to the throne, and the pattern of foreign manipulation of Iran's affairs was set.

X

Conclusions

In the late eighteenth and early nineteenth centuries, several different forces disrupted the status quo in Iran and its Caucasian marches. After decades of disunity and internecine warfare, a new dynasty overcame various local rulers to gather many fragments of the Safavi empire under a single centralized authority. This fit into a well-established cycle of empire building and dissolution. A more novel and ultimately more unsettling change was the permanent involvement of Russia in the affairs of this region. The shifting rivalries of the Napoleonic wars were also mirrored in this area, as France and Britain and, to a lesser degree, Russia tried to use pressure in this quarter to affect the outcome of the wars in Europe. Caught in the middle of this multifaceted rivalry were the inhabitants of the borderlands, who tried to find some balance between the ideal of maintaining their independence and the necessity of dealing with more powerful outside forces.

Russian expansion in this part of Asia, for all its momentous consequences, was more the product of accident than of a carefully considered master plan. A series of decisions of limited scope designed to meet specific circumstances achieved a cumulative power that was greater than the sum of the parts. Tentative, not particularly successful efforts in the reign of Catherine the Great to use parts of the Caucasus as a base of operations against the Ottoman Empire and as a commercial base (also including parts of Iran's Caspian coast) for increased trade with Asia were transformed into a crusade to uphold

162

Russian honor and combat Iranian barbarism. Russia's attitude stiffened precisely because its early efforts were poorly executed through inadequate preparation, insufficient and inaccurate knowledge of the region, and occasional lapses of interest in St. Petersburg. This produced a series of reversals that culminated in the collapse of Georgia—the very thing that Russia had promised to prevent—and the militant insistence of Iran's Qājār dynasty that it alone was the rightful sovereign of all of the eastern Caucasus. It was the challenge to the policies that Russia had so haphazardly pursued that stimulated Russia to pursue them with new vigor.

There was an attitude toward expansion that affected the overall climate in which these decisions were made, even though there was not always a direct impact. This had nothing to do with some legendary Russian drive to obtain warm-water ports or some grand design for the conquest of Asia. Instead, Russia, after a century of westernization, developed a colonialist outlook that was consciously imitative of Western overseas expansion. Exotic alien lands made attractive targets for colonization because it was believed that they could make their colonial master rich and because the colonial master could in return benefit the subject peoples by introducing them to civilization. Furthermore, all of this would prove that Russia, too, was as great and civilized an empire as those of western Europe.

Attempts to challenge any aspect of Russian expansion were short-lived failures. This is not surprising in light of the widespread belief at this time throughout Europe in the advantages of having colonies. Moreover, as Russian involvement increased, a change to a more restrained approach became unthinkable, a sign of dishonorable weakness. In this case, the threshold was passed probably in 1796, certainly no later than 1801. Even those who criticized certain aspects of the established policy differed on the issue of degree, not on fundamental doubts about the merits of all involvement in the Iranian sphere. That virtually doomed the critics' arguments to defeat since it was the very failure of earlier, more limited activities that had led to the escalation of Russian involvement. The great cost to Russia of conquering and administering the Caucasian borderlands only strengthened the expansionists' contention that a more limited approach was unthinkable.

The relationship between decision makers in St. Petersburg and officials in the field had a significant impact on the shaping and execution of Russian policy. Given the general lack of information about Iran and the Caucasian borderlands, as well as the difficulties of maintaining close supervision over distant subordinates, officials on the frontier were able to mold considerably opinion in St. Petersburg. They could portray their blunders as an enemy's wickedness or pass along misinformation that they themselves believed. Most important, they could use their position to do more or less what they wished, to create situations to enhance their military reputation or settle personal grievances and present St. Petersburg with a fait accompli. The usual reaction of the central authorities was to praise any such action that succeeded or that could be blamed on Asian treachery when it failed, thereby encouraging border officials to continue their methods of operation.

Russia launched its expansionist policy just at the time when a reunited Iranian state began an expansionist policy of its own. The Qājār dynasty did not consider its own actions as at all expansionist. Rather, the new government believed that it was continuing the reunification process it had begun with the extension of its authority beyond its power base along the southeast Caspian coast. The acquisition of the territory in the eastern Caucasus was especially significant to a government that already controlled the Iranian plateau because those northwestern marches had once been prosperous dominions of the Safavis. Even though the Safavis had been vanquished, Iranians still thought of legitimizing authority gained through force by association with some aspect of Safavi prestige. One way to do that was to claim to restore Iran to its Safavi dimensions. This put Iran on a collision course with Russian expansion. The way Russia pursued its objectives intensified Iranian opposition by appearing to threaten Qājār sovereignty over the central provinces as well. For several years, neither side seemed able to win. Then the weaknesses of Iranian methods of organizing and fighting a war combined with the disruptive effects of military reform to give victory to the Russians. When Iran attempted to recoup its losses in a second war, the Russian victory was even more decisive. The Iranian government was left defeated, humiliated, and less capable than ever to deal with the great challenges of a rapidly changing world. A long process of decline had begun, and its aftermath is with us still.

The inhabitants of the disputed provinces viewed this imperial conflict with at best cautious optimism. A few rulers, such as the last two kings of Georgia and the khan of Ganjeh, believed that one or the other empire would be a valuable ally against traditional rivals. More often, Caucasian rulers did not welcome the encroachments of either empire but, since they could not alter the fact, tried instead to turn it to advantage by seeking the most favorable alliance possible. This meant the preservation of autonomy to the greatest extent permitted and favored treatment at the expense of traditional rivals. What all the rulers found, even when they were initially well disposed toward Russia, was that Russian sovereignty was much more restrictive than the traditional pattern of dominance in the region. Rulers who openly opposed the Russians were ousted, but even those who agreed to Russia's terms lost most of their power and their territories were eventually annexed. Most ordinary inhabitants of the borderlands were less interested in the competing power plays than the desire not to be involved in any war. They were wary of the Russians because of a few instances of attacks on civilians and anti-Islamic measures, but that did not make them automatically pro-Iranian. The struggle to control this region devastated many parts of it. More than anything else, most Caucasians just wanted to be allowed to engage without disruption in the normal activities that enabled them to survive. Some tried to solve their problem by flight. Eventually, most of those who remained became so disenchanted with Russian rule that they looked to Iran as backers of their traditional leaders to free them from the Russians. However, this did not occur until the second war, when Iran's military weaknesses doomed it to defeat once Russia recovered from the initial shock of being caught off guard.

Iran, too, was caught in the midst of an imperial rivalry of sorts. Both France and Britain increased their involvement in Iranian affairs as a side effect of the Napoleonic wars in Europe. France toyed with using Iran as a route of march against the British possessions in India, something the British were determined to stop far west of the Indus. Both Western powers were interested in supporting the First Russo-Iranian War at times when one or the other was at war with Russia in Europe. This meant, of course, that both Western nations made alliances with Iran for reasons of their own that were quite different from Iran's reasons for being at war with Russia. Therefore, both countries encouraged the shah to continue the war and rendered military assistance only so long as such actions coincided with their interests in Europe. When France and, later, Britain made peace with Russia, support for Iran became a burden. Iran was left relying on assistance that it would no longer receive. French influence in Iran was negligible for a long time after the departure of its embassy in 1809. The British kept up diplomatic contacts, albeit on a limited scale, even after the rapprochement with Russia in 1812. This enabled Britain to have some influence over Iranian affairs even before the great revival of British interest in that quarter during the second half of the nineteenth century.

Even though this era was the one in which the preconditions for the "great game" were set, it is extremely important to note how different this formative period was from the later one. It is arguable that there was no Russian drive toward India, notwithstanding British fears on one, even during the "great game." It is certain that there was none during the formative period. Paul's attempt to conquer India was a temporary aberration motivated not by an ongoing obsession with India but by a specific crisis in Europe—the British threat to Russia in the Baltic. The undertaking was, in any case, very unpopular with the Russian elite and hastened the coup in which Paul was killed. Apart from that incident, Russian policy makers, including Paul, were interested in using parts of Iran and its borderlands to imitate the operations of the East India Company in the Subcontinent, not in trying to conquer those holdings via Iran or any other route. Most British officials during this era did not partake of the "great game" mentality either. Some, especially those in the company's service in India, were quick to see threats from many quarters, including Russia. However, this view did not hold sway in the highest councils. Britain sent embassies to Iran during this era because it was afraid of the French threat. When the French threat had passed and Russia broke with France, Britain relegated its involvement in Iranian affairs to a secondary plane, where it remained for roughly half a century. Only one element of the "great game" was obvious as early as 1828—the decreased ability of the Iranian government to govern the nation.

NOTES

ABBREVIATIONS

AGS Russia, State Council, *Arkhiv Gosudarstvennago Soveta* (5 vols., St. Petersburg, 1869-1904).

Akty Russia, Viceroyalty of the Caucasus, *Akty sobrannye kavkazskoiu arkheograficheskoiu kommissieiu* (12 vols., Tiflis, 1866-1904).

AKV M. S. Vorontsov, *Arkhiv Kniazia Vorontsova*, P. Bartenev, ed. (40 vols., Moscow, 1870-1895).

FO Great Britain, Public Record Office, Foreign Office Archives.

MAE France, Ministère des Affaires Étrangères—Correspondence Politique: Perse.

P&PGFR Great Britain, Commonwealth Relations Office, India Office, Persia and Persian Gulf Factory Records.

SIRIO *Sbornik Imperatorskago Russkago Istoricheskago Obshchestva.*

VPR Union of Soviet Socialist Republics, Ministry of Foreign Affairs, *Vneshniaia Politika Rossii*, series I (1801-1815) (7 vols., Moscow, 1970).

Notes

PREFACE

1. (2 vols., Paris, 1952).

2. V. P. Lystsov, *Persidskii pokhod Petra I, 1722-1723* (Moscow, 1951), pp. 15-17.

3. *Jange-e dah sāleh yā jange-e avval-e Irān bā Rus* (Tehran, 1315 Shamsi/1936-1937) and *Jang-e Irān va Rus 1826-1828* (Tehran, 1314 Shamsi/1934-1935).

4. *Tārikh-e ravābet-e siyāsi-ye Irān va Inglis dar qarn-e nuzdahom-e milādi* (Tehran, 1336 Shamsi/ 1957-1958).

5. D. M. Lang, *The Last Years of the Georgian Monarchy, 1658-1832* (New York, 1957); L. H. Rhinelander, Jr., "The Incorporation of the Caucasus into the Russian Empire: The Case of Georgia, 1801-1854," Ph.D. dissertation (Columbia University, 1972); G. A. Bournoutian, "Eastern Armenia on the Eve of the Russian Conquest: The Khanate of Erevan under the Governorship of Hoseyn Qoli Khan Qajar, 1807-1827," Ph.D. dissertation (University of California at Los Angeles, 1976); F. Kazemzadeh has discussed Russian involvement in the Caucasus since the fifteenth century in "Russian Penetration of the Caucasus," T. Hunczak, ed., *Russian Imperialism from Ivan the Great to the Revolution* (New Brunswick, 1974), pp. 239-63.

CHAPTER I

1. Catherine to V. A. Zubov (commander of the 1796 Russian expedition), February 19, 1796, N. F. Dubrovin, *Istoriia voiny i vladychestva russkikh na Kavkaze* (6 vols., St. Petersburg, 1871-1888), II, 69-78.

2. Manifesto of March 27, 1796, Dubrovin, III, 125-29.

3. S. M. Bronevskii (expediter of the Asian Department, Ministry of Foreign Affairs), "Zapiska kasatel'no nekotorykh vnushenii koi nebespoleznym pochitaetsia dovesti do svedeniia Abbas-mirzy" (No later than April 10 [22], 1807), *VPR*, III, 553.

CHAPTER II

1. This figure is a rough estimate made in the absence of adequate demographic records. K. F. Knorring (commander-in-chief of the Caucasus) to Tsar Alexander, August 28, 1801, *Akty*, I, 426.

2. Population estimates for these principalities are even more conjectural than for Georgia, especially since most estimates were made during the Russian conquest of the area at a time when there were substantial population shifts. M. A. Atkin, "The Khanates of the Eastern Caucasus and the Origins of the First Russo-Iranian War," Ph.D. dissertation (Yale University, 1976), pp. 81, 95, 98, 105, 109, 111, 112, 117, 122; Bournoutian.

3. Dubrovin, II, 29, 32, 34; P. G. Butkov, *Materialy dlia novoi istorii Kavkaza s 1722 po 1803* (3 vols., St. Petersburg, 1869), II, 142, 144.

4. Ahmedbeg Javānshir, "O politicheskom sushchestvovanii Karabakhskogo khanstva (s 1747 po 1805 god)," E. B. Shukiurzade, trans., *Istoriia Karabakhskogo khanstva* (Baku, 1961), p. 75; E. Pakravan, *Abbas Mirza* (2 vols., Tehran, 1958), I, 102.

5. Rezā Qoli Khān Hedāyat, *Rouzatos-Safā-ye Nāseri* (10 vols., Tehran, 1960), IX, 265, 267-68, 271; Knorring to Alexander, July 28, 1801, *Akty*, I, 426; Lang, pp. 226-29.

CHAPTER III

1. M. Raeff, "Patterns of Russian Imperial Policy toward the Nationalities," E. Allworth, ed., *Soviet Nationality Problems* (New York, 1971), pp. 24-29.

2. H. Brougham, *An Inquiry into the Colonial Policy of the European Powers* (2 vols., New York, 1970, facsimile reprint of Edinburgh 1803 edition), I, 2.

3. Catherine to Prince Potemkin, May 5, 1783, *SIRIO*, XVII (1880), 256; N. Grigorovich, ed., "Kantsler Kniaz' Aleksandr Andreevich Bezborodko," *SIRIO* (2 vols., XXVI [1879] and XXIX [1881]), XXVI, 444.

4. Rescript to Count A. G. Orlov (commander of Russian forces in the war against the Ottoman Empire, 1768-1774), March 22, 1771, *SIRIO*, I, 66.

5. Note of Chancellor I. A. Osterman and Bezborodko on the conditions for concluding peace with Turkey . . . . read in the council (State Council) December 16, 1788, Grigorovich, XXIX, 523.

6. M. Raeff, *Siberia and the Reforms of 1822* (Seattle, 1956), p. 6.

7. M. V. Lomonosov, "Dratkoe opisanie raznykh puteshestvii" (1763), *Polnoe sobranie sochinenii* (10 vols., Moscow and Leningrad, 1950-1959). VI, 421-23, 494, 497.

8. C. L. de Secondat, Baron de Montesquieu, *The Spirit of the Laws,* T. Nugent, trans., F. Neumann, ed. (New York, 1966), pp. 331, 334-35, 360-64, 367.

9. G. T. Raynal, *Histoire philosophique et politique des établissemens et du commerce des Européens dans les deux Indes*, 2nd ed. (10 vols., Geneva, 1780), I, 2, 133-34, 266, 449-54, 477-79, II, 21, 233-34, 263-66, III, 246 ff.

10. Ibid. II, 33-35, 96, III, 141-49, 167-70.

11. P. A. Zubov, *Shest'pisem o Gruzii i o Kavkaze* (Moscow, 1834), p. 60.

12. Catherine to Iv. V. Gudovich (commander of the Caucasian Line, the Russian fortifications in the northern Caucasus), September 4, 1795, and Catherine's ukase to V. A. Zubov (commander of the 1796 Iranian campaign), February 19, 1796, Dubrovin, III, 22, 69-78.

13. Bell's *Travels from St. Petersburg in Russia to Various Parts of Asia* was first published in Glasgow in 1763 and in Russian in St. Petersburg in 1776. One of the French works was entitled *Mémoires historiques et géographiques sur les pays situées entre la mer Noire et la mer Caspienne* (Paris, 1793). The second was translated into Russian as *Istoriia o persid-*

skom shakh Takhmasp Kuli Khane (3 eds., St. Petersburg, 1762, 1788, 1790). S. G. Gmelin, *Reise durch Russland* (3 vols., St. Petersburg, 1770-1774). J. A. Güldenstädt, *Reisen durch Russland und in die Caucasischen Gebürge* (2 vols., St. Petersburg, 1787-1791).

14. *Pobuditel'nyia prichiny posol'stva Karabakhskikh Melikov, s istoricheskim opisaniem otnositel'no, k Ego Imperatorskomu Velichestvu Petru Velikomu, i o izdannykh Imiannykh Ego Ukaz na sii obstoiatel'stva* (n.p., 1790).

15. Manifesto to the Caucasian and Iranian peoples, March 27, 1796, and ukase to V. A. Zubov (commander of the 1796 campaign), February 10, 1796, and V. A. Zubov to General Rimskii-Korsakov, October 10, 1796, Dubrovin, III, 67, 79, 127, 175, 177, 179, 182.

16. M. D. Chulkov, *Istoricheskoe opisanie Rossiiskoi kommertsii* (7 vols., St. Petersburg, 1781-1788), II, book 2, 185 ff., 256 ff., 270, 281 ff., 313, 331 ff., 388, 402 ff., 451 ff.

17. Catherine to Prince G. A. Potemkin, May 5, 1783, A. K. Grot, ed., "Bumagi Imperatritsy Ekateriny II," *SIRIO*, XXVII (1880), 256.

18. Catherine to V. A. Zubov, February 19, 1796, Dubrovin, III, 72-73.

19. Ibid., III, 73.

20. G. R. Derzhavin, "Na pokorenie Derbenta," *Stikhotvoreniia* (Leningrad, 1957), p. 239.

21. Chulkov, VII, 252.

22. Dubrovin, II, 183.

23. Butkov, II, 95.

24. G. A. Olivier, *Voyage dans l'empire Othman, l'Egypte, et la Perse* (3 vols., Paris, 1807), III, 176.

25. A. R. Ioannisian, "Russkaia diplomatiia i Armianskii vopros v 80 kh godakh XVIII stoletiia," *Voprosy istorii*, VI (1947), 98; Dubrovin, II, 29-41.

26. Ukase, April 19, 1793, Butkov, II, 287; ukase to V. A. Zubov, February 19, 1796, Dubrovin, III, 9, 76, 120; Gudovich's reports to St. Petersburg, May 7 and September 13, 1795, and Gudovich to Catherine, September 23 and 28, 1795, A. A. Tsagareli, *Gramoty i drugie istoricheskie dokumenty XVIII stoletiia otnosiashchiesia do Gruzii* (3 vols., St. Petersburg, 1891-1902), II, part ii, 89, 101-2, 108, 110.

27. F. V. Rostopchin (Bezborodko's assistant) to S. R. Vorontsov (Russian ambassador to Britain), February 22 and 24, 1796, *AKV*, VIII, 132, 137; Butkov, II, 359; Dubrovin, III, 93.

28. F. V. Rostopchin to S. R. Vorontsov, February 1, 1796, *AKV*, VIII, 124.

29. Ioannisian, "Russkaia diplomatiia," p. 99. (There was no discussion of establishing a corridor to the Black Sea as an alternative route. St. Petersburg consistently underestimated the desire or the ability of Iranian rulers to enforce a claim to the eastern Caucasus, but Ottoman claims to the western Caucasus and that empire's naval presence on the Black Sea were treated more warily.)

30. Catherine to V. A. Zubov, February 10, 1796, Dubrovin, III, 84.

31. Gudovich to P. A. Zubov, October 8, 1795, Dubrovin, III, 17, 54, 105, 134 ff.; 'Abbās Qoli 'Āqā Bakikhanov, *Giulistan-Iram* (Golestān-e Eram) (Baku, 1926), pp. 145-46; Derzhavin, pp. 255-59; "O Pokhode Rossiiskikh voisk v 1796 godu v Dagestan i Persiiu pod kommandoiu Grafa Valeriana Aleksandrovicha Zubova," *Otechestvenyia zapiski*, 1827, II, 303, 309.

CHAPTER IV

1. N. N. Beliavskii and V. A. Potto, *Utverzhdenie Russkago vladychestva na Kavkaze* (12 vols., Tiflis, 1901-1902), I, 18; Rostopchin to Vorontsov (initials unspecified), June 30, 1801, *AKV*, VIII, 291.

2. Session of the State Council, October 25, 1798, and Skibinevskii's memorandum, 1798, and Skibinevskii's memorandum, Session of the State Council, October 25, 1798, *AGS*, II, columns 681-83, 684-86, 704-5; Paul to Skibinevskii, July 27, 1800, *Akty*, I 678; Dubrovin, II, 200.

3. *Shest' pisem of Gruzii i o Kavkaze* (Moscow, 1834); *Podvigi Russkikh voinov v stranakh Kavkazskikh s 1800 po 1834 g.* (2 vols., St. Petersburg, 1835); *Kartina Kavkazskago kraia* (4 vols., St. Petersburg, 1834-1835).

4. Meetings of the Secret Committee, August 13, 1801, March 31, 1802, Grandduke Nikolai Mikhailovich, ed., *Graf Pavel Aleksandrovich Stroganov* (3 vols., St. Petersburg, 1903), II, 92, 205; Kochubei to Alexander, August 13, 1802, *AKV*, XIV, 176-78; V. A. Zubov, "Obshchee obozrenie torgovli s Azieiu," *Russki arkhiv*, 1873, book I, column 888; Dubrovin, III, 418-19.

5. Zubov, "Obshchee obozrenie," columns 885-87, 888, 892.

6. Alexander to P. D. Tsitsianov, September 26, 1802, *Akty*, II, 8.

7. Alexander to Ermolov, July 29, 1816, ibid., VI, part ii, 124.

8. Report of A. R. Vorontsov and V. P. Kochubei to State Council. June 24, 1801, *AGS*, III, column 1201.

9. Session of the State Council, August 8, 1801, *AGS*, III, part ii, columns 1196-97; meeting of the Secret Committee, August 13, 1801, Nikolai Mikhailovich, *Stroganov*, II, 93; Knorring to Alexander, July 28, 1801, *Akty*, I, 426; Butkov, II, 475-79; Lang, pp. 247-49.

10. Sessions of the State Council, December 17, 1800 and April 11, 1801, and report of A. R. Vorontsov and V. P. Kochubei, *AGS*, II, column 882, III part ii, columns 1189-90, 1203; Musin-Pushkin to Tsitsianov, February 22, 1804, A. P. Tormasov (commander-in-chief in the Caucasus) to Active State Counsellor Gur'ev, May 5, 1811, *Akty*, II, 204, IV, 69; Butkov, II, 502.

11. Sessions of the State Council, October 25, 1798, and December 17, 1800, *AGS*, II, columns 726, 831-32; Paul to *sardār* Bābā Khān (Fath 'Ali Shāh), March 23, 1799, and Paul to P. I. Kovalenskii (Russian political agent in Georgia), April 16, 1799, and Paul to the khans of Yerevan, Qarābāgh, and Ganjeh, August 3, 1800, and Paul to Knorring, January 23, 1801, and College of Foreign Affairs to Skibinevskii, July 27, 1800, and College of Foreign Affairs to Kovalenskii, April 16, 1799, *Akty*, II, 1145, I, 94-95, 108-9, 414, 680, II, 1149; Paul to Gudovich, January 5, 1797, Dubrovin, III, 200; A. V. Fadeev, *Rossiia i Kavkaz, pervoi treti XIX v.* (Moscow, 1960), p. 70.

12. Paul to V. P. Orlov, January 12, 1801, N. K. Shil'der, *Imperator Pavel Pervyi* (St. Petersburg, 1901), p. 418.

13. Paul to Gudovich, January 5, 1797, Dubrovin, III, 199.

14. N. E. Saul, *Russia and the Mediterranean, 1797-1807* (Chicago, 1970), p. 144.

15. College of Foreign Affairs to Kovalenskii, April 16, 1799, and Paul to Ebrāhim Khalil Khān of Qarābāgh, May 2, 1797, and Lazarev to Kalb 'Ali Khan of Nakhjavān, March 22, 1801, and Knorring to Lazarev, December 15, 1800, *Akty*, I, 94, II, 1143, I, 624, 630.

16. Paul to Kovalenskii, January 23, 1801, ibid., I, 414.

17. Paul to Gudovich, January 5, 1797, Dubrovin, III, 199-200.

18. Knorring to Paul, April 11, 1800, and Kovalenskii's observations of Georgia, August 1800, *Akty*, I, 678, 113.

19. Paul to Kovalenskii, April 16, 1799, and Paul to Skibinevskii, July 27, 1800, and Paul to *sardār* Bābā Khān, March 23, 1799, ibid., I, 96, 678, II, 1145.

20. Kovalenskii's observations on Georgia, and Paul to Kovalenskii, April 16, 1799, and Lieutenant Merabov (Paul's emissary to Fath 'Ali) to Kovalenskii, July 1800, and Lazarev to Knorring, August 25, 1800, ibid. I, 113, 95, II, 1161, I, 142.

21. Reference to a letter from Paul to Gudovich, 1797, and Knorring to Alexander, March 6, 1802, and Paul to Bābā Khān, March 23, 1799, and Paul to Kovalenskii, April 17, 1799, ibid., I, 688, II, 1145, I, 96; session of the State Council, November 11, 1798, *AGS*, II, column 726.

22. Paul to Bābā Khān, March 23, 1799, and Russian government's reply to Mirzā Sayyed Hasan (Fath 'Ali's emissary to Paul), n.d. (1799), and College of Foreign Affairs to Skibinevskii, July 27, 1800, *Akty*, II, 1145, 1146-47, I, 679, 82; sessions of the State Council, October 1798 and November 11, 1798, *AGS*, II, columns 683, 726-27.

23. Paul to Kovalenskii, April 16, 1799, and ukase of the College of Foreign Affairs, July 19, 1799, and Paul to Knorring, July 10, 1800, *Akty*, I, 96, II, 1149, 106-7.

24. Session of the State Council, December 17, 1800, *AGS*, II, columns 881-82; Lang, pp. 226, 228, 230-32, 235-36, 239-45; Rhinelander.

25. Hedāyat, IX, 328; M. F. Brosset, ed. and trans., *Histoire de la Géorgie depuis l'antiquité juqu'au XIXe siècle* (4 parts, St. Petersburg, 1849), II, part ii, 267; Giorgi had also made a very hesitant attempt to obtain the Porte's aid but changed his mind early in his negotiations with a border pasha, Lang, p. 228.

26. Saul, pp. 126-48; A. M. Stanislavskaia, *Russko-angliiskie otnosheniia i problemi Sredizemnomor'ia (1798-1807)* (Moscow, 1962), pp. 161-64.

27. M. A. Atkin, "The Pragmatic Diplomacy of Paul I: Russia's Relations with Asia, 1796-1801," *Slavic Review*, 38 (March 1979), pp. 60-74.

28. Sessions of the State Council, April 11 and 15, August 8, 1801, *AGS*, III, part ii, columns 1189-90, 1191-94, 1197-98.

29. Report of A. R. Vorontsov and V. P. Kochubei, June 24, 1801 (July 6, N.S.), ibid., III, part ii, columns 1200-1206.

30. Alexander to Knorring, September 12, 1801, Butkov, II, 503-4, 507.

31. Fadeev, p. 102.

32. Governor-General of India et al., meeting in council, January 30, 1808, P&PGFR, XXVIII, 39; N. B. Edmonstone (secretary to secret, political, and foreign departments of the governor generalship, Bengal) to Fath 'Ali Shāh, January 10, 1807, FO 60/1.

33. General P. A. Tolstoi (Russian ambassador to France) to N. P. Rumiantsev (foreign minister), October 26, 1807, and A. Caulaincourt (Napoleon's emissary to Alexander) to Napoleon, January 21, 1808, *VPR*, IV, 104-5, 177-78; A. Vandal, *Napoléon et Alexandre Ier* (3 vols., Paris, 1891-1896), I, 247-48, 282, 292 ff.; Caulaincourt to Napoleon, January 21, 1808, Nikolai Mikhailovich, *Les Relations diplomatiques de la Russie et de la France d'après les rapports des ambassadeurs d'Alexandre et de Napoléon, 1808-1812* (7 vols., St. Petersburg, 1905-1914), I, 72-73.

34. Session of the State Council, August 8, 1801, *AGS*, III, part ii, column 1197.

35. Manifesto of September 12, 1801, *Akty*, I 432-33.

36. Alexander to Tsitsianov, September 26, 1802, ibid., II, 8.

37. Alexander to Knorring, September 12, 1801, and Alexander to Tsitsianov, September 26, 1802, and Alexander to Knorring, April 23, 1802, and Alexander to Knorring, April 16, 1802, ibid., I, 436, 688, II, 8.

38. Alexander to Knorring, September 12, 1801, April 23, 1802, ibid., I, 436, 689.

39. Alexander to Tsitsianov, September 26, 1802, ibid., II, 7-8.

40. Meeting of the Secret Committee, March 31, 1802, Nikolai Mikhailovich, *Stroganov*, II, 205-5.

41. Alexander to Knorring, September 12, 1801, *Akty*, I, 436.

42. Alexander to Knorring, April 23, 1802, and Tsitsianov to Alexander, December 30, 1804, and Gudovich to Alexander, December 11, 1808, and January 11, 1809, ibid., I, 688-89, II, 621, III, 253, 511.

CHAPTER V

1. Stanislavskaia, p. 248; a longer statement of the Soviet view can be found in the essays "Azerbaidzhan" and "Formyi i metody natsional'no-kolonial'noi politiki tsarizma," B. A. Rybakov et al., eds., *Istoriia SSSR* (12 vols., Moscow, 1966-71), III, 669, IV, 380; the pro-expansionist view also permeates the works of P. A. Zubov, Dubrovin, and Beliavskii and Potto.

2. Knorring to Mohammad, April 18, 1802, and Kovalenskii's observations on Georgia, August 1800, and plea of the Qazzāqs to Knorring, 1802, and Knorring to Alexander, August 15 and 28, 1801, May 25, 1802, *Akty*, I, 619, 119, 593, 604, 427, 475.

3. Major-General Lazarev (commandant of the Russian garrison in Georgia) to Knorring, July 13, 1801, and December 5, 1802, and Javād to Kovalenskii, n.d. (1802), and Javād to Knorring, n.d., and Kalb 'Ali to the Armenian archbishop Hovannes, n.d., *Akty*, I, 618, 622, 607, 611-12, II, 634. Not surprisingly, many Georgians also expected Alexander to order a retreat from the Caucasus. S. A. Tuchkov, *Zapiski Sergeia Alekseevicha Tuchkova, 1766-1808* (St. Petersburg, 1908), p. 190.

4. Beliavskii and Potto, I, 23; M. O. Kosven and Kh. M. Khashaev, eds., *Istoriia geografiia i etnografiia Dagestana XVIII-XIX vv.* (Moscow, 1958), p. 208.

5. For example, there was F. F. Simonovich, who saw action in Tsitsianov's siege of Yerevan and went on to become military governor of the west Georgian principalities of Imeretia, Mingrelia, and Guria. Kosven and Khashaev, p. 156; see also pp. 172 and 228-29.

6. V. A. Potto, *Kavkazskaia voina* (4 vols., St. Petersburg, 1885-1888), I, 556-57; Beliavskii and Potto, II, 472-73; N. R. Rtishchev (commander-in-chief) to Alexander, January 28, 1813, and Active State Counsellor Malinskii (civilian governor of Georgia) to Major-General Portniagin (commander of Russian troops in Georgia), January 26, 1813, *Akty*, V, 700, 702-3. Michael Vorontsov, son of the ambassador to London (1801-1806) served briefly as a young officer under Tsitsianov's command. Forty years later, he returned as viceroy of the Caucasus (1844-1853).

7. Gudovich to N. Saltykov (president of the College of War), December 18, 1796, Dubrovin, III, 196; Beliavskii and Potto, II, 1; Gudovich to the commandant and all inhabitants of the citadel of Yerevan, October 4 and 17, 1808, and Gudovich to Mustafā Khān of Shirvān, December 12, 1806, and Gudovich to Foreign Minister Budberg, October 19 and December 6, 1806, *Akty*, III, 237, 239, 297-98, 393.

8. Beliavskii and Potto, I, 306, 309, II, 277, 285; Potto, I, 469-70, 499, 525; Tormasov to Rumiantsev, February 24, 1811, and Paulucci to Rtishchev, March 20, 1812, *Akty*, IV, 755, V. 52.

9. Beliavskii and Potto, I, 44.

10. J. Baddeley, *The Russian Conquest of the Caucasus* (New York, 1969, facsimile reprint of London 1908 edition), pp. 61-62.

11. Hedāyat, IX, 389.

12. Tuchkov, pp. 197, 208, 210, 215.

13. Tsitsianov to Alexander, February 10, 1803, and Tsitsianov to Kochubei, February 10, 1803, and Tsitsianov to Ja'far Qoli Khān (of Khoi), June 24, 1804, and Czartoryski to Tsitsianov, September 14, 1804, April 16 and 28, 1805, and Tsitsianov to Zavalishin, March 29, 1805, and Tsitsianov to Czartoryski, *Akty*, II, 19-20, 855, 824, 827, 620, 1027.

14. Kochubei to Tsitsianov, July 8, 1804, and Tsitsianov to Zavalishin, March 29, 1805, and Tsitsianov to Javād Khān, November 29, 1803, and Tsitsianov to Fath 'Ali Shāh, March 29, 1805, ibid., II, 51, 825, 826, 588; Beliavskii and Potto, I, 44, 129.

15. Tsitsianov to Javād, December 29, 1803, *Akty*, II, 591.

16. Tsitsianov to Soltān Begum, July 1, 1804, and Tsitsianov to Alexander, July 14, 1804, ibid., II, 856-58.

17. Tsitsianov to Alexander, April 27, 1803, ibid., II, 290.

18. Tsitsianov to Czartoryski, September 26, 1805, ibid., II, 1036-37; Tsitsianov stressed the same point on other occasions, for example, Tsitsianov to Alexander, April 27, 1803, ibid., II, 290; Beliavskii and Potto, I, 44.

19. Tuchkov, pp. 221, 223, 226, 228-29, 234, 243-44, 249; M. S. Vorontsov to S. R. Vorontsov, October 12, 1804, *AKV*, XXXVI, 99-103; Tsitsianov to Mohammad Khān, July 14, 1804, and Collegiate Assessor Lofitsskii (head of the civilian administration of Georgia) to Alexander, April 30, 1806, *Akty*, II, 615, III, 4-6; Lang, pp. 252-58; 'Abd or-Razzāq Domboli, *Ma'āser Soltāniyeh* (Tehran, 1392 Qomri/1972-73), pp. 97-98, 110-14, 117-20.

20. Tsitsianov to Czartoryski, September 14, 1804; see also Tsitsianov to Alexander, August 15, 1804, *Akty*, II, 619-20, 811; Beliavskii and Potto, I, 156.

21. Alexander to Tsitsianov, November 8, 1804, and Czartoryskii to Tsitsianov, November 15, 1804, *Akty*, II, 620-21, 1021; Beliavskii and Potto, I, 157; Caulaincourt to Napoleon, February 22, 1809, Nikolai Mikhailovich, *Relations diplomatiques*, III, 100.

22. Tsitsianov to Alexander, December 30, 1804, and Tsitsianov to Czartoryski, April 16, 1805, ibid., II, 621-22, 1027.

23. Alexander to Tsitsianov, March 19 and 20, 1803, February 5, 1804, March 22, 1805, and Czartoryski to Tsitsianov, April 28 and July 26, 1805, and Tsitsianov to Alexander, March 12, April 27, 1803, June 17, 1805, undated letter (June 1805), and Tsitsianov to Czartoryski, April 7 and 16, June 17, August 13, 1805, *Akty*, II, 289-91, 594, 610, 782-83, 826, 827, 829, 830-31, 841, 847, 1024, 1027.

24. Tsitsianov to Zavalishin, March 29, June 17, and August 17, 1805, and Tsitsianov to Fath 'Ali Shāh, March 29, 1805, ibid., II 824-26, 832, 848; Domboli, pp. 158-59.

25. Lofitsskii to Alexander, April 30, 1806, and Gudovich to Foreign Minister A. Ia. Budberg, April 4, 1807, *Akty*, III, 3-7, 16; Dubrovin, V, 12-15.

26. Tsitsianov to Alexander, April 7, 1805, and January 10, 1806, *Akty*, II, 701, 1041.

27. Tsitsianov to Javād, November 29 and December 29, 1803, and Javād to Tsitsianov, n.d. (December 1803), *Akty*, II, 588-91.

28. Domboli, pp. 109-10; Hedāyat, IX, 389-90; Mirzā Jamāl Javānshir Qarābāghi, *Istoriia Karabaga* (Baku, 1959), p. 136; Brosset, II, part ii, 279-90; Tsitsianov to A. R. Vorontsov, January 13, 1804, and Tsitsianov to Alexander, May 29, 1804, and Ughurlu Āqā (a son of Javād) to Alexander, n.d., *Akty*, II, 592, 594-95, 601; Beliavskii and Potto, I, 88-90; P. A. Zubov, *Podvigi Russkikh voinov v stranakh Kavkazskikh s 1800 po 1834 g.* (2 vols., St. Petersburg, 1835), I, part i, 51.

29. Tuckhov, p. 215; Zubov, *Podvigi*, I, part i, 43; J. von Klaproth, *Travels in the Caucasus and Georgia Performed in the Years 1807 and 1808*, F. Shoberl, trans. (London, 1814), p. 222.

30. Tsitsianov to Alexander, May 29, 1804, and Tsitsianov to Javād, December 9, 18, and 28, 1803, and Tsitsianov to the Armenians of Ganjeh, November 30, 1803, *Akty*, II, 601, 590-91.

31. Tsitsianov to A. R. Vorontsov, January 13, 1804, ibid., II, 592.

32. Dubrovin, IV, 143.

33. Beliavskii and Potto, I, 94-95; similar threats were made to other khans. Tsitsianov to Mohammad Khān of Yerevan, June 14, 1804, and Tsitsianov to Ebrāhim Khalil Khān of Qarābāgh, January 8 and February 4, 1804, and Tsitsianov to Zavalishin, March 29, 1805, *Akty*, II, 615, 696, 825.

34. Domboli, p. 110; Hedāyat, IX, 390; Beliavskii and Potto, I, 94; Dubrovin, IV, 143; Tsitsianov to the Executive Expedition, March 3, 1804, and Tsitsianov to the *Akhund* (a low-ranking religious leader) of Elizavetpol', May 14, 1805, and anonymous, secret report on Elizavetpol', 1812, *Akty*, II, 597, 285, V, 542.

35. Paulucci to 'Abbās Mirzā, February 20, 1812, and Paulucci to Rumiantsev, April 7, 1812, *Akty*, V, 119-20.

36. Beliavskii and Potto, I, 95; Alexander to Tsitsianov, February 5, 1805, *Akty*, II, 593.

37. T. Alcock, *Travels in Russia, Persia, Turkey, and Greece in 1828-29* (London, 1831), pp. 31, 34; R. Ker Porter, *Travels in Georgia, Persia, Armenia, Ancient Babylonia, etc., during the Years 1817, 1818, 1819, and 1820* (2 vols., London, 1821) I, 120, 122; Skibinevskii to Knorring, February 26, 1802, and unsigned petition of the Muslim clergy of Tbilisi to Alexander, n.d., *Akty*, I, 640, II, 285; R. Gordon, "Journal of Robert Gordon in Transcaucasia and from Tiflis to Moscow," Aberdeen Papers, vol. 179, British Museum, Additional Manuscripts, 43,217.

38. Colonel Kariagin to Tsitsianov, March 14, 1804, and proclamation by Tsitsianov to the Armenians of Qarābāgh, n.d. (1805), and report of the elders and inhabitants of Shushā, 1806, *Akty*, II, 696, 833, III, 341; Hedāyat, IX, 390; Domboli, p. 109.

39. Dubrovin, IV, 469, V, 64, 75-76; Tsitsianov to Ebrāhim Khalil, July 20, 1805, and Colonel Aseev (commandant of the Shushā garrison) to Tormasov, July 20, 1810, and Tsitsianov to Major Rebinder, January 20, 1806, *Akty*, II, 815, IV, 560-61, II, 659.

40. Tsitsianov to Mostafā, April 13, August 15, September 24, October 8, November 9, 12, 14, and 15, and Mostafā to Tsitsianov, four undated letters (1805), and Tsitsianov to Ebrāhim Khalil Khān of Qarābāgh, September 2 and November 9, 1805, and Tsitsianov to Major Tarasov (Tsitsianov's emissary to Mostafā), March 7, 1805, and Tsitsianov to Alexander, December 22, 1805, *Akty*, II, 661-67, 669-71, 673, 675-76.

41. Tsitsianov to Hāshem Beg (brother of the khan of Shirvān), December 16, 1805, and January 6, 1806, and Tsitsianov to Alexander, January 9 and March 31, 1803, and Tsitsianov to Hosein Qoli, January 31, February 1 and 2, 1806, ibid., II, 641-42, 673-79, 745-46, 781, 729; Bakikhanov, pp. 152, 155.

42. M. A. Atkin, "The Strange Death of Ebrāhim Khalil Khān of Qarābāgh," *Iranian Studies*, 12 (1979).

43. Bakikhanov, pp. 148, 153-54; Āqā Fath Karim, "Kratkaia istoriia Shekinskikh khanov," F. Babaev, ed., *Iz istorii Shekinskogo khanstva* (Baku, 1958), pp. 51-52; Hāji Seyyed 'Abd ol-Hamid, "Rodoslovnaia Shekinskikh khanov i ikh potomkov," F. Babaev, ed., *Iz istorii Shekinskogo khanstva* (Baku, 1958), p. 61; Salim to Tsitsianov, April 2, 1804, and two undated letters (1805), and Salim to Kariagin, April 1804, and Tsitsianov to Salim, May 26, 1804, February 13, March 7 and 22, July 2, 1805, and Kariagin to Salim, n.d. (1805), and Tsitsianov to Alexander, May 22, 1805, *Akty*, II, 637-38, 641, 642-43, 644-45, 646, 650, 655.

44. Salim to the commandant of Elizavetpol', 1806, *Akty*, III, 272.

45. Procurator of the Supreme Government of Georgia Plaskin to Active State Counselor Litvinov, July 22, 1806, ibid., III, 268; Salim to Alexander, n.d. (1806), and Gudovich to Nesvetaev, December 7, 1806, and imperial patent of December 10, 1806, *Akty*, III, 268-69, 271; Bakikhanov, p. 157; Dubrovin, V, 84-87.

46. Bakikhanov, p. 155; Mir Mostafā Khān of Tālesh to Tsitsianov, undated letters (1802, 1804), and Lieutenant Cheleev (commander of Russian troops in Tālesh) to Repin, November 24, 1809, and Tsitsianov to Mirzā Mohammad Beg (messenger from Mir Mostafā), December 7, 1802, and Tsitsianov to Mir Mostafā, June 9, 1804, April 23 and June 9, 1805, and Gudovich to Mir Mostafā, March 27, 1809, and Mir Mostafā to Tormasov, n.d. (1809), and Tormasov to Repin, June 23 and September 26, 1809, and February 5, 1810, and Repin to Tormasov, July 8, 1809, and Tormasov to Mir Mostafā, September 14 and December 2, 1809, and July 4, 1810, and Tormasov to Rumiantsev, September 14, 1809, and Tormasov to Cheleev, November 20, 1809, and March 18, 1810, and Gur'ev (commandant of Baku) to Gudovich, March 31, 1807, and Lieutenant Captain Stepanov (in Tālesh) to Gudovich, October 9, 1808, and Mir Mostafā to Repin, n.d. (1809) and November 13, 1811, and Paulucci

to Rumiantsev, November 18, 1811, *Akty*, II, 748, 751, 752, III, 305, 354, 362, 363, IV, 291, 577-79, 582-83, 585-87, 589-92, 595-96, V, 140, 141.

47. J. Campbell, "The Russo-Persian Frontier, 1810," *Journal of the Royal Central Asian Society*, XVIII (1931), 227-28; J. J. Morier, "Diary," 6 vols., British Museum, Additional Manuscripts, 33,839-44, IV f. 117; Beliavskii and Potto, II, 479-83, 487-98; Cheleev to Tormasov, September 10 and 19, 1809, and March 7, 1810, and (Caspian) Fleet Lieutenant Nekliudov (in Tālesh) to Cheleev, March 30 and July 1, 1810, and Captain Veselago (commander of a squadron off the west coast of the Caspian) to Paulucci, December 16, 1811, and Veselago to Kotliarevskii, August 20, 1812, and Active State Counselor Malinskii (civil governor of Georgia) to Major-General Portniagin (commander of Russian troops in Georgia), January 26, 1813, and Rtishchev to Gorchakov, January 6 and 9 and April 9, 1813, and Rtishchev to Alexander, January 28, 1813, *Akty*, IV, 582, 584-85, 592-93, V, 141, 633, 697, 698, 700, 702-3, 710-11.

CHAPTER VI

1. Czartoryskii to Ambassador A. Ia. Italinskii, August 18, 1804, *VPR*, I, 126.

2. I. A. Guseinov et al., eds., *Istoriia Azerbaidzhana* (3 vols., Baku, 1958-1963), II, 5; A. R. Ionnisian, *Prisoedinenie Zakavkaz'ia k Rossii i mezhdunarodnye otnosheniia v nachale XIX stoletiia* (Yerevan, 1958), pp. xxv, 68-70.

3. Ioannisian, *Prisoedinenie*, p. 51.

4. Political and commercial treaties between Iran and Great Britain, January 1801, C. U. Aitchison, ed., *A Collection of Treaties, Engagements, and Sunnuds Relating to India and Neighboring Countries*, 2nd ed. (14 vols., Calcutta, 1929-1933), XII, 41-45; Skibinevskii to Knorring, May 1, 1801, *Akty*, I, 683-84.

5. R. M. Savory, "Safavid Persia," P. M. Holt, A. K. S. Lambton, and B. Lewis, eds., *The Cambridge History of Islam* (2 vols., Cambridge, 1970), I, 403.

6. J. Malcolm, *A History of Persia* (2 vols., London, 1815), II, 53.

7. J. R. Perry, "The Last Safavids, 1722-1773," *Iran*, IX (1971), 59-69.

8. Hedāyat, IX, 269.

9. Ibid., IX, 269-72, 285.

10. H. Algar, *Religion and the State in Iran, 1785-1906* (Berkeley and Los Angeles, 1969), p. 56.

11. Hāji Ebrāhim to Kovalenskii, n.d. (1800), *Akty*, I, 97; italics added.

12. Ibid., I, 97.

13. Fath 'Ali to the elders of the Samukh district (of Georgia), 1803, and Fath 'Ali to the inhabitants of Kakheti, Zo'l-Hejjeh 1218 (March-April 1804), and Fath 'Ali to the inhabitants of Tbilisi, n.d. (1804), and Fath 'Ali to Prince P'arnaoz, two undated letters (1804), ibid., II, 802-3, 804, 812-17.

14. John Malcolm to the Earl of Mornington (Marquis Richard Wellesley, governor general of the British East India Company's Indian territories), April 22, 1800, P&PGFR, XXII, 146.

15. Hedāyat, IX, 289.

16. Domboli, p. 109.

17. Hedāyat, IX, 389.

18. Hedāyat, IX, 389.

19. Mirzā Shafi' to Tsitsianov, May 23, 1804, *Akty*, II, 808; Samuel Manesty (East India Company resident at Basra) to Marquis Wellesley, July 31, 1804, P&PGFR, XXIV (pages unnumbered).

20. Tsitsianov to Mirzā Shafi', May 27, 1804, *Akty*, II, 808-9.

21. Tuchkov, pp. 197, 208, 210.

22. Tsitsianov to Alexander, April 27, 1803. *Akty*, II, 289.

23. Tsitsianov to Kochubei, Septermber 30, 1804, and Tsitsianov to Czartoryski, August 13, 1805, ibid., II, 812-13, 847.

24. M. S. Vorontsov to S. R. Vorontsov, October 12, 1804, *AKV*, XXXVI, 93.

25. Czartoryski to Tsitsianov, September 27 and November 15, 1804, and Tsitsianov to Kochubei, September 30, 1804, and Tsitsianov to Alexander, n.d. (1805), and Tsitsianov to Czartoryski, June 17 and August 13, 1805, *Akty*, II, 812-13, 830, 831, 847.

26. Czartoryski to Tsitsianov, September 27, 1804, ibid., II, 1020.

27. Hedāyat, IX, 390; Domboli, pp. 95-96, 110.

CHAPTER VII

1. Potto, I, 453-54; Beliavskii and Potto, I, 209-13; Dubrovin, IV, 446-47; Lofitsskii to Alexander, report on conditions in Georgia, 1801-1805, and Kariagin to Tsitsianov, June 27, 1805, *Akty*, III, 6, II, 833-34.

2. Baddeley, p. 77.

3. Lord Gower (British ambassador to St. Petersburg) to Charles James Fox (foreign secretary), April 14, 1805, FO 65/62, f. 154; Caulaincourt to Napoleon, February 5, 1809, Archives Nationales, AF IV, 1698, dossier 3; Alexander to Gudovich, January 7, 1807, and notes of S. M. Bronevskii (expeditor, Asian Department, Ministry of Foreign Affairs) to Count A. N. Saltykov, n.d. (probably November 1808), *VPR*, I, 470, IV, 413; Gudovich to Saltykov, December 11, 1808, and Gudovich to Chancellor Rumiantsev, October 30, 1808, *Akty*, III, 264-65, 498.

4. Caulaincourt to Napoleon, October 12, 1808, Nikolai Mikhailovich, *Relations diplomatiques*, II, 280.

5. Caulaincourt to Napoleon, February 5, 1809, Archives Nationales, AF IV, 1698, dossier 3.

6. Nebol'sin to Tormasov, July 15, 1810, *Akty*, IV, 560.

7. Tsitsianov to Alexander, March 9, and October 19, 1805, and Tsitsianov to Admiral Paul Chichagov (acting naval minister), Januray 29, 1805, ibid., II, II, 798, 741, 735-36.

8. G. T. Keppel, *Personal Narrative of a Journey from India to England* (London, 1827), pp. 275-76, 290; J. F. Gamba, *Voyage dans la Russie méridionale et particulièrement dans les provinces situées au-delà du Caucase* (2 vols., Paris, 1826), II, 327-28, 332; W. Monteith, *Kars and Erzeroum* (London, 1856), p. 36; Lofitsskii to Alexander, report on conditions in Georgia, and Rozhnov (vice-governor of the Caucasus) to Gudovich, July 25, 1806, and Gudovich to Alexander, March 15, 1807, and Gudovich to Kochubei, September 28, 1807, and General of the Infantry Bulgakov (inspector of the Caucasian Line) to Prince Kurakin, April 7, 1808, *Akty*, 6, 52, 433, 53, 55-56; Brosset, II, part ii, 299; Beliavskii and Potto, II, 297-98; Dubrovin, V, 452.

9. Collegiate Counselor Sokolov (St. Petersburg's special investigator of the unrest in Georgia) to A. R. Vorontsov, September 1, 1802, and Tsitsianov to Alexander, February 10, 1803, and November 28, 1805, and Active State Counselor Litvinov to Gudovich, January 15, 1807, and Gudovich to Rumiantsev, n.d. (probably July 1808), and Tormasov to Active Sceret Counselor Gur'ev, August 2, 1810, and Paulucci to the minister of Police, October 1, 1811, *Akty*, II, 14, 18-19, 299, III, 13-14, 479-80, 43, V, 51-52; P. A. Jaubert, *Voyage en Arménie et en Perse* (Paris, 1821), p. 299; Beliavskii and Potto, II, 290, 345; Dubrovin, V, 69; Fadeev, p. 135.

10. M. S. Vorontsov to S. R. Vorontsov, October 12, 1804, *AKV*, XXXVI, 98; J. von Klaproth, *Tableau historique, géographique et ethnographique du Caucase et des provinces limitrophes entre la Russie et la Perse* (Paris, 1827), p. 110; Baddeley, p. 95; Sokolov to A. R. Vorontsov, 1802, and Lofitsskii to Alexander, April 30, 1806, *Akty*, II, 5-6, III, 3-7; Beliavskii and Potto, II, 277-82; Dobrovin, V, 421-22, 454; J. -B. Dumas, ed., *Un Fourrier de Napoléon vers l'Inde, les papiers du Lieutenant-Général Trézel*, 2nd ed. (Paris, 1915), p. 80.

11. Tsitsianov to Alexander, July 1, 1805, and Gudovich to Alexander, January 11, 1809, *Akty*, II, 835, III, 510: Beliavskii and Potto, I, 87; Dubrovin, VI, 24; Potto, I, 419, 525, 527.

12. Gudovich to Nesvataev, August 2, 1806, and Nesvataev to Gudovich, August 9, 1806, and Guodvich to Alexander, October 29 and December 11, 1808, and Gudovich to Major-General Akhverdov, October 25, 1808, *Akty*, III, 88-89, 243-46, 252-55, 241; Caulaincourt to Napoleon, February 22, 1809, Nikolai Mikhailovich, *Relations diplomatiques*, III, 100-101; R. Strachey, "Diary of a Journey from Moscow to the Caucasus" (1806), Somerset Record Office, vol. VII; Dumas, p. 75; Beliavskii and Potto, I, 251-57, 303-6.

13. (There is one report that 'Abbās Mirzā arranged the murder of a Russian who had served as an officer in the Iranian army when that man announced his intention to return to Russia after the war.) Captain Charles Christie (head of the infantry in 'Abbās's British-trained army) to General John Malcolm (ambassador from the governor-general in Bengal to Iran), October 16, 1810, India Office, Home Miscellaneous Series, 736, pp. 318-19; W. Price, "Journal of the Embassy to Persia" (The Ouseley mission), British Museum, Additional Manuscripts, 19,270, f. 70; C. Masson, journal of his trip to Iran (1830), India Office, Miscellaneous European Manuscripts, E 163 (Masson Manuscripts, "Journals and Travels," II), f. 31; Porter, *Travels in Georgia*, I, 349; P. M. R. Aucher-Éloy, *Relations de voyages en Orient de 1830 à 1838*, P. A. Jaubert, ed. (Paris, 1843), pp. 415-16; R. C. M. (R. C. Money), *Journal of a Tour in Persia during the Years 1824 and 1825* (London, 1828), pp. 151-52; J. M. Tancoigne, *A Narrative of a Journey into Persia* (London, 1820), p. 317; Keppel, p. 272; T. B. Armstrong, *Journal of Travels in the Seat of War* (London, 1831), p. 112; A. Dupré, *Voyage en Perse fait dans les années 1807, 1808, et 1809* (2 vols., Paris, 1819), II, p. 234; Nesvetaev to Gudovich, November 4, 1807, and Rtishchev to Gorchakov, January 9, 1813, and Rtishchev to Rumiantsev, July 31, 1813, *Akty*, III, 236, V, 698, 727; Dubrovin, IV, 446-47; Beliavskii and Potto, II, 298, 476, n. 1.

14. Tsitsianov to Czartoryski, July 10, 1804, and Gudovich to Alexander, September 15, 1807, and Gudovich to Rumiantsev, September 15, 1807, and Tormasov to the minister of war, January 16, 1811, *Akty*, II, 1030, III, 100, 707, IV, 187-89; Beliaveskii and Potto, I, 197, II, 270-71, 296; Dubrovin, IV, 436-37, V, 19, 228-29, 234.

15. W. Hollingberry, *A Journal of Observations Made during the British Embassy to the Court of Persia in the Years 1799, 1800* and *1801* (Calcutta, 1814), p. 83; G. Drouville, *Voyage en Perse fait en 1812 et 1813*, 1st ed. (2 vols., St. Petersburg, 1819), II, 104, 111-12; Malcolm, *History of Persia*, II, 496; J. -E. Driault, "La Mission Gardanne en Perse (1807-1809) d'après les Archives nationales et les Archives du ministère des affaires étrangères," *Revue d'histoire moderne et contemporaine*, II (1900-1901), 132; M. S. Vorontsov to S. R. Vorontsov, October 12, 1804, *AKV*, XXXVI, 99; J. J. Morier, *Journey through Persia, Armenia and Asia Minor to Constantinople* (London, 1812), p. 281; Tancoigne, pp. 152, 246-47; Dupré, II, 291-93; Pakravan, I, 158; Drouville, 1st ed., II, 107-14; W. Freygang and F. K. Freygang, *Letters from the Caucasus and Georgia* (London, 1823), p. 271.

16. A. Gardane, *Mission du Général Gardane en Perse sous le premier empire* (Paris, 1865), p. 226; Morier, "Diary," IV, f. 117; Rtishchev to Gorchakov, January 6 and 19, April 9, 1813, *Akty*, V, 697, 698, 710-11; Campbell, pp. 227-28; Bournoutian, pp. 15-17 et passim.

17. H. Jones (Brydges), *Account of the Transactions of His Majesty's Mission to the court of Persia in the Years 1807-1811* (2 vols., London, 1834), I, 256.

18. Bakikhanov, P. 160; Active State Counselor Litvinov (serving in the civil administration of Georgia) to Gudovich, August 17, 1806, *Akty*, III, 226-27.

19. Tormasov to Lieutenant-General Repin (commandant of Baku), May 24, 1809, and Prince Alexander (of Georgia), two letters, to Hosein Qoli Khān of Yerevan and Mirzā Bozorg (chief vizier to 'Abbās Mirzā), 1813, *Akty*, IV, 639, V, 369.

20. Domboli, p. 199; Jones, *Transactions*, I, 312, 314-15; declaration by the sons of Sādeq Khān (leader of the Sheqaqi Kurds, executed by the order of Fath 'Ali Shāh in 1800), n.d., and report from Ahmad Khān (governor of Tabriz) to Tsitsianov, n.d., and Tsitsianov to Ahmad Khān, February 8, 1805, and Tsitsianov to 'Abbās Qoli Khān of Qarādāgh (across the Aras from Qarābāgh), n.d. and Tsitsianov to Alexander, June 17, 1805, and Major-General Nebol'sin to Gudovich, December 30, 1808, and Gudovich to Mir Mostāfā Khān (Tālesh), and Gudovich to Captain Stepanov (Caspian fleet), n.d. (1808), and Colonel Aseev (commandant of Shushā garrison) to Gudovich, December 28, 1808, and Jehāngir Khān Sheqaqi to Gudovich, n.d., and Nazar 'Ali Khān (Shāhsevan) to Tormasov, n.d., and "Some Information about the Aisors" (Assyrian Christians), *Akty*, II, 801-2, 823-24, 829-30, III, 291, 362, 502-4, 683-84, 690.

21. J. Macdonald (Kinneir), *A Geographical Memoir of the Persian Empire* (London, 1813), pp. 26-27; Algar, *Religion*, pp. 36, 79.

22. Dupré, II, 294-97; Drouville, 1st ed., II, 109; Driault, p. 132; M. von Kotzebue, *Narrative of a Journey into Persia in the Suite of the Imperial Russian Embassy in the Year 1817* (London, 1819), p. 280; A. Debidour, "Le Général Fabvier, sa vie et ses écrits," *Annales de l'Est* (1887), p. 328.

23. Malcolm, *History of Persia*, II, 297-98.

24. Domboli, p. 197.

25. Drouville, 1st ed., II, 115-17, 154; Macdonald, pp. 33-34; Jaubert, *Voyage*, pp. 274-75, 278; Kotzebue, p. 288; Tormasov to Rumiantsev, September 10, 1809, and Nebol'sin to Tormasov, July 15, 1810, *Akty*, IV, 693, 560; Major D'Arcy (commander of 'Abbās's British-trained artillery) to Gore Ousely (British ambassador to Iran), February 16, 1812, FO 60/6.

26. Macdonald, p. 35; Campbell, p. 237; Malcolm, *History of Persia,* II, 497, 497 n., 498; Morier, "Diary," IV, f. 40; J. J. Morier, *A Second Journey through Persia, Armenia, and Asia Minor to Constantinople* (London, 1818), p. 215; Drouville, 1st ed., II, 97-98; B. Wilbraham, *Travels in the Transcaucasian Provinces of Russia* (London, 1839), p. 63; C. Bélanger, *Voyage aux Indes-Orientales par le norde de l'Europe, les provinces du Caucase, la Géorgie, l'Arménie et la Perse pendant les ann*ees 1825-1829 (3 vols., Paris, 1834), II, 402, n. 1.

27. Jaubert, *Voyage*, p. 277; Freygang and Freygang, p. 275; Morier, "Diary," IV, ff. 52-53; Drouville, 1st ed., II, 100-102; "Names and Account given of themselves by four Russians from Muskat on their arrival at Bombay," March 28, 1811, India Office, microfilm reel 647 (correspondence with R. Dundas).

28. Jones to Adair (British ambassador to the Ottoman Empire), May 20, 1809, and Stratford Canning (British ambassador to the Ottoman Empire) to Jones, August 1, 1810, and Ouseley to Stratford Canning, December 17, 1811, FO 60/2, 3, 10; Stratford Canning to Ouseley, March 8, 1812, FO 181/8; Jones, *Transactions*, I, xxvi, n. 18, 400-401; Morier, "Diary," IV, ff. 59, 104; Morier, *Second Journey*, pp. 221-23; W. Monteith, "Routes in Azerbaijan, Kurdistan and Armenia, 1811-1829," India Office, Miscellaneous European Manuscripts, B 24, pp. 18-19.

29. Malcolm to Lord Minto (governor-general of the East India Company's domains in India), October 6, 1810, FO 95/8/6.

30. Malcolm to the Earl of Mornington, April 22, 1800, P&PGFR, XX, 133; Jones, *Transactions,* I, 242-43, 329-30; Price, f. 66; Tancoigne, p. 101; F. Adamiyat, "The Diplomatic Relations of Persia with Britain, Turkey, and Russia, 1815-1830," Ph.D. dissertation (University of London, 1949), pp. 15-18.

31. Pakravan, I, 12-13.

32. Morier, "Diary," IV, f. 59; Morier, *Second Journey,* pp. 195-97; E. Frederick, "Persian Journal, 1801" (sic., 1810), India Office, Miscellaneous European Manuscripts, D 111, pp. 109-10; Jones, *Transactions,* I, 248-49; W. Ouseley, *Travels in Various Countries of the East* (3 vols., London, 1821), III, 347-49; Jaubert, *Voyage,* pp. 211-13; Dupré, II, 239-41; Drouville, 1st ed., I, 47, II, 2; Malcolm to Minto, October 6, 1810, FO 95/8/6; Pakravan, I, 22-29.

33. Henry Willock (chargé d'affaires in Iran) to George Canning (foreign secretary), April 1, 1823, and Dr. Cormick (British physician who treated 'Abbās) to Dr. J. Campbell (another British physician who treated 'Abbās), August 7, 1833, India Office, Political and Secret, Persia, XXXVII, 117, XLIX, 637-38; Campbell to Jones, March 13, 1812, Kentchurch Court Papers, National Library of Wales, #9015; Jones, *Transactions,* I, 250, 259, 353; Porter, *Travels in Georgia,* I, 249-50, 282; R. Mignan, *A Winter Journey through Russia, the Caucasian Alps, and Georgia thence to Koordistan* (2 vols., London, 1839), I, 173-75; Ouseley, III, 400; Morier, *Journey, pp. 279-80, 282, 283;* Morier, "Diary," IV, ff. 41-42, 56; Tancoigne, pp. 76, 318; Bélanger, II 353-57; Olivier, III, 87; Jouannin (member of Gardane mission to Iran) to the minister of external relations, June 8, 1809, MAE, XII, f. 38; P. A. Jaubert, notes on his mission to Iran, May 1807, Archives Nationales IV, 1705, dossier 1; Malcolm to Minto, October 6, 1810, FO 95/8/6; J. B. Fraser, *Travels and Adventures in the Persian Provinces on the Southern Banks of the Caspian Sea* (London, 1826), pp. 305-7, 310-11; Pakravan, I, 29.

34. Jaubert, *Voyage,* pp. 170-71.

35. Morier, "Diary," III, ff. 36, 109; Price, f. 67; Kotzebue, pp. 160-61; Domboli, pp. 218-19; Malcolm to Minto, October 6, 1810, FO 95/8/6; Jones to Minto, October 5, 1809, and Jones to Stratford Canning, November 14, 1810, and Gore Ouseley to Minto, October 6, 1811, FO 60/2,3,6; Samuel Manesty (East India Company resident in Basra) to chairman of the court of directors (of the East India Company), July 18, 1804, P&PGFR, XXIV; Frederick, p. 110; Jaubert, *Voyage,* pp. 213-25; C. Gardane (French ambassador to Iran) to Champagny, August 5, 1808, MAE, X, f. 165; Jones, *Transactions,* I, 294.

36. Substance of a *farmān* (decree) by Fath 'Ali Shāh to Jones, FO 248/22, p. 5; Cormick to Malcolm, May 6, 1811, India Office, Home Miscellaneous Series, 736, p. 354; Morier, "Diary," III, ff. 80-87; Jones, *Transactions,* I, 283; Jaubert, *Voyage,* p. 215; Drouville, 2nd ed. (2 vols., Paris, 1825), I, 214.

37. J. H. Lovett (East India Company resident at Bushire [Bushehr], Iran) to N. B. Edmonstone (secretary to the governor-general, India), October 20, 1805, and Malcolm to the Earl of Mornington, April 22, 1800, and Jones to Minto, April 13 and July 3, 1809, P&PGFR, XXII, 133, XXIX A, XXVI, 307-12, 183-84; Jones, *Transactions,* I, 286-87, 377-79, 402, 404; Jaubert, *Voyage,* pp. 434, 437, 439; Ouseley, III, 337, 370; Malcolm, *History of Persia,* II, 471-81; Morier, *Journey,* pp. 109-10, 236-39; Mignan, I, 399-400; J. B. Fraser, *An Historical and Descriptive Account of Persia from the Earliest Ages to the Present,* (Edinburgh, 1834), p. 314; Tancoigne, p. 152.

38. Domboli, pp. 179-80; Macdonald, pp. 149, 151, 153-54; Morier, *Journey,* pp. 266, 270-71, 279, 283, 284; Tancoigne, pp. 67, 80-81; Jaubert, *Voyage,* pp. 168-69, 172-73, 358; Fraser, *Travels,* I, 8; Bournoutian, pp. 87-88.

39. Jones to Minto, April 13, 1809, P&PGFR, XXVI, 182; Jones, *Transactions,* I, 282-83, 290, 403; G. Ouseley to (Richard) Wellesley, August 25, 1812, Wellesley Papers, British Museum, Additional Manuscripts, 37,285, ff. 290-91; Dupré, II, 239.

40. E. Ingram, "An Aspiring Buffer-State: Anglo-Persian Relations in the Third Coalition, 1804-1807," *The Historical Journal*, XVI (1973), 509-10.

41. Tuchkov, pp. 221 et passim; M. S. Vorontsov to S. R. Vorontsov, October 12, 1804, *AKV*, XXXVI, 99-103; Domboli, pp. 112-20; Tsitsianov to Prince Teneshev, July 7, 1804, and Tsitsianov to Alexander, August 15 and December 30, 1804, and Tsitsianov to Czartoryski, September 14, 1804, and Lofitsskii to Alexander, April 30, 1806, *Akty*, II, 809-11, 619, III, 5.

42. Jones to Wellesley, July 26, 1810, FO 60/3; Nebol'sin to Tormasov, June 29, July 8 and 25, September 18, 1810, and Aseev to Tormasov, May 27, September 25 and 29, 1810, and Tormasov to Nebol'sin, July 2, 1810, *Akty*, IV, 720-21, 558-59, 561-62, 741, 715, 721, 742-43, 744-45; Dubrovin, V, 44-46, 215-16, 347-50.

43. G. Ouseley to Minto, May 12, 1812, FO 60/6; Tormasov to Rumiantsev, September 10, 1809, *Akty*, IV 696.

CHAPTER VIII

1. Political and commercial treaties between Iran and Britain, January 1801, Aitchison, XII, 37-45.

2. Harford Jones, report, January 7, 1807, and Mirzā Bozorg to Jones, n.d. (1805), and company resident at Baghdad to Mirzā Bozorg, October 19, 1805, and Mirzā Rezā Qoli (chancellor of Iran) to the resident at Baghdad, February 2, 1805, and Fath 'Ali Shāh to King George III, 1809, FO 60/1, 2; Manesty to (Richard) Wellesley, February 21, July 2 and 18, 1804, and Manesty to the chairman of the court of directors (of the East India Company), July 18, 1804, and Manesty to Viscount Castlereagh (president of the board of control of the East India Company), September 23, 1804, and Mirzā Rezā Qoli Khān to the resident at Baghdad, 1805, and Lovett to Manesty, December 1, 1803, and N. B. Edmonstone to William Ramsay (secretary to the court of directors), July 9, 1804, P&PGFR, XX, XXIV, XXXI; Fath 'Ali Shāh to Mohammad Nabi Khān (ambassador to the governor-general, India), n.d. (1806), and Edmonstone to Fath 'Ali, January 10, 1807, Kentchurch Court papers, National Library of Wales, #8412 and #8413.

3. Warren to Lord Hawkesbury, February 17 and August 30, 1804, FO 65/54, f. 118, 65/55, ff. 367-69.

4. Lord Gower to Charles James Fox, April 14, 1806, FO 65/62, ff. 153-54.

5. Letter from the Iranian government to the French government, 1217 A.H. (1802-1803), and Mirzā Mohammad Rezā to Napoleon, n.d., and C. Gardane to Napoleon, January 21, 1808, Archives Nationales, AF IV, 1686, dossiers, 1, 2; Manesty to Mirzā Rezā Qoli, n.d. (probably late 1804), P&PGFR, XXIV; Treaty of Finkenstein, May 4, 1807, J. C. Hurewitz, ed., *Diplomacy in the Near and Middle East* (2 vols., Princeton, 1972), I, 77-78.

6. Fath 'Ali to Napoleon, n.d. (probably 1806), Archives Nationales, AF IV, 1705, dossier 1.

7. Domboli, p. 213.

8. Tancoigne, pp. 313, 315-17; C. Gardane, precis of an audience with Fath 'Ali, May 4, 1808, and convention concluded by Gardane and Mirzā Shafi', January 21, 1808, MAE, X, f. 28, XIV, ff. 16-17; Bélanger, II, 394-96; P. A. L. Gardane, *Journal d'un voyage dans la Turquie d'Asie et la Perse fait en 1807 et 1808* (Paris and Marseilles, 1809), p. 39; Debidour, pp. 329-40; Dupré, II, 298-300.

9. Drouville, 1st ed., II, 126-27; Porter, *Travels in Georgia*, II, 587.

10. Captain Lamy (engineer in charge of fortification projects), report on initial Russo-Iranian hostilities near Khoi, October 13, 1808, MAE, X, f. 302; Ja'far 'Ali Khān (company informant in Shirāz) to Jones, n.d. (1808), and Jones to Minto, April 13 and July 3,

1809, and Jones to Robert Dundas, July 17, 1809, P&PGFR, XXV, 197-98, XXVI, 180-82, 295-96, 310-11; Cormick to Malcolm, May 1, 1812, India Office, Home Miscellaneous Series, 736, p. 438; C. Gardane to Champagny, October 25, 1808, Gardane, *Mission*, p. 210; Bélanger, II, 373, 396, 402-2; Debidour, p. 343; Drouville, 1st ed., II 125, 129, 135, 139-40; A. Delrieu, "Une Ambassade française à la cour de Perse sous l'empire 1808," *Revue britannique*, XX (1854), 200; Jones, *Transactions*, I, 309, 355, 390-91; Morier, *Second Journey, pp. 211-15, 311; Morier, "Diary," IV*, f. 48; Malcolm, *History of Persia*, II, 499-500.

11. Napoleon to Fath 'Ali, January 17, 1807, Archives Nationales, AF IV, 1705, dossier 1.

12. Gudovich to Budberg, September 17, 1806, and Alexander to Gudovich, October 4, 1806, *Akty*, III, 419, 420-21.

13. Fath 'Ali to Napoleon, 1807, and C. Gardane to Ministry of Foreign Affairs, April 5 and 24, 1808, and C. Gardane, precis of audience with Fath 'Ali, May 4, 1808, MAE, IX, ff. 218-19, X, ff. 4, 17-19, 27; C. Gardane to Champagny, June 2, 1808, and C. Gardane, precis of an audience with Fath 'Ali, February 8, 1809, Gardane, *Mission*, pp. 167-70, 275-77; Champagny to Caulaincourt, February 23, 1809, Nikolai Mikhailovich, *Relations diplomatiques*, VII, 105; copy of a declaration by C. Gardane to the Iranian government, December 17, 1807, P&PGFR, XXVI, 113; Driault, pp. 126, 135, 142, 145, 148, 152.

14. Napoleon to Fath 'Ali, January 17 and March 14, 1807, MAE, IX, ff. 103-4; memorandum by S. M. Bronevskii, n.d. (no later than April 1807), *VPR*, III, 553-55; Nesvetaev to Glazenap, July 18, 1806, and Gudovich to Budberg, December 6, 1806, and Nesvetaev to Gudovich, September 19, 1807, and Gudovich to Major Stepanov (bearer of a letter from Gudovich to the shah), February 12, 1807, and Gudovich to Rumiantsev, March 7, 1808, and Budberg to Gudovich, March 8 and April 21, 1807, and Gudovich to 'Abbās, March 25, 1808, and Rumiantsev to Gudovich, December 20, 1807, and Gudovich to Alexander, October 29, 1808, and 'Abbās to Gudovich, n.d. (1808), and Mirzā Shafi' to Gudovich, n.d. (1808), and Rumiantsev to Gudovich, August 4, 1808, and Gudovich to Rumiantsev, September 2, 1808, *Akty*, III, 416-17, 425-26, 235, 430, 432, 435-36, 444-46, 242, 449-51, 456-60, 461-64, 485-86.

15. Félix Lajard (third secretary of the Gardane mission) to Champagny, November 17, 1808, and Joseph Jouannin (French consul in Iran) to the Ministry of Foreign Affairs, August 21, 1809, and Fath 'Ali to Napoleon, 1809, and C. Gardane, precis of an audience with Fath 'Ali, January 24, 1809, and Fath 'Ali to Napoleon, February 16, 1809, MAE, X, f. 384, XI, ff. 29-31, 84-85, XII, ff. 151-53, 216-20; Champagny to Napoleon, November 8, 1808, Archives Nationales, AF IV, 1697, dossier 5, 1686, dossier 1; Caulaincourt to Napoleon, February 20, 1808, and Caulaincourt to Champagny, August 9, 1808, Nikolai Mikhailovich, *Relations diplomatiques*, I, 153-54, II, 271-72; Jones to Canning, April 4, 1809, FO 60/2.

16. Charles Pasley (member of Malcolm's 1808 mission) to Edmonstone, August 18, 1808, and Malcolm to Minto, August 15, 1808, and Minto to Malcolm, August 12, 1808, FO 248/2, 101-29, 248/3, 29-49, 248/9, 68-89; Malcolm to Jones, March 15, 1810, FO 60/3.

17. Jones to Minto, May 18, 1809, and Mirzā Shafi' to Canning, n.d. (1809), FO 60/2; Jones to Minto, November 3, 1808, FO 248/11; preliminary treaty between Britain and Iran, March 12, 1809, Aitchison, XII, 45-46; Jones, *Transactions*, I, 136-37, 139.

18. Minutes of a meeting between James Morier (member of the Jones mission) and Fath 'Ali on April 9, 1809, and Jones to Canning, May 2 and August 28, 1809, and Jones to Minto, December 10, 1809, and Mirzā Shafi' and Mirzā Bozorg to Jones, n.d. (1809), and Mirzā Bozorg to Jones, n.d. (1810), and Malcolm to the Secret Committee, May 20, 1810, and Malcolm to Jones, March 3, 1810, FO 60/2, 3, 4; Jones to Robert Dundas, March 16, 1809, and Jones to Minto, July 3, 1809, and Dr. Andrew Jukes (translator for the Jones mission) to Pasley, April 19, 1809, and Minto to Fath 'Ali, January 30,

1809, P&PGFR, XXVI, 85-87, 99-100, 302-2, XXX, 288-92, XXIX A; Minto to Jones, October 31, 1808, and Jones to Minto, November 1, 1808, and Malcolm to Minto, July 22, 1810, and Malcolm to Edmonstone, July 22, 1810, and Jukes to Malcolm, March 26 and 27, April 5, 1810, and Wellesley to Jones, April 21, 1810, FO 248/2, 11, 16, 18; 'Abbās to Jouannin, n.d. (1810), Fath 'Ali to Napoleon, two letters, n.d. (1810, 1811), and C. Gardane to the Ministry of Foreign Affairs, April 24, 1808, MAE, X, f. 19. XIII, ff. 59-60, 65-73, XV, f. 59; treaty between Britain and Iran, March 14, 1812, Aitchison, XII, 48-53; Jones, *Transactions*, I, 202-4.

19. Jones, *Transactions*, I, 271; Malcolm to Minto, October 6, 1810, FO 95/8/6; Malcolm to Jones, July 15, 1810, and G. Ouseley to Minto, January 17, 1812, FO 60/3, 6; G. Ouseley to Wellesley, April 21, 1811, British Museum, Additional Manuscripts, 37, 285, f. 256.

20. G. Ouseley to Minto, December 10, 1811, P&PGFR, XXXI; Cormick to Malcolm, March 10, 1811, May 1, 1812, and an undated latter (1812), and Christie to Malcolm, May 29, 1811, India Office, Home Miscellaneous Series, 736, pp. 341-42, 366, 438, 461-62; J. Sutherland (secretary to the Jones mission) to Jones, February 21, 1812, National Library of Wales, Kentchurch Court Papers, #9009; G. Ouseley to Wellesley, April 21, 1811, British Museum, Additional Manuscripts, 37, 285, ff. 256-57; Jones to Wellesley, October 16 and November 4, 1810, and G. Ouseley to Wellesley, January 21, 1811, FO 60/3, 6; Jonathan Duncan (company official, Bombay) to Jones, January 16, 1811, and "Roll of British Officers and Non-Commissioned Officers serving in Persia," February—July 1812, and "Invoice of Military Stores . . . . ," January 31, 1811, and Lindesay to G. Ouseley, December 17, 1812, FO 248-25, 31, pp. 126-27, 130-31, 174; Porter, *Travels in Georgia*, II, 587; Price, f. 124; Ouseley, III, 394, 399; Drouville, 1st ed., II, 125-27, 129-30, 135; Campbell, pp. 223-24; Malcolm, *History of Persia*, II, 499-500; Morier, "Diary," IV, f. 69, 78-79; Morier, *Second Journey*, pp. 210, 212, 226-27, 274; Jones, *Transactions*, I, 290-92.

21. Jones to Wellesley, November 5, 1810, and G. Ouseley to Wellesley, February 29, 1812, and D'Arcy to G. Ouseley, February 16, 1812, FO 60/3, 6; Cormick to Malcolm, February 29, 1812, India Office, Home Miscellaneous Series, 736, pp. 433-35; Campbell to Jones, March 13, 1812, National Library of Wales, Kentchurch Court Papers, #9015; Bakikhanov, p. 160; Campbell, pp. 225-26; Paulucci to Alexander, March 27, 1812, *Akty*, V, 177.

22. Domboli, pp. 291-99, Hedāyat, IX, 482-85; Cormick to Malcolm, November 23, 1812, India Office, Home Miscellaneous Series, 736, pp. 450-58; Campbell, pp. 228-30; Morier, "Diary," IV, ff. 105-12; Rtishchev to Kotliarevskii, October 15, 1812, and Rtishchev to Active State Counselor Malinskii (civil governor of Georgia), October 26, 1812, and Rtishchev to Rumiantsev, October 31, 1812, and Rtishchev to Alexander, November 21, 1812, and Rtishchev to Gorchakov, November 22, 1812, *Akty*, V, 678, 683-84, 690, 692-93, 695.

23. Malinskii to Major-General Portniagin (commander of Russian troops in Georgia), January 26, 1813, and Rtishchev to Gorchakov, January 6 and 9 and April 9, 1813, and Rtishchev to Alexander, January 28, 1813, *Akty*, V, 700, 697-98, 710-11, 702-3.

24. Morier, "Diary," IV, ff. 112-22; Drouville, 1st ed., II, 131, 143-48; G. Ouseley to George Brown (governor of Bengal), December 20, 1812, and Minto to G. Ouseley, November 28, 1812, FO 248/29, 31, p. 135; G. Ouseley to Minto, May 12, 1812, and G. Ouseley to Castlereagh, January 16, 1813, and G. Ouseley to Minto, June 11, 1813, FO 60/6, 8; Cormick to Malcolm, February 22, 1813, India Office, Home Miscellaneous Series, 736, pp. 463-65; Rtishchev to Gorchakov, July 12, 1813, *Akty*, V, 581-82; Beliavskii and Potto, II, 501.

25. Tormasov to Michael Barclay de Tolly (minister of war), July 28, 1810, and Tormasov to 'Abbās, April 28, 1810, and Tormasov to Rumiantsev, May 26 and July 3, 1810, 'and Rumiantsev to Tormasov, April 7, 1810, and 'Abbās to Tormasov, n.d. (1810), and

Rtishchev to Alexander, May 19, 1812, and Rumiantsev to Rtishchev, April 7 and June 23, 1812, and Rtishchev to Rumiantsev, July 27, 1812, and Rtishchev to Major-General Akhverdov (Russian negotiator in peace talks with Iran, September 1812), September 25, 1812, and Rtishchev to Rumiantsev, September 25 and October 31, 1812, *Akty*, IV 183, 593-94, 595, 709-12, 706-7, 713, V, 590-92, 649-50, 654-57, 668-75, 687; Jones to Adair, May 20, 1809, February 13, and April 1, 1810, and Jones to Minto, May 18, 1809, and Jones to Mirzā Shafiʻ, October 4, 1809, FO 60/2, 3: "Memorandum of Conferences on the subject of Baron Wrede's Mission" (Vrede was the Russian negotiator in the peace talks with Iran in 1810), n.d. (1810), and Jones to Admiral Drury (commander-in-chief of the British navy in Indian waters), October 15, 1810, and G. Ouseley to Minto, October 19, 1812, FO 248/16, 19, 29; Fath ʻAli to G. Ouseley, 1227 A.H. (1812), and G. Ouseley to Castlereagh, August 10, 1812, and G. Ouseley to Rtishchev, August 10, 1812, and account of meeting between Akhverdov and Mirzā Abu ʼl-Qāsem (Iranian negotiator at peace talks, 1812), September 27, 1812, and Morier to G. Ouseley, October 6, 1812, FO 60/7; Jones, *Transactions*, I, xv, xxvii-xxxi; Morier, "Diary," IV, ff. 50, 55, 57-58, 81.

26. G. Ouseley to Castlereagh, July 10, 1813, FO 60/8.

27. G. Ouseley to Castlereagh, December 30, 1812, January 16, March 13, September 28, and October 30, 1813, and February 16, 1814, and G. Ouseley to Minto, June 30, 1813, and G. Ouseley to Rtishchev, July 10, 1813, and Fath ʻAli to the Prince Regent, n.d. (1813), and G. Ouseley to William Hamilton (undersecretary of state for foreign affairs), April 4, 1815, FO 60/7, 8, 9, ff. 37-38, 43-46, FO 60/10, ff. 21-24; G. Ouseley to Wellesley, August 25, 1812, British Museum, Additional Manuscripts, 37,285, ff. 290-91; Rumiantsev to Rtishchev, August 9, 1813, and Rtishchev to Rumiantsev, May 23 and September 9, 1813, and Rtishchev to G. Ouseley, May 8, July 14, and August 24, 1813, *Akty*, V, 716-17, 722-23, 727-28, 729-32; Rtishchev to Rumiantsev, January 5 (17), 1813, *VPR*, VI, 19-20.

28. G. Ouseley to Castlereagh, July 10, 1813, FO 60/8.

29. Rtishchev to Alexander, October 14, 1813, *Akty*, V, 737-47; Treaty of Golestān, October 12 (24), 1813, *VPR*, VIII, photographic inset following p. 403.

CHAPTER IX

1. Tsitsianov to Alexander, May 22, 1805, and Gudovich to Budberg, November 14, 1806, and Tormasov to Mahdi Qoli Khān, May 10, 1810, and Mahdi Qoli Khān to Prince Abkhazov, June 21, 1827, and Paskevich to Foreign Minister Karl Nessel'rode, February 25, 1828, and Baron Rozen (commander-in-chief in the Caucasus) to Count Chernishev, March 3, 1832, and Nessel'rode to Rozen, June 4, 1836, *Akty*, II, 703, III, 338, IV, 551-52, VII, 458-59, VIII, 492, 479-80, see also VI, part 1, v; Gamba, II, 285; A. Sh. Mil'man, *Politicheskii stroi Azerbaidzhana v XIX-nachale XX vekov* (Baku, 1966), p. 65.

2. Paulucci to Lieutenant-General Repin (commandant of Baku), February 1812, and Paulucci to the minister of police, March 10, 1812, and anonymous secret report on Elizavetpol', 1812, *Akty*, V, 139, 20-21, 543; Gamba, II, 304; Mil'man, pp. 62-63, 69, 90-91, 95-96; Guseinov et al., II, 20-22.

3. Bulgakov to Gudovich, November 13, 1806, and plea of the Armenians of Elizavetpol' to Court Counselor Ivanov (customs director of the port of Astrakhan), July 18, 1809, and Budberg to Gudovich, November 14, 1809, and Tormasov to Repin, March 31, 1809, January 1, 1810, and register of Qobbeh's revenue under Sheikh ʻAli Khān, February 15, 1810, and Tormasov to Rumiantsev, June 22, 1810, and Akhverdov to Tormasov, December 12, 1810, and Paulucci to Mahdi Qoli Khān, December 5, 1811, and Paulucci to Lieutenant Colonel Parfenov, December 21, 1811, and minister of finances to Paulucci, January 30, 1812, and Treasury Expedition (of Georgian administration) to Rtishchev, June 11, 1812,

Akty, III, 350, 703, IV, 96, 489-90, 651, 648-49, 652-53, V, 18-19, 118, 130, 201; Gamba, II, 285, 294-99.

4. Budberg to Gudovich, December 4, 1806, and Gudovich to minister of education, July 27, 1807, and Gudovich to Kurakin, April 11, 1809, and anonymous secret report on Elizavetpol', 1812, and Rozen to Chernyshev, July 31, 1832, *Akty*, III, 351, 27, 359, V, 543, VIII, 496; A. Haxthausen, *Transcaucasia* (London, 1854), pp. 183, 442, 442 n.; Gamba, II, 294; Henry Willock (British chargé d'affaires in Iran) to George Canning (foreign minister), November 24, 1823, India Office, Political and Secret, Persia, XXXVI, 27; Qarābāghi, p. 59; Javānshir, pp. 61-62; Bakikhanov, pp. x-xi; Klaproth, *Tableau historique*, p. 149, Kh. Kh. Stewen, "Mémoire sur les provinces qui avoisinent le Caucase, tiré du voyage fait au Caucase en 1810 par le conseller de college Stewen," *Le Moniteur universel*, February 28, 1812, p. 240; Mil'man, p. 69; Guseinov et al., II, 20-21, 29-32; Akademiia Nauk SSSR, Institut Istorii, *Kolonial'naia politika Rossiiskogo tsarisma v Azerbaidzhane v 20-60-kh gg. XIX v.* (2 vols., Moscow, 1936-1937), I, 9.

5. Gudovich to State Treasurer Golubtsev, October 17, 1807, and Gudovich to Treasury Expedition (of Georgian administration), May 8, 1808, and Gudovich to Akhverdov, February 26, 1806, and Gudovich to Mostafā Khān of Shirvān, December 16, 1806, and Aseev to Gudovich, July 19, 1808, and Gudovich to Mahdi Qoli Khān of Qarābāgh, February 13, 1809, and Gudovich to Nesvetaev, May 9, 1808, and Tormasov to Aseev, April 22, 1809, and Aseev to Tormasov, August 15 and September 28, 1810, and Major General Stal' to Paulucci, September 30, 1811, and Ja'far Qoli Khān of Shakki to Paulucci, n.d. (1812), and Lisanevich to Rtishchev, October 7, 1812, and Rtishchev to 'Abbās Mirzā, May 8, 1815, *Akty*, III, 228-30, 299, 347, 467, IV, 489, 562-63, 566, V, 115, 125, 676, 759; Strachey, "Diary," VIII (pages unnumbered); Gamba, II, 159; Dupré, II, 265; Morier, "Diary," IV, f. 85, and *Second Journey*, pp. 227-28; Dubrovin, VI, 49; Beliavskii and Potto, I, 156; Guseinov et al., II, 22-23; Bournoutian, pp. 51, 58, 68.

6. Petition of the Muslim inhabitants of Tiflis (Tbilisi), n.d., and Tsitsianov to the *akhund* (low-level religious leader) of Elizavetpol', May 14, 1805, and anonymous secret report on Elizavetpol', 1812, *Akty*, II, 285, V, 542; Henry Willock to George Canning, November 24, 1823, India Office, Political and Secret, Persia, XXXVI, 27-28; Gordon, f. 19; Porter, *Travels in Georgia*, I, 122; Alcock, pp. 31, 34; Keppel, p. 290; A. M., "Slovenost' Shakh Gusein," *Severnaia Pchela* (1830), #112, #113 (pages unnumbered); I. Berezin, *Puteshestvie po Dagestanu i Zakavkaz'iu* (Kazan, 1850), part II, 37-38, part III, 18.

7. Gur'ev to Gudovich, March 7, 1808, and Repin to Tormasov, February 7, 1811, and Tormasov to Captain Veselago (of the Caspian fleet), February 11, 1810, and Rtishchev to Alexander, July 30, 1813, *Akty*, III, 358, IV, 92, 752-53, V, 340-41; K. Arsen'ev, *Nachertanie statistiki Rossiiskago gosudarstva* (2 parts, St. Petersburg, 1818), part I, 162-63; Bélanger, II, 83-85; Berezin, part I, 11, III, 114; E. de Cazalès, "Des Etablissemens russes dans l'Asie occidentale—guerres du Caucase," *Revue des deux mondes*, III (1838), pp. 601-2; Klaproth, *Tableau historique*, pp. 115, 117, 149, 169-70; Gamba, II, 149-50, 305, 328; M. K. Rozhkova, "Iz istorii ekonomicheskoi politiki Rossiiskogo Tsarizma v Zakavkaz'e," *Istorisheskie zapiski*, XVIII (1946), 169.

8. Nessel'rode's thoughts on establishing a border with Persia," n.d. (probably 1816), and Alexander's instructions to Ermolov, July 29, 1816, and Ermolov to Alexander, January 9, 1817, and Nessel'rode to Ermolov, March 13 and May 25, 1817, and Ermolov to Nessel'rode, October 1817, *Akty*, VI, part 2, 117, 122-27, 142, 147-48, 151, 177-79; J. E. Alexander, *Travels from India to England* (London, 1827), pp. 271-74; Claudius James Rich (company resident in Baghdad) to Secret Department (India), January 2, 1818, and Rich to president and governor in council (India), October 26, 1819, India Office, Political and Secret, Persia, XXXIII, 29, 223a-24a.

9. Alexander, pp. 288-89; Stephen Shairp (British consul-general in St. Petersburg) to George Hammond, September 19, 1805, and Gower to Fox, April 14, 1806, and Charles Stuart (British minister plenipotentiary in St. Petersburg) to Fox, July 31, 1806, and Stuart to Lord Viscount Howick, January 14 and 17, 1807, and Foreign Office to Lord Cathcart (British ambassador in St. Petersburg), July 24, 1812, and Cathcart to Castlereagh, FO 65/59, ff. 185-87, 65/62, ff. 153-54, 65/63, f. 69, 65/67, ff. 43-44, 46-48, 65/78, pp. 9-10, 65/80, ff. 151, 163; Moira to Morier, June 3 and October 13, 1815, FO 248/35, pp. 19-27, 32.

10. Treaty between Britain and Iran, November 25, 1814, Aitchison, XII, 53-56; unsigned (sender was a ranking official in the Foreign Office) to Morier, January 9, 1815, FO 60/10, ff. 37-38.

11. Cormick to Malcolm, May 20 and December 3, 1814, India Office, Home Miscellaneous Series, 736, pp. 497-98, 508; Alexander, pp. 76-78, 80-81; G. Fowler, *Three Years in Persia* (2 vols., London, 1841), II, 185-92; D'Arcy to Morier, December 11, 1814, FO 248/32, pp. 117-19; Willock to Lord Amhurst (governor-general, India), March 30, 1824, and Willock to George Canning, February 12, 1825, and June 27, 1826, India Office, Political and Secret, Persia, XXXVI, 259-61, XXXVIII, 64, 68-69, XXXIX, ff. 202-3.

12. Alexander, pp. 276-79; Macdonald to chairman and other members of the Secret Committee, October 28, 1826, India Office, Political and Secret, Persia, XXXIX, 761; Adamiyat, pp. 15-21, 28.

13. Fraser, *Travels*, pp. 308-9; Drouville, 1st ed., II, 126; J. Johnson, *A Journey from India to England through Persia*, (London, 1818), pp. 121-13, 214-15; Alexander, pp. 172, 216; Fowler, II, 145-48; Algar, *Religion*, pp. 85-89; G. Ouseley to Castlereagh, April 19, 1815, and Morier to Castlereagh, May 25, 1815, FO 60/10, ff. 25, 72; extract from Willock's journal, July 3, 1826, and Macdonald to chairman and other members of the Secret Committee of the court of directors, October 28, 1826, India Office, Political and Secret, Persia, XXXIX, ff. 279-80, 753-61; Jehāngir Mirzā, *Tārikh-e Nou*, A. Eqbāl, ed. (Tehran, 1327/1948), pp. 5-7; Hedāyat, IX, 644-47.

14. Willock to George Canning, August 18, 1826, and Captain Macdonald to the chairman and other members of the Secret Committee of the court of directors, September 6, 1826, May 10, and August 20, 1827, and Macdonald to George Swinton (secretary to the Political Department, India), January 16, July 22, and November 1, 1827, and Lieutenant George Willock (Henry Willock's brother), "A detail of occurrences in Tabreez since the 24th October to the 5th November 1827," and Lieutenant-Colonel William Monteith (member of the British mission in Iran), "Memorandum on the Siege of Erivan by the Russian Troops," December 17, 1827, India Office, Political and Secret, Persia, XXXIX, 407-11, 543-58, XL, 55-58, 567-78, 385, 589-91, XLI, 69-77, 177-95, 661-63; Alexander, pp. 189-91, 279-87; Fowler, II, 148-66; Fraser, *Account of Persia*, pp. 276-77; Mignan, I, 92, 107-8; Jehāngir Mirzā, pp. 9-93; Hedāyat, IX 647-66, 667-79.

15. Political and commercial treaties of Torkmānchāi, February 10 (22), 1828, Hurewitz, I, 96-101; "Translation of a Bond Granted by Abbas Mirza, Prince-Royal of Persia, to Lieutenant-Colonel Macdonald, British Envoy," 1828, Aitchison, XII, 57; Fowler, II, 169-71.

16. Fowler, I, 264, II, 61, 74; Adamiyat, p. 33; H. Algar, "An Introduction to the History of Freemasonry in Iran," *Middle Eastern Studies*, VI (1970), 276-77; H. F. Farmayan, "The Forces of Modernization in Nineteenth-Century Iran: A Historical Survey," W. R. Polk and R. L. Chambers, eds., *Beginnings of Modernization in the Middle East* (Chicago, 1968), pp. 120-24.

BIBLIOGRAPHY

Bibliography

ARCHIVAL MATERIALS

France

Archives Nationales, Paris:

AF IV 1686, dossiers, 1, 2, 3, 4.
AF IV 1697, dossier 5.
AF IV 1698, dossier 3.
AF IV 1699, dossier 3.
AF IV 1705, dossier 1.

Ministère des Affaires Étrangères, Archives, Paris:

Correspondence Politique—Perse, vols. VIII-XV.
Mémoires et Documents—Perse, vols. I, III, IV, VI, VII.
Mémoires et Documents—Russie, vol. XXXV.

Great Britain

British Museum, London:

Gordon, R., "Journal of Robert Gordon in Transcaucasia and from Tiflis to Moscow," Aberdeen Papers, vol. 179, Additional Manuscripts, 43, 217.
Jones (Brydges), H., "Letters and Papers," vol. II, Additional Manuscripts, 41, 768.
Layard Papers, vol. CCXI, Additional Manuscripts, 39,141.
Morier, J. J., "Diary," 6 vols., Additional Manuscripts, 33,839-44.
Porter, R. Ker, "Travels in the Caucasus, Georgia, Persia, Armenia," 2 vols., Additional Manuscripts, 14,758.
Price, W., "Journal of the Embassy to Persia," Additional Manuscripts, 19,270.
Wellesley Papers, series II, vols. X, XI, XII, Additional Manuscripts, 37,283-85.

Commonwealth Relations Office, India Office, London:

Correspondence with Robert Dundas, microfilm reel 647.
Frederick, E., "Persian Journal 1801" (sic., 1810), Miscellaneous European Manuscripts, D 110, D 111.

Home Miscellaneous Series, vols. 470-72, 474, 477-79, 504, 591, 733, 736-737.
Masson, C., "Journals and Travels," II, Miscellaneous European Manuscripts, E 163.
Monteith, W., "Routes in Azerbaijan, Kurdistan and Armenia, 1811-1829," Miscellaneous
European Manuscripts, B 24.
Oriental History and Antiquities, Miscellaneous Manuscripts, C 9.
Persia and Persian Gulf Factory Records, G/29, vols. 20-31.
Persian Gulf Territories, R/15/1/0, vols. 4-15.
Political and Secret, Persia, vols. 2, 31, 33-40, 42-50.

National Library of Scotland, Edinburgh:
Melville Papers, MSS 59, 1071.

National Library of Wales, Aberystwyth:
Kentchurch Court Papers.

Public Record Office, Foreign Office, London:
FO 60, vols. 1-10.
FO 65, vols. 46, 54-55, 57-59, 62-64, 66-69, 71-72, 76-80, 84.
FO 78, vol. 5.
FO 95/8, vol. 6.
FO 181, vols. 6, 8.
FO 248, vols. 2-3, 5-9, 11-14, 16, 18-19, 21-25, 27-35.

Public Records Office, War Office, London:
WO 1, vol. 623.

Somerset Record Office, Taunton:
Papers of Richard Charles Strachey, vols., VI-VIII.

PUBLISHED DOCUMENTS

Aitchison, C. U., ed., *A Collection of Treaties, Engagements, and Sunnuds Relating to India and Neighboring Countries*, 2nd ed. (14 vols., Calcutta, 1929-1933), XII.
Arkhiv Grafov Mordvinovikh, V. A. Bil'bassov, ed. (10 vols., St. Petersburg, 1901-1903), V.
Bartenev, P., ed., "Iz Zapisok Grafa E. F. Komarovskago," *Ocemnadtsatyi vek* (4 vols., 1869), I, 386-419.
Broglie (Duc de), "La Politique de la Russie en 1800 d'après un document inédit," *Revue d'histoire diplomatique*, 1889, pp. 1-12.
"Bumagi Imperatritsky Ekateriny II," A. K. Grot, ed., *SIRIO*, XXVII (1880).
Dehérain, H., "Lettres inédites de membres de la mission Gardane en Perse (1807-9)," *Revue de l'histoire des colonies françaises,* XVI (1923), 249-82.
"Diplomaticheskiia snosheniia Rossii s Frantsiei v epokhu Napoleona I," A. S. Trachevskii, ed., *SIRIO*, LXX (1890), LXXXII (1892), LXXXVIII (1893).
Gardane, A., *Mission du Général Gardane en Perse sous le premier empire* (Paris, 1865).
Grigorovich, N., ed., "Kantsler Kniaz' Aleksandr Andreevich Bezborodko," *SIRIO*, XXVI (1879) and XXIX (1881).
Hurewitz, J. C., ed., *Diplomacy in the Near and Middle East* (2 vols., Princeton, 1972), I.
Karatygin, P. P., ed., "Proekt russko-frantsuzskoi ekspeditsii v Indiiu 1800 g.," *Russkaia starina*, VIII (1873), 401-10.
Maikov, P. M., ed., "Pis'ma A. A. Bezborodka grafu P. A. Rumiantsovu, 1777-1793 gg.," *Starina i Novizna*, book 3 (1900), 160-311.

Nikolai Mikhailovich (Grandduke), ed., *Graf Pavel Aleksandrovich Stroganov* (3 vols., St. Petersburg, 1903), II, III.

"Pis'ma grafa F. V. Rastopchina k Kniaziu P. D. Tsitsianovu (1803-1806)," *Deviatnadtsatyi vek*, 1872, book II, 1-113.

"Pis'ma k grafu P. S. Potemkinu," Russkii Arkhiv, 1879, book VIII, columns 429-41.

"Posol'stvo grafa P. A. Tolstogo v Parizhe v 1807 i 1808," N. K. Shil'der, ed., *SIRIO*, LXXXIX (1893).

Russia, State Council, *Arkhiv Gosudarstvennago Soveta* (5 vols., St. Petersburg, 1869-1904), I-III.

Russia, Viceroyalty of the Caucasus, *Akty sobrannye kavkazskoiu arkheograficheskoiu kommissieiu* (12 vols., Tiflis, 1866-1904), I-VIII.

Tolstoi, Iu. V., ed., "Proekt russko-frantsuzskoi ekspeditsii v Indiiu," *Russkaia starina, XV (1878), 216-17.*

Tsagareli, A. A., *Gramoty i drugie istoricheskie dokumenty XVIII stoletiia otnosiashchiesia do Gruzii* (3 vols., St. Petersburg, 1891-1902), II, part ii.

Union of Soviet Socialist Republics, Ministry of Foreign Affairs, *Vneshniaia Politika Rossii*, series I (1801-1815) (7 vols., Moscow, 1970).

Vorontsov, M. S., *Arkhiv Kniazia Vorontsova*, P. Bartenev, ed. (40 vols., Moscow, 1870-1895), VIII, IX, XIII, XIV, XXIV, XV, XXXVI.

Wilson, G., ed., "Some Hitherto Unpublished Dispatches of Captain John Malcolm," *Journal of the Royal Central Asian Society*, XVI (1929), 428-44.

MEMOIRES, TRAVELERS' ACCOUNTS, AND CONTEMPORARY ESSAYS

A. M., "Slovenost' Shakh Gusein," *Severnaia Pchela* (1830) numbers 112, 113.

Alcock, T., *Travels in Russia, Persia, Turkey, and Greece in 1828-29* (London, 1831).

Alexander, J. E., *Travels from India to England* (London, 1827).

Armstrong, T. B., *Journal of Travels in the Seat of War* (London, 1831).

Aucher-Éloy, P. M. R., *Relations de voyages en Orient de 1830 à 1838*, P. A. Jaubert, ed. (Paris, 1843).

Bélanger, C., *Voyage aux Indes-Orientales par le nord de l'Europe, les provinces du Caucase, la Géorgie, l'Arménie et la Perse pendant les années 1825-1829* (3 vols., Paris, 1834).

Bell, J., *Travels from St. Petersburg in Russia to Various Parts of Asia* (2 vols., Edinburgh, 1788).

Berezin, I., *Puteshestvie po Dagestanu i Zakavkaz'iu* (Kazan, 1850).

Brougham, H., *An Inquiry into the Colonial Policy of the European Powers* (2 vols., New York, 1970, facsimile reprint of Edinburgh 1803 edition).

Buckingham, J. S., *Travels in Assyria, Media, and Persia* (London, 1829).

Campbell, J., "The Russo-Persian Frontier, 1810," *Journal of the Royal Central Asian Society*, XVIII, (1931), 223-32.

Caulaincourt, A. A. L., *Mémoires* (3 vols., Paris, 1933), I.

Chardin, J., *Voyages du Chevalier Chardin en Perse, et autres lieux de l'Orient*, L. Langlés, ed. (10 vols., Paris, 1811).

Chulkov, M. D., *Istoricheskoe opisanie Rossiiskoi kommertsii* (7 vols., St. Petersburg, 1781-1788), II, book 2, VII, book 2.

Danibegov, R., *Puteshestvie v Indiiu* (Moscow, 1815).

Derzhavin, G. R., *Stikhotvoreniia* (Leningrad, 1957).

Drouville, G., *Voyage en Perse fait en 1812 et 1813*, 1st ed., (2 vols., Paris, 1825).

Dumas, J. -B., ed., *Un Fourrier de Napoléon vers l'Inde, les papiers du Lieutenant-Général Trézel*, 2nd ed. (Paris, 1915).

Dupré, A., *Voyage en Perse fait dans les années 1807, 1808, et 1809* (2 vols., Paris, 1819).

"Extracts from the Travels of Pietro delle Valle in Persia," J. Pinkerton, ed., *A General Collection of the Best and Most Interesting Voyages and Travels in All Parts of the World* (17 vols., London, 1811), IX.

Forster, G., *A Journey from Bengal to England* (2 vols., London, 1798).

Fowler, G., *Three Years in Persia* (2 vols., London, 1841).

Fraser, J. B., *Narrative of a Journey into Khorassan* (2 vols., London, 1825).

————, *Travels and Adventures in the Persian Provinces on the Southern Banks of the Caspian Sea* (London, 1826).

————, *Travels in Koordistan, Mesopotamia* (London, 1826).

————, *A Winter's Journey from Constantinople to Tehran* (London, 1838).

Freygang, W., and Freygang, F. K., *Letters from the Caucasus and Georgia* (London, 1823).

Gamba, J. F., *Voyage dans la Russie méridionale et particulièrement dans les provinces situées au-delà du Caucase, fait depuis 1820 jusqu'en 1824* (2 vols., Paris, 1826).

Gardane, P. A. L., *Journal d'un voyage dans la Turquie d'Asie et la Perse fait en 1807 et 1808* (Paris and Marseilles, 1809).

Gmelin, S. G., *Reise durch Russland* (3 vols., St. Petersburg, 1774).

Haxthausen, A., *Transcaucasia* (London, 1854).

Hollingberry, W., *A Journal of Observations Made during the British Embassy to the Court of Persia in the Years 1799, 1800 and 1801* (Calcutta, 1814).

Jaubert, P. A., *Voyage en Arménie et en Perse* (Paris, 1821).

Johnson, J., *A Journey from India to England through Persia* (London, 1818).

Jones, (Brydges), H., *Account of the Transactions of His Majesty's Mission to the Court of Persia in the Years 1807-1811* (2 vols., London, 1834).

Keppel, G. T., *Personal Narrative of a Journey from India to England* (London, 1827).

Klaproth, J. von, *Tableau historique, géographique et ethnographique du Caucase et des provinces limitrophes entre la Russie et la Perse* (Paris, 1827).

————, *Travels in the Caucasus and Georgia Performed in the Years 1807 and 1808*, F. Shoberl, trans. (London, 1814).

Kosven, M. O., and Khashaev, Kh. M., eds., *Istoriia geografiia i etnografiia Dagestana XVIII-XIX vv.* (Moscow, 1958).

Kotov, F. A., *Khozhdenie kuptsa Fedota Kotova v Persiiu* (Moscow, 1958).

Kotzebue, M. von, *Narrative of a Journey into Persia in the Suite of the Imperial Russian Embassy in the Year 1817* (London, 1819).

Lerch, J. J., "Auszug aus dem Tagebuch von eine Reise, welche D. Lerche von 1733 bis 1735 aus Moscau nach Astrachan und in die auf Westseite des Caspischen Sees belegene Länder, gethan hat," *Magazin für die neue Historie und Geographie*, III (1769), 1-44.

————, "Nachricht von der zweiten Reise nach Persien," *Magazin für die neue Historie und Geographie*, X (1776), 365-476.

Lomonosov, M. V., "Kratkoe opisanie raznykh puteshestvii" (1763), *Polnoe sobranie sochinenii* (10 vols., Moscow and Leningrad, 1950-1959), VI, 414-98.

Lumsden, T., *A Journey from Merut in India to London through Arabia, Persia, etc.* (London, 1822).

Lyall, R., *Travels in Russia, the Krimea, the Caucasus and Georgia* (2 vols., London, 1825).

Macdonald (Kinneir), J., *A Geographical Memoir of the Persian Empire* (London, 1813).

————, *Journey through Asia Minor, Armenia, and Koordistan in the Years 1813 and 1814* (London, 1818).

Malcolm, J., *Sketches of Persia* (London, 1845).

Marschall von Bieberstein, F., *Tableau des provinces situées sur la côte occidentale de la mer Caspienne entre les fleuves Terek et Kour* (St. Petersburg, 1798).

Masson, C. F., *Mémoires secrets sur la Russie* (4 vols., Amsterdam and Paris, 1800-1803).

Mémoires posthumes du feldmaréchal Comte de Stedingk, General Björnstjerna, ed. (3 vols., Paris, 1845), II.

Mignan, R. *A Winter Journey through Russia, the Caucasian Alps, and Georgia, thence into Koordistan* (2 vols., London, 1839).

Monteith, W., "Journal of a Tour through Azerbijan and the Shores of the Caspian," *Journal of the Royal Geographical Society*, III (1833), 1-58.

—————, *Kars and Erzeroum* (London, 1856).

Montesquieu, C. L. de Secondat, Baron de, *The Spirit of the Laws*, T. Nugent, trans., F. Neumann, ed. (New York, 1966).

Morier, J. J., *Journey through Persia, Armenia and Asia Minor to Constantinople* (London, 1812).

—————, *A Second Journey through Persia, Armenia and Asia Minor to Constantinople* (London, 1818).

—————, "Some account of the Iliyats or Wandering Tribes of Persia Obtained in the Years 1814 and 1815," *Journal of the Royal Geographical Society*, VIII (1937), 230-42.

Neopatras, Kh., "Ob"iasnenie," *Russkii arkhiv*, 1873, book I, columns 863-76.

Olearius, A., *The Voyages and Travels of the Ambassadors from the Duke of Holstein, to the Great Duke of Muscovy, and the King of Persia*, J. Davies, trans. (London, 1672).

Olivier, G. A., *Voyage dans l'empire Othman, l'Egypte et la Perse* (3 vols., Paris, 1807).

"O Pokhode Rossiiskikh voisk v 1796 godu v Dagestan i Persiiu pod komandoiu Grafa Valeriana Aleksandrova Zubova," *Otechestvenyia zapiski* (1827), 127-68, 266-314.

"O Pokhode sukhim putem v Ost-Indiiu," *Vestnik Evropy* (June 1808), 174-78.

"Otryvok iz puteshestviia po Zakavkaz'iu v 1828, 1829, i 1830 godakh," *Severnaia Pchela* (1840), number 255, 1019-20.

Ouseley, W., *Travels in Various Countries of the East* (3 vols., London, 1821).

"Overland Route through Persia," *Asiatic Journal* (1823), 6-8.

Porter, R. Ker, *Travels in Georgia, Persia, Armenia, Ancient Babylonia, etc., during the Years 1817, 1818, 1819, and 1820* (2 vols., London, 1821).

R. C. M. (R. C. Money), *Journal of a Tour in Persia during the Years 1824 and 1825* (London, 1828).

Raynal, G. T., *Histoire philosophique et politique des etablissemens et du commerce des Européens dans les deux Indes*, 2nd ed. (10 vols., Geneva, 1780).

Rottiers, B. E. A., *Itinéraire de Tiflis à Constantinople* (Brussels, 1829).

Rousseau, J. B., *Extrait de l'itinéraire d'un voyage en Perse par la voie de Bagdad* (Paris, 1813).

Spilman, J., *A Journey through Russia into Persia by Two English Gentlemen* (London, 1742).

Steven, Kh. Kh., "Mémoire sur les provinces qui avoisinent le Caucase, tiré du voyage fait au Caucase en 1810 par le conseller de college Stewen," *Le Moniteur universel*, February 12, 1812, p. 162; February 21, 1812, p. 212; February 28, 1812, p. 240; March 8, 1812, pp. 269-70.

Tancoigne, J. M., *A Narrative of a Journey into Persia* (London, 1820).

Teule, J. C., *Pensées et notes critiques extraites du journal de mes voyages dans l'empire du Sultan dans les provinces Russes, Géorgiennes, et Tartars et dans le royaume de Perse* (2 vols., Paris, 1842), II.

Tuchkov, S. A., *Zapiski Sergeia Alekseevicha Tuchkova 1776-1808* (St. Petersburg, 1908).

Wagner, M., *Travels in Persia, Georgia, and Koordistan* (3 vols., London, 1856).

Wilbraham, R., *Travels in the Transcaucasian Provinces of Russia* (London, 1839).

CHRONICLES

'Abd ol-Hamid, Hāji Seyyed, "Rodoslovnaia Shekinskikh khanov i ikh potomkov," F. Babaev, ed., *Iz istorii Shekinskogo khanstva* (Baku, 1958), pp. 55-63.

Asef, Mohammad Hashem, *Rostam ot-Tavārikh*, M. Moshiri, ed. (Tehran, 1348/1969).

Bagrationi, D., *Istoriia Gruzii*, A. A. Rogav, ed. (Tbilisi, 1971).

Bakikhanov, 'Abbās Qoli 'Āqā, *Giulistan-Iram* (Golestān-e Eram), (Baku, 1926).

Batonishvili, V., *Obozrenie istorii Gruzinskago naroda (St. Petersburg, 1814)*.

Brosset, M. F., ed. and trans., *Histoire de la Géorgie depuis l'antiquité jusqu'au XIXe siècle* (4 parts, St. Petersburg, 1849), II, part ii.

Domboli, 'Abd or-Razzāq, *Ma'āser Soltāniyeh* (Tehran, 1392 Qomri/1972-1973), a translation of the portion dealing with events up to 1811 was made by Harford Jones Brydges, *The Dynasty of the Kajars* (London, 1833).

Eskandar, Monshi, *Tārikh-e 'Alam Ārā-ye 'Abbāsi* (2 vols., Tehran, 1334-1335/1955-1956).

Hedāyat, Rezā Qoli Khān, *Rouzat os-Safā-ye Nāseri*, addition to the chronicle of Mir Khānd (10 vols., Tehran, 1960), IX.

Javānshir, Ahmedbeg, "O politicheskom sushchestvovanii Karabakhskogo khanstva (s 1747 po 1805 god)", E. B. Shukiurzade, trans., *Istoriia Karabakhskogo khanstva* (Baku, 1961).

Jehāngir, Mirzā, *Tārikh-e Nou*, A. Eqbāl, ed. (Tehran, 1327/1948).

Karim, Āqā Fath (probable author), "Kratkaia istoriia Shekinskikh khanov," F. Babaev, ed., *Iz istorii Shekinskogo khanstva* (Baku, 1958), pp. 41-53.

Qarābāghi, Mirzā Jamāl Javānshir, *Istoriia Karabaga* (Baku, 1959).

Tadhkirat al-Muluk, V. Minorskii, ed. and trans., E. J. W. Gibb Memorial, New Series, XVI, (London, 1943).

BIBLIOGRAPHIES

Beskrovnyi, L. G., *Ocherki po istochnikovedeniiu voennoi istorii Rossii* (Moscow, 1957).

Dubrovin, N. F., *Istoriia voiny i vladychestva russkikh na Kavkaze* (6 vols., St. Petersburg, 1871-1878), I.

Elwell-Sutton, L. P., *A Guide to Iranian Area Study* (Ann Arbor, 1952).

Farmayan, H. F., *Iran* (Washington, D. C., 1951).

Kosven, M. O., "Materialy po istorii etnograficheskogo izucheniia Kavkaza v russkoi nauke," *Kavkazskii etnograficheskii sbornik*, I (1955), 265-374; II (1958), 139-274; III (1962), 158-281.

Miansarov, M. M., *Bibliographia Caucasia et Transcaucasia* (St. Petersburg, 1874-1876).

Sabā, M., *Bibliographie de l'Iran* (Paris, 1936).

Storey, C. A., *Persian Literature* (2 vols., London, 1927-1971), I, section ii, fasciculus 2.

Sverchevskaia, A. K., *Bibliografiia Irana* (Moscow, 1967).

Wainwright, M. D., and Matthews, N., *A Guide to Western Manuscripts and Documents in the British Isles Relating to South and Southeast Asia* (London, 1965).

Wilson, A. T., *A Bibliography of Persia* (Oxford, 1930).

SECONDARY SOURCES

Abdullaev, F., *Iz istorii russko-iranskikh otnoshenii i angliiskoi politiki v Irane v nachale XIX v.* (Tashkent, 1971).

Abdullaev, G. B., "Iz istorii Azerbaidzhana vo vtoroi polovine XVIII v.," *Trudy Institut Istorii* (Baku, 1960), XIV, 52-112.

Abrahamian, E., "Oriental Despotism: The Case of Qajar Iran," *International Journal of Middle Eastern Studies*, V (1974), 3-31.

Adamczyk, T., *Fürst G. A. Potemkin* (Berlin, 1936).

Adamiyat, F., "The Diplomatic Relations of Persia with Britain, Turkey, and Russia, 1815-1830," Ph.D. dissertation (University of London, 1949).

Adonts, M. A., *Ekonomicheskoe razvitie vostochnoi Armenii v XIX veke* (Yerevan, 1957).

Akademiia Nauk SSSR, Institut Istorii, *Kolonial'naia politika Rossiiskogo tsarizma v Azerbaidzhane v 20-60 kh gg. XIX v.* (2 vols., Moscow, 1936-1937), I, 5-32.

Algar, H., "An Introduction to the History of Free masonry in Iran," *Middle Eastern Studies*, VI (1970), 276-96.

————, *Religion and State in Iran 1785-1906* (Berkeley and Los Angeles, 1969).

Allen, W. E. D., *A History of the Georgian People: From the Beginning down to the Russian Conquest in the Nineteenth Century* (London, 1932).

Anderson, M. S., *Britain's Discovery of Russia, 1552-1815* (New York, 1958).

————, *The Eastern Question, 1774-1923* (London, 1966).

Araratskii, A., "Svedenii o pokhode grafa Zubova v Zakavkaz'e," *Sbornik Gazety Kavkaz,* 1847, pp. 67-84.

Arasteh, A. R., *Man and Society in Iran* (Leiden, 1964).

Arsen'ev, K., *Nachertanie statistiki Rossiiskago gosudarstva* (2 parts, St. Petersburg, 1818).

Artamonov, L. K., *Severnyi Azerbaidzhan* (Tiflis, 1890).

Ashraf, A., "Historical Obstacles to the Development of a Bourgeoisie in Iran," M. A. Cook ed., *Studies in the Economic History of the Middle East* (London, 1970), pp. 308-32.

"Aslanduz," *Severnaia Pchela*, 1834, number 276, 1203.

Atkin, M. A., "The Khanates of the Eastern Caucasus and the Origins of the First Russo-Iranian War," Ph.D. dissertation (Yale University, 1976).

————, "The Pragmatic Diplomacy of Paul I: Russia's Relations with Asia, 1796-1801," *Slavic Review*, 38, number 1 (March 1979), 60-74.

————, "The Strange Death of Ebrāhim Khalil Khān of Qarābāgh," *Iranian Studies*, 12 (1979).

Avery, P. W., "An Enquiry into the Outbreak of the Second Russo-Persian War, 1826-1828," C. E. Bosworth, ed., *Iran and Islam* (Edinburgh, 1971), pp. 17-45.

————, *Modern Iran* (New York, 1965).

————, and Simmons, J. B., "Persia on a Cross of Silver, 1880-1890," *Middle Eastern Studies*, X (1974), 259-86.

Baddeley, J., *The Russian Conquest of the Caucasus* (New York, 1969, facsimile reprint of London 1908 edition).

Bakhash, S., "The Evolution of the Qajar Bureaucracy: 1779-1879," *Middle Eastern Studies*, VII (1971), 139-68.

Balaian, B. P., "Prisoedinenie Zakavkaz'ia k Rossii v obveshchenii sovremennoi iranskoi istoriografii," *Kratkie soobshcheniia Instituta Narodov Azii Akademii Nauk SSSR*, number 73 (1963), Trudy sessii po voprosam istorii i ekonomiki Afganistana, Irana, Turtsii, 192-97.

Banani, A., *The Modernization of Iran* (Stanford, 1961).

Baratov (Prince), "Kratkoe obozrenii glavneishikh prichin padeniia Gruzinskago tsarstva," *Sbornik Gazety Kavkaz*, 1848, pp. 87-96.

Bartol'd, V. V., *Istoriia izucheniia vostoka v Evrope i Rossii* (Leningrad, 1925).

————, "K istorii Derbenta," *Sochineniia* (8 vols., Moscow, 1963-1973), II, part i, 786-87.

————, "Mesto prikaspiiskikh oblastei v istorii musul'manskogo mira," *Sochineniia* (8 vols., Moscow, 1963-1973), II, part i, 750-72.

Bearce, G. D., *British Attitudes toward India 1784-1858* (London, 1961).

Beely, H., "A Project of Alliance with Russia in 1802," *English Historical Review*, XLIX (1934), 497-502.

Beliavskii, N. N., and Potto, V. A., *Utverzhdenie Russkago vladychestva na Kavkaze* (12 vols., Tiflis, 1901-1902), I, II.

Bennigsen, A., "Peter the Great, the Ottoman Empire, and the Caucasus," *Canadian American Slavic Studies*, VIII (1974), 311-18.

Berdzenishvili, N. A.; Dzhakhishvili, I. A.; and Dzhanashia, S., *Istoriia Gruzii* (2 vols., Tbilisi, 1946), I.

Bezobrazov, P. V., *O snosheniiakh Rossii s Frantsiei* (Moscow, 1892).

Bilbassoff, B. (Bil'bassov, V. A.), *Geschichte Katharina II* (2 vols., Berlin, 1891-1893).

Binā, A. A., *La Question iranienne au debut du XIXeme siècle* (Paris, 1939).

"Biographical Sketch of His Late Royal Highness Abbas-Mirza," *Journal of the Royal Asian Society*, I (1834), 322.

Biographie nouvelle des contemporains ou dictionaire historique raisoné (20 vols., Paris, 1820-1825).

Bournoutian, G. A., "Eastern Armenia on the Eve of the Russian Conquest: The Khanate of Erevan under the Governorship of Hoseyn Qoli Khan Qajar, 1807-1827," Ph.D. dissertation (University of California at Los Angeles, 1976).

Bronevskii, S. M., *Noveishiia geografocheskiia i istoricheskiia izvestiia o Kavkaze* (2 parts, Moscow, 1823).

Brunn, G., *Europe and the French Imperium, 1799-1814* (New York, 1938).

Buchan, J., ed., *The Baltic and Caucasian States (London, 1923)*.

Butkov, P. G., *Materialy dlia novoi istorii Kavkaza s 1722 po 1803* (3 vols., St. Petersburg, 1869).

Byhan, A., *La Civilization caucasienne*, G. Montandon, trans., (Paris, 1936).

Cazalès, E. de, "Des Etablissemens russes dans l'Asie occidentale—Guerres du Caucase," *Revue des deux mondes*, II (1838), 770-829; III (1838), 585-626, 772-806.

Chahan de Cirbied, J., *Détails sur la situation actuelle du royaume de Perse* (Paris, 1816).

Crawford, D. G., *Roll of the India Medical Service 1615-1930* (London, 1930).

Curzon, G. N., *Persia and the Persian Question* (2 vols., London, 1892).

Daniel, N., *Islam, Europe, and Empire* (Edinburgh, 1966).

Davies, C. C., "Rivalries in India," J. O. Lindesay, ed., *The Old Regime, 1713-1763*, in *The New Cambridge Modern History* (14 vols., Cambridge, 1957-1979), VII, 541-65.

Debidour, A., "Le Général Fabvier, sa vie et ses ecrits," *Annales de l'Est* (1887), pp. 3-33, 310-48.

Deherain, H., "Les Preliminaires de l'alliance franco-persane sous le Premier Empire," *Académie des sciences coloniales, comptes rendues des séances,* VI (1925-1926), 241-52.

Delrieu, A., "Une Ambassade francaise à la cour de Perse sous l'empire 1808," *Revue britannique*, XX (1854), 175-220.

Dickson, M. B., "The Fall of the Safavi Dynasty," *Journal of the American Oriental Society*, LXXXII (1962), 503-17.

Dictionary of National Biography (63 vols., London, 1885-1900).

Dodwell, H. H., et al., *The Cambridge History of India*, 3rd Indian reprint (5 vols., Delhi, 1963-1968), V.

Dorn, B., "Geschichte Schirwans unter den Statthaltern und Chanen von 1558-1820," *Mémoires de l'Académie impériale des sciences de St-Petersbourg*, VIeme série, sciences politiques, histoire, philologie, V (1845), 317-434.

Driault, J. -E., "La Mission de Gardanne en Perse (1807-1809) d'après les Archives nationales et les Archives du ministère des affaires étrangerès," *Revue d'histoire moderne et contemporaine*, II (1900-1901), 121-55.

―――, "Napoléon à Finkenstein," *Revue d'histoire diplomatique (1899)*, 404-62.

―――, *La Politique orientale de Napoléon, Sébastiani et Gardane (1806-1808)* (Paris, 1904).

Druzhinina, E. I., *Severnoe Prichernomor'e v 1775-1800 gg.* (Moscow, 1959).

Dubrovin, N. F., *Istoriia voiny i vladychestva russkikh na Kavkaze* (6 vols., St. Petersburg, 1871-1888).

Edwards, H. S., *Russian Projects against India from Czar Peter to General Skobeleff* (London, 1885).

Ellis, E. R. I., "British Policy toward Persia and the Defense of India 1798-1807," Ph.D. dissertation (University of London, 1968).

Encyclopaedia of Islam, 1st ed. (Leidon and London, 1913-1934), 2nd ed. (Leiden and London, 1960+).

F. M., *Memoir of the Right Honorable Sir John McNeil* (London, 1910).

Fadeev, A. V., *Rossiia i Kavkaz, pervoi treti XIX v.* (Moscow, 1960).

————, *Rossiia i vostochnyi krizis 20-kh godov XIX veka* (Moscow, 1952).

Farmayan, H. F., "The Forces of Modernization in Nineteenth-Century Iran: A Historical Survey," W. R. Polk and R. L. Chambers, eds., *Beginnings of Modernization in the Middle East* (Chicago, 1968), pp. 119-51.

————, "Observations on Sources of Study of Nineteenth- and Twentieth-Century Iranian History," *International Journal of Middle East Studies*, V (1974), 32-49.

Fisher, A. W., "Enlightened Despotism and Islam under Catherine II," *Slavic Review*, XXVII (1968), 542-53.

————, *The Russian Annexation of the Crimea 1772-1783* (Cambridge, 1970).

Florovskii, A. V., "K istorii ekonomicheskikh idei v Rossii v XVIII v.," *Nauchnye trudy Russkago narodnago universiteta v Prage*, I (1928).

Fraser, J. B., *An Historical and Descriptive Account of Persia from the Earliest Ages to the Present* (Edinburgh, 1834).

Foust, C. M., *Muscovite and Mandarin: Russia's Trade with China and its Setting* (Chapel Hill, 1969).

Gaffarel, P., "La Mission en Perse du Général Gardane sous Napoléon I," *La Revue politique et littéraire*, II^(ème) série, XXXIII (1878), 773-79.

Gagemeister, Iu., *O rasprostranenii Rossiiskago gosudarstva s edinoderzhaviia Petra I-go do smerti Aleksandra I-go* (St. Petersburg, 1835).

Gerhard, D., *England und der Aufstieg Russlands* (Berlin, 1933).

Geyer, D., *Der russische Imperialismus* (Göttingen, 1977).

Griffiths, D. M., "Russian Court Politics and the Question of an Expansionist Foreign Policy under Catherine II, 1762-1783," Ph.D. dissertation (Cornell, 1967).

Grimsted, P. K., *The Foreign Ministers of Alexander I* (Berkeley and Los Angeles, 1969).

Grunebaum, G. E. von, "The Structure of the Muslim Town," *Islam* (London, 1955), pp. 141-58.

Grunwald, C. de, *Les Alliances franco-russes* (Paris, 1965).

————, *Trois siècles de diplomatie russe* (Paris, 1945).

Guseinov, I. A., et al., eds., *Istoriia Azerbaidzhana* (3 vols., Baku, 1958-1963), I, II.

Hambly, G. R. G., "An Introduction to the Economic Organization of Early Qajar Iran," *Iran* II (1964), 69-81.

Haumant, E., *La Culture francaise en Russie* (Paris, 1910).

Heckscher, E., *Mercantilism*, M. Shapiro, trans. (2 vols., London, 1935).

Holditch, T. *The Gates of India* (London, 1910).

Hopkins, D., *The Danger to British India from French Invasion and Missionary Establishments* (London, 1809).

Hösch, E., "Das sogenannte 'Griechische Projekt' Katharinas II," *Jahrbücher für Geschichte Osteuropas*, XII (1964), 168-206.

Hurani, A. H., and Stern, S. M., *The Islamic City* (Oxford, 1970).

Ibragimbeili, Kh. M., *Rossia i Azerbaidzhan v pervoi treti XIX veka* (Moscow, 1969).

Igamberdiev, M. A., *Iran v mezhdunarodnykh otnosheniiakh pervoi treti XIX v.* (Samarkand, 1961).

Ingram, E., "An Aspiring Buffer-State: Anglo-Persian Relations in the Third Coalition, 1804-1807," *The Historical Journal*, XVI (1973), 509-33.

Ioannisian, A. R., *Prisoedinenie Zakavkaz'ia k Rossii i mezhdunarodnye otnosheniia v nachale XIX stoletiia* (Yerevan, 1958).

————, "Russkaia diplomatiia i Armianskii vopros v 80-kh godakh XVIII stoletiia," *Voprosy istorii*, VI (1947), 94-105.

Ismailov, M., "Ob uchastii Azerbaidzhantsev v russko-iranskikh i russko-turetskikh voinakh pervoi treti XIX v.," *Trudy Instituta istorii i filosofii Akademii Nauk Azerbadzhanshoi SSR*, IV (1954), 5-19.

Iu-va, "Materialy dlia biografii General-leitnanta Knorringa," *Sbornik Gazety Kavkaz* (1848), 259-63.

Ivanov, M. S., *Ocherk istorii Irana* (Moscow, 1952).

Jaubert, P. A., "Histoire persane de la dynastie des Kadjars," *Journal asiatique*, XIII (1834), 122.

Kafengauz, B., *Vneshniaia politika pri Petre I* (Moscow, 1942).

Karpovich, M. M., "Kommentarii: eshche o russkom messianizme," *Novyi Zhurnal*, LIV (1958), 271-89.

Kaye, J. W., *The Life and Correspondence of Major General Sir John Malcolm* (2 vols., London, 1856).

Kazemzadeh, F., *Russia and Britain in Persia, 1864-1914* (New Haven, 1968).

————, "Russia and the Middle East," I. J. Lederer, ed., *Russian Foreign Policy* (New Haven, 1962), pp. 489-530.

————, "Russian Penetration of the Caucasus," T. Hunczak, ed., *Russian Imperialism from Ivan the Great to the Revolution* (New Brunswick, 1974), pp. 239-63.

Kaziev, M. A., ed., *Azerbaidzhan* (Baku, 1960).

Keddie, N. R., "The Iranian Power Structure and Social Change 1800-1969: An Overview," *International Journal of Middle East Studies*, II (1971), 3-200.

Kellenbenz, H., "Der russische Transithandel mit dem Orient im 17 und zu Beginn des 18 Jahrhunderts," *Jahrbücher für Geschichte Osteuropas*, XII (1965), 481-98.

Kelly, J. B., *Britain and the Persian Gulf, 1795-1850* (Oxford, 1968).

Kiniapina, N. S., *Vneshniaia politika Rossii pervoi poloviny XIX v.* (Moscow, 1963).

Koebner, R., *Empire* (New York, 1961).

Krausse, A., *Russia in Asia* (London, 1899).

Lambton, A. K. S., "Impact of the West on Iran," *International Affairs*, XXXIII (1957), 12-25.

————, *Landlord and Peasant in Persia* (London, 1969).

————, "Persian Trade under the Early Qajars," D. S. Richards, ed., *Islam and the Trade of Asia—A Colloquium* (Oxford, 1970), pp. 215-44.

Lang, D. M., *The Last Years of the Georgian Monarchy, 1658-1832* (New York, 1957).

Lapidus, I. M., *Middle Eastern Cities* (Berkeley and Los Angeles, 1969).

Lebedev, V. I., "Posol'stvo Artemiia Volynskogo v Persiiu," *Izvestiia Akademii Nauk SSSR*, V (1948), 528-39.

Lensen, G. A., ed., *Russia's Eastward Expansion* (Englewood Cliffs, 1964).

Le Strange, G., *The Lands of the Eastern Caliphate* (Cambridge, 1905).

Lichtheim, G., *Imperialism* (New York, 1971).

Lockhart, L., *The Fall of the Safavi Dynasty and the Afghan Occupation of Persia* (Cambridge, 1958).

————, *Nadir Shah* (London, 1938).

————, "The 'Political Testament' of Peter the Great," *Slavonic and East European Review*, XIV (1935-1936), 438-41.

Luxenburg, N., "Russian Expansion into the Caucasus and the English Relationship Thereto," Ph.D. dissertation (University of Michigan, 1957).

Lystsov, V. P., *Persidskii pokhod Petra I 1722-1723*, (Moscow, 1951).

McConnell, A., "Abbé Raynal and a Russian Philosophe," *Jahrbücher für Geschichte Osteuropas*, XII (1964), 499-512.

Mahmud, M., *Tārikh-e Ravābet-e Siyāsi-ye Irān va Englis dar Qarn-e Nuzdahom-e Milādi* (Tehran, 1336/1957-1958).

Malcolm, J., *A History of Persia* (2 vols., London, 1815), II.

Mancall, M., *Russia and China: Their Diplomatic Relations to 1728* (Cambridge, Mass., 1971).

Markova, O. P., "O proiskhozhdenii tak nazyvaemogo grecheskogo proekta (80-e gody XVIII v.)," *Istoriia SSSR*, IV (1954), 52-78.

————, *Rossiia, Zakavkaz'e i mezhdunarodnye otnosheniia v XVIII veke* (Moscow, 1966).

————, *Vosstanie v Kakhetii v 1812 g.* (Moscow, 1951).

Marriott, J. A. R., *The Eastern Question*, 4th ed. (Oxford, 1967).

Mauro, F., *L'Expansion européen 1600-1870* (Paris, 1964).

Mel'gunov, G., "Pokhod Petra Velikago v Persiiu," *Russkii Vestnik*, CIX (1874), 5-60.

Meredith, C., "The Qajar Response to Russia's Military Challenge 1804-1828," Ph.D. dissertation (Princeton, 1973).

Meskhia, S. A., *Istoriia Gruzii* (Tbilisi, 1968).

Miliutin, D. A., *Istoriia voiny 1799 goda*, 2nd ed. (3 vols., St. Petersburg, 1857), II, III.

Mil'man, A. Sh., *Politicheskii stroi Azerbaidzhana v XIX-nachale XX vekov* (Baku, 1966).

Minto (Countess), *Lord Minto in India* (London, 1880).

Mohrenschildt, D. S. von, *Russia in the Intellectual Life of Eighteenth Century France* (New York, 1972).

Nakhai, M., *L'Évolution politique de l'Iran* (Paris, 1938).

Nikolai Mikhailovich (Grandduke), *Imperator Aleksandr I* (2 vols., St. Petersburg, 1912).

Nolde, B., *La Formation de l'Empire Russe* (2 vols., Paris, 1952), II.

Nouvelle biographie général (46 vols., Paris, 1853-1866).

Okun', S. B., *Ocherki istorii SSSR konets XVIII—pervaia chetvert' XIX veka* (Leningrad, 1956).

————, *Rossiisko-amerikanskaia kompaniia* (Moscow-Leningrad, 1939).

"Our Political Relations with Persia," *Calcutta Review*, XVII (1849), 1-63.

P. P., "Kniaz' Platon Aleksandrovich Zubov," *Russkaia starina*, XVII (1876), 691-726.

Pakravan, E., *Abbas Mirza* (2 vols., Tehran, 1958).

Pelenski, J., "Muscovite Imperial Claims to the Kazan' Khanate: A Case Study in the Emergence of Imperial Ideology," Ph.D. dissertation (Columbia, 1967).

Perry, J. R., "Forced Migration in Iran during the Seventeenth and Eighteenth Centuries," manuscript of an article.

————, "Iran, Russia and the Caucasus 1747-1797," paper presented to the International Conference of Orientalists (Paris, 1973).

————, "The Last Safavids, 1722-1773," *Iran*, IX (1971), 59-69.

"Persia," *Blackwood's Edinburgh Journal*, XXI (1827), 158-68.

Petschauer, P., "The Education and Development of an Enlightened Absolutist: The Youth of Catherine the Great, 1729-1762," Ph.D. dissertation (New York University, 1969).

Philips, C. H., *The East India Company 1784-1834* (Manchester, 1961).

Poole, R. S., *The Coins of the Shahs of Persia* (London, 1887).

Potto, V. A., *Kavkazskaia voina* (4 vols., St. Petersburg, 1885-1888).

Quadflieg, G., *Die Russische Expansions Politik von 1774 bis 1914* (Berlin, 1914).

Quzānlu, J., *Jang-e Dah Sāleh yā Jang-e Avval-e Irān bā Rus* (Tehran, 1315/1936).

Rabino, H. L., *Coins, Medals, and Seals of the Shahs of Iran, 1500-1941* (Hertford, 1945).

————, "Coins of the Shahs of Persia," *Revue du Monde Musulman*, XXVI (1914), 111-27.

————, "Coins of the Shahs of Persia, Part II," *The Numismatic Chronicle*, fourth series, XI (1911), 176-96.

————, "Les Provinces Caspiennes de la Perse, le Guilan," *Revue du monde musulman*, XXXII (1916-1917).

————, *Mazandaran and Astarabad*, E. J. W. Gibb Memorial, New Series, VII (London, 1928).

————, "Rulers of Gilan," *Journal of the Royal Asian Society*, 1920, part 3, 277-96.

Raeff, M., "Patterns of Russian Imperial Policy toward the Nationalities," E. Allworth, ed., *Soviet Nationality Problems* (New York, 1971), pp. 22-42.

————, *Siberia and the Reforms of 1822* (Seattle, 1956).

————, "Staatsdienst, Aussenpolitik, Ideologien," *Jahrbücher für Geschichte Osteuropas*, VII, (1959), 145-81.

Rahman, F., "Revival and Reform in Islam," P. M. Holt, A. K. S. Lambton, and B. Lewis, eds., *The Cambridge History of Islam* (2 vols., Cambridge, 1970) II, 632-56.

Ramazani, R. K., *The Foreign Policy of Iran* (Charlottesville, 1966).

Rauch, G. von, *Russland: staatliche Einheit und nationale Vielfalt* (Munich, 1953).

Rawlinson, H., *England and Russia in the East* (London, 1875).

Rhinelander, L. H., Jr., "The Incorporation of the Caucasus into the Russian Empire: The Case of Georgia, 1801-1854," Ph.D. dissertation (Columbia University, 1972).

Rogger, H. *National Consciousness in Eighteenth-Century Russia* (Cambridge, Mass., 1960).

Rozhkova, M. K., "Iz istorii ekonomicheskoi politiki Rossiiskogo Tsarizma v Zakavkaz'e," *Istoricheskie zapiski*, XVIII (1946), 169-200.

Rubenshtein, N. L., "Vneshniaia torgovlia Rossii i russkoe kupechestvo vo vtoroi polovine XVIII v.," *Istoricheskie zapiski*, LIV (1955), 343-61.

Russkii biograficheskii slovar' (25 vols., St. Petersburg, 1896-1913).

Rybakov, B. A., et al., eds., *Istoriia SSSR* (12 vols., Moscow, 1966-1971), III, IV.

Sarkizyanz, E., *Geschichte der orientalischen Völker Russlands bis 1917* (Munich, 1961).

————, "Russian Imperialism Reconsidered," T. Hunczak, ed., *Russian Imperialism from Ivan the Great to the Revolution*, pp. 45-81.

Saul, N. E., *Russia and the Mediterranean 1797-1807* (Chicago, 1970).

Savory, R. M., "Safavid Persia," P. M. Holt, A. K. S. Lambton, and B. Lewis, eds., *The Cambridge History of Islam* (2 vols., Cambridge, 1970), I, 394-429.

Scheidman, J. L., "The Proposed Invasion of India by Russia and France in 1801," *Journal of Indian History*, XXXV (1957), 167-75.

Ségur, L. P., *Mémoires ou souvenirs et anecdotes* (2 vols., Paris, 1826).

Semenev, L. S., "K istorii russko-persidskie otnoshenii pervoi treti XIX v.," *Nauchnyi doklady Vysshei Shkoly, Istoricheskie nauki*, I (1958), 52-65.

Semenov, A., *Izuchenie istoricheskikh svedenii o rossiiskoi vneshnei torgovle i promyshlennosti* (St. Petersburg, 1859).

Shadman, S. F., "The Relations of Britain and Persia, 1800-1815," Ph.D. dissertation (University of London, 1937).

Shaw, S. J., *Between Old and New: The Ottoman Empire under Sultan Selim III, 1789-1807* (Cambridge, Mass., 1971).

Sheil, M., *Glimpses of Life and Manners in Persia* (London, 1856).

Shil'der, N. K., *Imperator Aleksandr Pervyi* (4 vols., St. Petersburg, 1903).

————, *Imperator Pavel Pervyi* (St. Petersburg, 1901).

Shopen, I. I., *Istoricheskii pamiantnik sostoianiia Armianskoi oblasti v epokhu ee prisoedineniia k Rossiiskoi imperii* (St. Petersburg, 1852).

Shumigorskii, E. S., *Imperator Pavel I* (St. Petersburg, 1907).

Siassi, A. A., *La Perse au contact de l'Occident* (Paris, 1931).

"Sokrashennoe izvlechenie iz liubopytnykh zapisok o proizshestviiakh v Persii i Gruzii sluchivshikhsia v iskhode minuvshago stoletiia," *Vestnik Evropy*, XXXII, number 6 (1807) 149-56.

Solov'ev, O. F., *Iz istorii russko-indiiskikh sviazei* (Moscow, 1958).

Solov'ev, S. M., *Istoriia Rossii* (11 vols., Moscow, 1959-1963), V, VI.

————, "Petr Velikii na Kaspiiskom more," *Vestnik Evropy*, II (1868), 163-202.

Sorel, A., *The Eastern Question in the Eighteenth Century* (New York, 1969).

Stanislavskaia, A. M., *Russko-angliiskie otnosheniia i problemy Sredizemnomor'ia (1798-1807)* (Moscow, 1962).

Swietochowski, T. A., "Modernization Trends and the Growth of National Awareness in Nineteenth Century Russian Azerbaijan," Ph.D. dissertation (New York University, 1968).

Sykes, P., *A History of Persia*, 3rd ed. (2 vols., London, 1930), II.

Szeftel, M., "La Formation et l'evolution de l'empire Russe jusqu'en 1918," *Russian Institutions and Culture up to Peter the Great* (London, 1975), pp. 422-32.

Tapper, R. L., "The Shahsavans of Azerbaijan," Ph.D. dissertation (University of London, 1972).

Ter-Gukasov, G., *Ekonomicheskie i politicheskie interesy Rossii v Persii* (St. Petersburg, 1916).

Thornton, A. P., *Doctrines of Imperialism* (New York, 1965).

Tompkins, S. R., and Moorhead, M. L., "Russia's Approach to America," *The British Columbia Historical Quarterly*, XIII (1949), 55-66, 231-55.

Trachevskii, A. S., "L'Empereur Paul et Bonaparte," *Revue d'histoire diplomatique*, III (1889), 281-86.

Upton, J. M., *The History of Modern Iran: An Interpretation* (Cambridge, Mass., 1960).

Ustrialov, N. G., *Russkaia istoriia* (4 vols., St. Petersburg, 1840).

Vandal, A., *Napoléon et Alexandre Ier* (3 vols., Paris, 1891-1896).

Vernadsky, G., *The Tsardom of Muscovy 1547-1682* (2 parts, New Haven, 1964).

Veselago, F. F., *Ocherk Russkoi morskoi istorii* (2 vols., St. Petersburg, 1875), I.

Vibart, H. M., *The Military History of the Madras Engineers and Pioneers* (2 vols., London, 1881).

Watson, R. G., *A History of Persia from the Beginning of the Nineteenth Century to the Year 1858* (London, 1866).

Wilson, C. H., "The Growth of Overseas Commerce and European Manufacture," J. O. Lindesay, ed., *The Old Regime 1713-1763*, in *The New Cambridge Modern History* (14 vols., Cambridge, 1957-1979), VII, 27-49.

Yapp, M. E., "Establishment of the East India Company Residency at Baghadad, 1798-1806," *Bulletin of the School of Oriental and African Studies*, XXX (1967), 323-36.

Zevakin, E. S., "Persidskii vopros v russko-evropeiskikh otnosheniiakh XVII v.," *Istoricheskie zapiski*, VIII (1940), 129-62.

Zubov, P. A., *Kartina Kavkazskago kraia* (4 vols., St. Petersburg, 1834-1835).

————, *Podvigi Russkikh voinov v strannakh Kavkazskikh s 1800 po 1834 g.* (2 vols., St. Petersburg, 1835).

————, *Shest'pisem o Gruzii i o Kavkaze* (Moscow, 1834).

Zubov, V. A., "Obshchee obozrenii torgovli s Azieiu," *Russkii arkhiv*, 1873, book I, columns 879-94.

————, "Pi'smo," *Russki arkhiv*, 1873, book I, columns 876-79.

INDEX

Index

'Abbās (the Great) (Safavi shah), 49
'Abbās (Mirzā) (Qājār): commands Iranian
army in First Russo-Iranian war, 82, 108,
109, 114-15, 138; employment of Russian
deserters, 106-7; character, 115, 117;
support for military Westernization, 128-
29, 135, 136, 159; favors continuing war
with Russia (*1813*), 139; attitude toward
peace negotiations (*1812*), 141; reference
to in Russo-Iranian peace (*1813*), 143;
succession to throne, 152; snubbed by
Ermolov, 153; eagerness for war (*1820s*),
154, 145-57; opposes peace with Russia
(*1828*), 159; later years, 160
'Abbāsābād: construction, 127; capture by
Russians, 158
(Mirzā) 'Abd ol-Vahhāb: head of Fath 'Ali's
chancellery, 114; increased power (*1819*
on), 156
Abkhazia: Tsitsianov wants to take, 74; submission to Russia, 102
(Mirzā) Abu'l-Hasan: Iranian negotiator at
Golestan, 143, 144; embassy to St. Peter'sburg, 152; increased power (*1819* on),
156
(Mirzā) Abu'l-Qāsem, 156
Academy of Sciences (Russia), 28
Afghans, 58, 113. *See also* Mahmud (Ghalzai)
and Zaman (Dorrāni)

Alexander (Bagration prince), 109
Alexander I (tsar): policy toward the Caucasus and Iran, 46, 47, 51, 63-65; advised
by Zubov brothers, 48, 49-50; reliance
on information from Armenians, 50; decision to annex Georgia, 50-51, 60-62,
63; seeks peace at start of reign, 60; and
French proposal to invade India, 62, 63;
opinion of Fath 'Ali Shāh, 63-64; and
Tsitsianov, 71-72, 77, 78-79, 80, 84-85;
on Russia civilizing the Caucasus, 75;
seeks peace with Iran (*1806-1808*), 101;
claims Russia controls Yerevan and Nakhjavān, 131; on territorial concessions to
Iran after *1813*, 153; news of death
reaches Iran, 157
Alexei Mikhailovich (tsar), 3
'Ali Khān, 112
'Ali Morād (Zand khan), 37
America (North), 26
Anzali: Russian commercial interest in, 33,
34, 43, 48, 52, 57; Russo-Qājār rivalry
over, 35; Paul refuses to fortify Russian
base at, 56
Āqā Mohammad (Qājār shah): Caucasian
campaign (*1795*), 6, 10, 19-20, 39, 45;
negative Russian opinion of, 6, 7, 32, 48;
rise to power, 9-10; relations with Russia,
33, 34-35, 37, 38, 40, 44, 54-55, 56; con-

207